Teacher Education in Challenging Times

Teacher education is experiencing a period of dramatic and arguably irrevocable change within a wider context of turbulence in the English education system. With contributions from a range of teacher educators and academics in the field, *Teacher Education in Challenging Times* presents sustainable, robust and informed responses to the challenges posed by the current unrest in the education sector.

This book considers the nature of teacher professionalism, the nurturing of truly collaborative partnerships between universities, schools and other agencies, and developments in practice with tangible impact for children and young people. Drawing on important research and illustrations of policy and practice from England and other countries, chapters present a series of counter-cultural ideas, principles and practices that respond to pressing challenges facing educators in a range of contexts. Positive and forward-looking, this book offers a robust defence of the present need for high-quality teacher education in challenging times.

This book is a timely contribution to an international debate about the future of teacher education and should be of key interest to academics, researchers and postgraduate students in the fields of teacher education, philosophy and sociology of education, policy and politics of education, and pedagogy. It will also appeal to a range of practitioners, including trainers, local authority officers, professional groups, educational service providers, and educational and school improvement consultants.

Philip M. Bamber is Associate Professor in the Faculty of Education at Liverpool Hope University where he is Head of the Department of Education Studies. His research interests include transformative learning, (global) citizenship and values in education. He is currently Associate Director of TEESNet, the UK Teacher Education for Equity and Sustainability Network. Philip has led and participated in research funded by the Department for International Development, European Union, Higher Education Academy, Church of England, OXFAM and the Porticus Foundation.

Jane C. Moore is the Head of Teacher Education and Director of the Professional Doctorate at Liverpool Hope University. Her research interests include teacher education, teacher identity and school leadership and professionalism. She has presented at a range of international conferences and published in the *European Journal of Teacher Education*. Her recent and current research with colleagues has involved collaboration with a large number of schools and teachers in projects that are designed to have a positive and tangible impact on practice and educational outcomes.

Routledge Research in Teacher Education

The Routledge Research in Teacher Education series presents the latest research on Teacher Education and also provides a forum to discuss the latest practices and challenges in the field.

A full list of titles in this series is available at: https://www.routledge.com/series/RRTE. Books in the series include:

Teacher Education in Taiwan
State Control vs. Marketization
Edited by Sheng-Keng Yang and Jia-Li Huang

Critical Feminism and Critical Education
An Interdisciplinary Approach to Teacher Education
Jennifer Gale de Saxe

The Use of Children's Literature in Teaching
A Study of the Politics and Professionalism Within Teacher Education
Alyson Simpson

LGBTQ Curriculum and Heteronormativity in the Classroom
Democratic Education as Social Change
Steven Camicia

Teacher Education in Challenging Times
Lessons for Professionalism, Partnership and Practice
Edited by Philip M. Bamber and Jane C. Moore

Teacher Education in Challenging Times
Lessons for professionalism, partnership and practice

Edited by Philip M. Bamber
and Jane C. Moore

LONDON AND NEW YORK

First published 2017
by Routledge

2 Park Square, Milton Park, Abingdon, Oxfordshire OX14 4RN
711 Third Avenue, New York, NY 10017

Routledge is an imprint of the Taylor & Francis Group, an informa business

First issued in paperback 2017

Copyright © 2017 selection and editorial matter, Philip M. Bamber and Jane C. Moore; individual chapters, the contributors

The right of the editors to be identified as the authors of the editorial material, and of the authors for their individual chapters, has been asserted in accordance with sections 77 and 78 of the Copyright, Designs and Patents Act 1988.

All rights reserved. No part of this book may be reprinted or reproduced or utilised in any form or by any electronic, mechanical, or other means, now known or hereafter invented, including photocopying and recording, or in any information storage or retrieval system, without permission in writing from the publishers.

Notice:
Product or corporate names may be trademarks or registered trademarks, and are used only for identification and explanation without intent to infringe.

British Library Cataloguing in Publication Data
A catalogue record for this book is available from the British Library

Library of Congress Cataloging in Publication Data
Names: Bamber, Phil, editor. | Moore, Jane C., editor.
Title: Teacher education in challenging times: lessons for professionalism, partnership and practice/edited by Philip M. Bamber and Jane C. Moore.
Description: New York, NY: Routledge, 2016.
Identifiers: LCCN 2016006600 | ISBN 9781138943360
(hardcover) | ISBN 9781315672519 (electronic)
Subjects: LCSH: Teachers—Training of. | Teachers—Professional relationships. | Teachers—Training of—England.
Classification: LCC LB1707. T399 2016 | DDC 370.71/1—dc23
LC record available at https://lccn.loc.gov/2016006600

ISBN: 978-1-138-94336-0 (hbk)
ISBN: 978-0-8153-6447-4 (pbk)

Typeset in Galliard
by Keystroke, Station Road, Codsall, Wolverhampton

Contents

List of contributors	xi
Foreword	xvii
SUSAN GROUNDWATER-SMITH	
Acknowledgements	xix
Abbreviations	xxi

Introduction	1

PHILIP M. BAMBER AND JANE C. MOORE

Overview 1
Professionalism 4
Partnership 6
Practice 8
Conclusion 10
References 10

PART I	
Professionalism	13

1 **Today's university challenge: maintaining and strengthening professional jurisdiction for the preparation of teachers**	15

SUE CRONIN

Introduction: how have we ended up here? 15
The features of a teacher educator 16
The features of the professional 17
Key questions for the university teacher educator 17
Conclusion 26
References 27

vi *Contents*

2 Building professionals and elevating the profession? The work of university-based initial teacher educators in Aotearoa New Zealand

29

DAVID A.G. BERG, ALEXANDRA C. GUNN,
MARY F. HILL AND MAVIS HAIGH

Introduction 29
A brief history of initial teacher education in New Zealand 30
Policy and ITE provision 32
Work of Teacher Educators–New Zealand Research
* (WoTE-NZ) 33*
Consequences of the bifurcation of teacher educator work 36
Conclusion 37
References 38

International vignette 1: teacher education in Wales

41

SUSAN WYN JONES AND JOHN LEWIS

Background 41
The current position of ITET in Wales 41
The future 42
References 42

3 Teaching as contemplative

44

JOHN SULLIVAN

Introduction 44
Acknowledging the active dimension of teaching 44
Connotations of contemplation 46
Education in light of Buber and Freire 50
The contemplative as counter-weight to some cultural
* assumptions about teaching 51*
Conclusion 56
References 56

4 Education for shalom: dimensions of a relational pedagogy

58

JOHN SHORTT

Introduction: the need to reconnect with purpose 58
Shalom and knowing of the third kind 60
Persons in relation 61
Partnership with the otherness of the world 63
Conclusion: teaching for shalom 65
References 67

Contents vii

5 Is being critical enough? 69
RUTH PILKINGTON

Introduction 69
Professional learning 72
Professional capital in teaching 75
An organisational solution 77
References 79

PART II
Partnership 81

6 Working at the intersection: partnerships as participatory mechanisms for disruption 83
TINA COOK

Introduction: intersection – a place where two or more
roads meet 83
Defining partnership 84
Uncritical approaches to partnership working: an example 85
Partnerships with parents: form and function 86
Challenge within partnerships: the purpose of mutual critique 88
Developing generative partnerships: the role of challenge,
conflict and collaboration 89
Conclusion: partnerships as spaces for critique and
communicative action 91
References 92

7 Student partnership and a university legitimation crisis 94
MORGAN WHITE

Introduction 94
Voice and authority 94
What is authority? 95
Freedom and the passions 96
Authority of the philosopher king 97
The Roman tradition 98
Revolution and foundations in the present 99
World turned upside down 100
Authority in the seminar 101
The authoritative tutor 102
Conclusion 103
References 103

viii *Contents*

8 Teacher development through professional partnership: harnessing the power of professional learning communities 105

GEOFF BAKER

Introduction 105
Teacher development and professional networks 105
Conceptualising professional communities 107
The research project 108
The research tool 108
Discussion 109
Conclusion 112
References 112

9 The changing role of the teacher in multi-agency work 115

ELIZABETH PARR

Introduction 115
The study 117
Context 118
Theories of multi-agency development and learning 119
Discussion 120
Conclusion 122
References 123

10 Partnership and teacher formation for global social justice 126

PHILIP M. BAMBER AND ANDREA BULLIVANT

Introduction 126
Global education for global social justice 127
Global education as a process of becoming 128
Partnership for global social justice in practice: nurturing
*   Wider Perspectives in Education in England 130*
Case study of teacher formation 1: community engagement through
*   church international evenings 132*
Case study of teacher formation 2: the ongoing impact of community
*   engagement 133*
Conclusion 134
References 135

International vignette 2: working in partnership for Learning for Sustainability in Scotland 137

BETSY KING AND GARY JOHNSTONE

References 140

Contents ix

PART III
Practice   141

11 **Subject knowledge enhancement courses a decade on:**
    redefining professional knowledge in mathematics
    teacher education   143
    MARY STEVENSON

    Introduction 143
    SKE background and context 144
    Discussion of literature and relationship to practice 144
    Mathematics knowledge as an active process 145
    Understanding mathematics in depth 146
    The SKE at Liverpool Hope University 147
    The SKE as a site for the interplay between subject
        matter knowledge and pedagogical content
        knowledge 148
    Implications for practice: deficits in traditional
        degree routes to teacher education and the
        place of the SKE 148
    Conclusion 151
    References 152

12 **Challenging dyslexia**   155
    OWEN BARDEN

    Introduction 155
    Labelling 156
    Biologising dyslexia 158
    Ideology of literacy 160
    Conclusion 162
    References 164

13 **An issue of social justice: bullying in schools**   166
    BABS ANDERSON

    Introduction 166
    An overview of bullying research 167
    The research project 168
    The findings 169
    Issues for practice 171
    Conclusion: an alternative view 172
    References 173

x   *Contents*

**14 Contemporary learners need enlightened environments:
technology, student agency and emergent learning**   175

SUSAN RODRIGUES

Introduction 175
*Changes in education policy, classroom practice and digital
    development 176*
The role of student agency in formal learning milieus 180
A place for emergent learning 181
Conclusion 182
References 183

**15 The Hope Challenge: a new model of partnership
for school improvement**   187

JANE C. MOORE, MICHELLE PEARSON AND SUE CRONIN

Introduction 187
The existing school improvement landscape 189
The Hope Challenge – principles and projects 191
Conclusion 195
References 195

Conclusion   197

KEITH CRAWFORD

References 205

Index   207

Contributors

Babs Anderson has extensive experience within the school sector of education. An experienced primary teacher, she has also worked as a consultant for Knowsley Healthy Schools programme, supporting schools in their work in gaining accreditation, with a particular interest in emotional health and well-being. She is presently a lecturer at Liverpool Hope University in the Early Childhood Department within the Faculty of Education, where she maintains her interest in holistic well-being. Much of her research is in this field, including children's peer relationships and their collaborations.

Geoff Baker is Principal of Cromer Academy, an 11–16 secondary school in North Norfolk, and Visiting Fellow in the Department of Education Studies at Liverpool Hope University. His research is concerned with teacher development, values based leadership, the history of education and curriculum innovation. He was awarded a Winston Churchill Fellowship in 2015 to complete a comparative study of approaches to school leadership in Finland and China. His papers can be found in a diverse range of publications and he has written or edited seven books including his monograph *Reading and Politics in Early Modern England* (Manchester University Press, 2013) and the edited collection *Arts and Humanities Academics in Schools: Mapping the Pedagogical Divide* (Bloomsbury Academic Press, 2013) with Andrew Fisher.

Philip M. Bamber is Head of Department of Education Studies at Liverpool Hope University. His research is concerned with transformative education, service-learning, education for citizenship and values in education. He was awarded the International Association of University Presidents International Education Faculty Achievement Award in 2013 for leadership in research and teaching in global citizenship. He is Associate Director of TEESNet, the UK Network for Teacher Education for Equity and Sustainability. His papers can be found in *Education, Citizenship and Social Justice, Journal of Beliefs and Values, Journal of Curriculum Studies* and *Journal of Transformative Education.*

Owen Barden is a Lecturer in Disability and Education at Liverpool Hope University. He has previously worked as a teacher and teacher educator in sixth-form, further and higher education. As a practitioner, Dr Barden focused on xii *Contributors*

teaching students labelled with dyslexia in tertiary education and on training other teachers to do the same. Dr Barden has published on relationships between dyslexia, identity and literacy practices, and on research methods for capturing digitally mediated classroom learning. He is currently particularly interested in exploring emerging digitally mediated literacy practices and the impact of these new literacies on how we conceptualise dyslexia.

David A. G. Berg is a former primary school teacher and deputy head teacher. He has worked in teacher education in New Zealand and England. His research interests include teacher self-efficacy beliefs, assessment and initial teacher education. David is a Lecturer and Associate Postgraduate and Distance Coordinator (Education Studies) at the College of Education, University of Otago, Dunedin, New Zealand.

Andrea Bullivant is an Associate Lecturer in the Faculty of Education at Liverpool Hope University where she leads a course for trainee primary teachers called Wider Perspectives in Education. She also works for Liverpool World Centre, a Development Education Centre (DEC) and a member of the national consortium of DECs, and is Director of TEESNet, the UK Network for Teacher Education for Equity and Sustainability. Andrea is co-author of a number of chapters and papers on global learning and is interested in the learning process for people's critical engagement in and with global society which she is pursuing through PhD research with Lancaster University.

Tina Cook is a Reader in Inclusive Methodologies and Faculty Ambassador for Impact (Northumbria University) and Visiting Professorial Fellow (Liverpool Hope University). At the core of her work is a focus on inclusive practice in research. Using qualitative research, particularly collaborative/participatory action research, she seeks ways of facilitating the inclusion, as research partners, of those who might generally be excluded from research that concerns their own lives. Her methodological approach centres on ways of fore-fronting voices of those directly involved in a situation as a means of improving the quality of their lives. She has published on both methodological issues in relation to the quality of participatory research approaches and issues related to research in practice. She is an Executive Committee Member of the International Collaboration for Participatory Health Research, an Editor of the *International Journal of Educational Action Research* and founder member of the Participatory Research Network, UK.

Keith Crawford is Adjunct Professor of Education in the School of Education at Macquarie University, Sydney, Australia. He has been engaged in teacher education programmes for over 25 years. He is particularly interested in interdisciplinary work that draws upon the traditions and methodologies of sociology, history, the political sciences, ideological, political and socio-cultural perspectives on curriculum and schooling. He has published work on citizenship education and historical and sociological analyses of the school curriculum. He currently serves on the editorial advisory boards of several journals including

Citizenship, Social and Economic Education, Journal of International Social Studies, Journal of Social Studies Research and *The Social Educator.*

Sue Cronin is currently Deputy Head of the School of Teacher Education at Liverpool Hope University. She started her teaching career in Liverpool as a secondary mathematics teacher and taught in a variety of schools before joining the local authority supporting mathematics departments across the city. Since joining Liverpool Hope, Sue has worked on a variety of programmes linked to teacher education including Secondary PGCE Leader, Coordinator of Mathematics Education and Director of School Direct programmes. Her main research interests are around the areas of teacher education, mathematics education and creativity.

Susan Groundwater-Smith is an Honorary Professor in the Faculty of Education and Social Work at the University of Sydney. She has published extensively on matters related to practitioner research and the nexus between the academy and the field of practice in education as demonstrated in Groundwater-Smith et al. (2013) *Facilitating Practitioner Research* (Routledge, 2013). Most recently she has turned her attention to participative research with children and young people, including in her publications *Engaging with Student Voice in Research, Education and Community: Beyond Legitimation and Guardianship* (with N. Mockler; Springer, 2015) and *Participatory Research with Children and Young People* (with S. Dockett and D. Bottrell; Sage, 2015). She is deeply committed to the services of educational research and inquiry in the interests of an emancipatory agenda as opposed to engaging in work that serves the current neoliberal ethos.

Alexandra C. Gunn teaches and researches in early childhood, inclusion, assessment and teacher education. Formerly an early childhood teacher, Alex's work centres on social justice, teachers' beliefs and practices, and the production and disruption of taken-for-granted norms. Alex is a Senior Lecturer and Associate Dean (Teacher Education) in the College of Education, University of Otago, Dunedin, New Zealand.

Mavis Haigh's professional background includes secondary science and biology teaching and teacher education, both pre-service and postgraduate. Her research interests are pre-service teacher education, particularly research around assessment of the practicum and teaching for equity, and the professional learning of teacher educators. Mavis is an Associate Professor in the Faculty of Education, University of Auckland, New Zealand.

Mary F. Hill was a primary teacher and deputy principal before becoming a teacher educator and academic. She teaches pre-service teachers and postgraduate students mostly in subjects aligned with her research interests of educational assessment, professional learning and teacher education. Mary is an Associate Professor in the Faculty of Education, University of Auckland, New Zealand.

xiv *Contributors*

Gary Johnstone started his teaching career as a teacher of geography and modern studies in the 1980s. He held a number of promoted posts in Glasgow and Inverclyde. In 2001, Gary joined the Advisory Service in Renfrewshire Council as Education Adviser with responsibility for mathematics and social subjects. In 2004, Gary joined North Ayrshire Council as Senior Adviser, moving to Quality Improvement Manager and Senior Manager where his responsibilities included curriculum development, quality improvement and continuing professional development. Within the Association of Directors of Education in Scotland (ADES), Gary was a member of the executive, co-chair of the Performance and Improvement Network and member of the Board of the Virtual Staff College Scotland. Gary joined Education Scotland as HMI in March 2013. In addition to his inspection duties, Gary was the Lead Officer for Leadership and Teacher Education, Subject Specialist Inspector for geography and Link Inspector to the University of the West of Scotland and the Open University. He is now Area Lead Officer for Three Scottish Local Authorities.

Susan Wyn Jones is a Senior Lecturer in the School of Education at Bangor University, Wales. Since 2014, she has been Deputy Head of School, Director of Teaching and Learning and Director of Student Engagement for the school. She sits on the curriculum and assessment working group of the Royal Society of Chemistry and is interested in promoting effective teaching practices which ensure every child makes progress and fulfils their true potential. She has research students working in the field of numeracy and science, scientific literacy and embedding digital competency. She has papers published on the professional development needs of teachers.

Betsy King is the Development Manager of Scotland's Regional Centre of Expertise in Education for Sustainable Development, Learning for Sustainability Scotland, hosted within the Moray House School of Education, University of Edinburgh. The centre is an open network where members and partners come together to undertake collaborative projects, research and advocacy that push forward Learning for Sustainability practice and policy in Scotland. She has a long-standing commitment to Learning for Sustainability. She is a former geography teacher, and worked at the Peak National Park Centre, for the University of Papua New Guinea and for an number of NGOs in the UK, most recently for WWF Scotland. She is a member of the UK Network for Teacher Education for Equity and Sustainability (TEESNet) Steering Group.

John Lewis is a Senior Lecturer in Science Education at the School of Education at Bangor University, Wales. He taught science at a range of secondary schools across North Wales before becoming the biology tutor at Bangor University. He currently teaches on the secondary PGCE programme and his research interests include the implementation and effectiveness of numeracy and literacy strategies in schools.

Jane C. Moore is the Head of Teacher Education and Director of the Professional Doctorate at Liverpool Hope University. Her research interests include teacher education, teacher identity and school leadership and professionalism. She has presented at a range of international conferences and published in the *European Journal of Teacher Education*. Her recent and current research with colleagues has involved collaboration with large numbers of schools and teachers in projects that are designed to have a positive and tangible impact on practice and educational outcomes.

Elizabeth Parr is currently a professional tutor in Initial Teacher Education at Liverpool Hope University with responsibility for postgraduate School Direct programmes. She also has experience as a primary school teacher across Key Stages 1 and 2 in schools across the northwest of England. Elizabeth is currently studying for a Doctorate of Education at the University of Manchester. Her research concerns community-oriented primary schools and she has thus far considered international approaches to this idea as well as the experiences of educational professionals who work in these settings. She intends to further develop her research by considering the characteristics of professionals' perceptions and practices in community-oriented schools.

Michelle Pearson taught as a primary school teacher for over ten years with senior management responsibility and curriculum leadership expertise in literacy in a wide variety of schools across the northwest. She has experience working in EYFS through to Year 6. Before working at LHU, Michelle was appointed as a literacy consultant for two authorities working in partnership with schools to raise standards in literacy. She has also been an independent consultant working in international schools researching and developing literacy teaching.

Ruth Pilkington is a National Teaching Fellow (2014). She has gained a national profile for her research and innovative use of dialogue as a means of assessing and recognising the professional learning of HE academics (cf. Appleby and Pilkington, *Developing Critical Professional Practice in Education*, NIACE, 2014). Her approach to dialogue has been adopted by a number of institutions for their CPD frameworks and resulted in national recognition and external work. She works as Professorial Teaching Fellow at Liverpool Hope University and part-time for the HE Academy, York. She also acts as educational consultant for a number of UK institutions. Ruth's career route into academic development built on national project leadership and development of professional learning and employability skills within the HE sector. Invited to lead the postgraduate certificate in learning and teaching in HE at University of Central Lancashire, she applied her skills in assessment, professional education and activity-based, reflective learning as leader of a suite of professional education programmes embracing PG Certificates, a Masters in Education (MEd Professional Practice in Education) and an EdD award.

Susan Rodrigues obtained her DPhil in chemical education from the University of Waikato, New Zealand, in 1993. Since then she has continued to research the role of context on student learning in chemistry. In the last 20 years that has come to include exploring and reporting on teacher education and the use of technology in science education.

xvi *Contributors*

John Shortt is Professorial Fellow in Christian Education at Liverpool Hope University and Senior Adviser to the European Educators' Christian Association (EurECA). He taught mathematics at secondary level for 19 years. He is co-author with David I. Smith of *The Bible and the Task of Teaching* (2000) and author of *Bible-Shaped Teaching* (2014). He was the founding editor of *Journal of Education and Christian Belief* (now *International Journal of Christianity & Education*) and the first director of the Charis Project for promoting spiritual and moral development across the curriculum based at the Stapleford Centre, Nottingham. He has also been a visiting professor at Calvin College in Grand Rapids, Michigan. He maintains a website at johnshortt.org for those who teach.

Mary Stevenson is a Senior Lecturer at Liverpool Hope University, where she has held the roles of Head of Mathematics for five years and then Coordinator of Mathematics Education for six years. Her work spans undergraduate and postgraduate mathematics and mathematics education programmes. Currently Mary leads the mathematics subject knowledge enhancement (SKE) and PGCE courses and also runs a CPD programme for qualified teachers. Mary has a particular interest in the nature of subject knowledge for mathematics teaching and has conducted research in this area. Before moving to Liverpool Hope University in the late 1990s, Mary taught mathematics in a sixth-form college and three secondary schools in the northwest of England. She was Head of Mathematics in two of the schools.

John Sullivan was, from 2002–2013, Professor of Christian Education at Liverpool Hope University, where he is now an Emeritus Professor. He is also Visiting Professor in Theology and Education at Newman University, Birmingham. He has taught, from classroom teacher to head teacher level, in several secondary schools, served in senior leadership roles in a local education authority and has substantial teaching experience, both at undergraduate and postgraduate levels and in supervising doctoral research in universities. Author and editor of 7 books and more than 70 chapters on religion and education, he is interested in the mutual bearing on each other of theology and education and also in continuing professional development.

Morgan White has taught philosophy and various social science subjects at A level. He has also taught social and political philosophy and the philosophy of education at various British universities. He is presently writing a book, *Towards a Political Theory of the University*, which explores the diminished democratic potential of contemporary universities.

Foreword

Susan Groundwater-Smith

Bob Dylan reminded us in his song 'The Times They Are A-Changin' that time never stands still. Indeed, it is ironic that the song was first performed in 1963, just one month before the assassination of US President John F. Kennedy, making great change in those political times. But what is remarkable about these early years of a new millennium is not that change is taking place, but that the rate of change is accelerating at breathtaking speed. This claim is well set out by Hartmut (2015), who writes of three categories of change in modern life: the speeding up of technology-based convergences; changes in transportation, communication and production; and social change in terms of cultural knowledge, personal relationships and social institutions. It is to the last of these that I refer. In recent years, education systems from all parts of our world have been affected by the rapid rise of neoliberal ideology, which has led to the commodification of critical social provisions in the public space. Education is now an industry, based upon a market logic, whether delivered through schools, universities or other tertiary providers manufacturing what Connell (2013, p.109) has named as a knowledge base 'in a closed loop that does not allow other kinds of knowledge to enter policy debate'.

However, in a more optimistic vein, when writing of logics of practice, Rizvi and Lingard (2010) challenge readers to consider how the neoliberal imaginary has shaped education policy and practices around the world and have sought to shed light on new ways to conceive of engaging in such a volatile environment, suggesting that many of the older approaches are insufficient and that new tools and ways of thinking will need to be employed, allowing for a 'new global imagination' (p.3). This is precisely what is sought by the many contributors to *Teacher Education in Challenging Times*.

Chapters variously address policy and ideological shifts in relation to the complex task of preparing teachers within national agendas that veer to the instrumental and pragmatic. Writers insist on moving beyond 'training' both those engaged in initial teacher education and those already practising in the field and instead adopt a form of carefully conceived professional education in which teachers may be seen as 'contemplative practitioners' in the many and varying education sectors. The chapters propose not only the challenges that are to be faced in relation to professional educational practices but also how a range of solutions might xviii *Foreword*

be applied, drawing upon a variety of discourses from the philosophical to the sociological. Discourses can be defined not only as ways of *thinking* and producing meaning but also as *practices* that, in effect, are formed by such habits of mind. They are more often than not 'steeped in historicity and sedimented meanings, such that their meanings stick and are frequently irreconcilable' (Youdell, 2010, p.314). In the context of this collection of writing, educational practices are continually evaluated and contested.

Practical matters such as the development of generative partnerships are mooted along with a concurrent critique of the ways in which standards frameworks and regimes have dominated a form of teacher professional learning that is crudely technical rather than liberatory; pragmatic rather than idealistic. Authors make a plea, instead, for authentic participative engagement. The richness of the chapters lies in the range of issues that they embody in relation to what we understand 'practice' to be and in their insistence upon solutions that are firmly based in principles of social justice and ethicality.

Some years ago, I wrote of the notion of universities being safe places for unsafe ideas (Groundwater-Smith, 2007): 'places that allow consensual values themselves to be made problematic without fear or favour' (p.57). If the neoliberal agenda seeks to provide a one-size-fits-all solution to the world's many complex and difficult problems, then that is a consensus that deserves to be vigorously and thoroughly fought in our universities. Texts such as *Teacher Education in Challenging Times* are designed to do just that.

References

Connell, R. (2013). The neoliberal cascade and education: an essay on the market agenda and its consequences. *Critical Studies in Education*, 54(2), 99–112.

Groundwater-Smith, S. (2007). Questions of quality in practitioner research: universities in the 21st century – the need for safe places for unsafe ideas. In: P. Ponte and B. Smit (eds), *The Quality of Practitioner Research*, pp.57–64. Rotterdam: Sense Publishers.

Hartmut, R. (2015). *Social Acceleration: A New Theory of Modernity*. Translated by J. Tretho-Mathys. New York: Columbia University Press.

Rizvi, F. and Lingard, B. (2010). *Globalizing Education Policy*. London: Routledge.

Youdell, D. (2010). Pedagogies of becoming in an end of the line 'special' school. *Critical Studies in Education*, 51(3), 313–324.

Acknowledgements

This book is a direct result of two seminar series held in the Faculty of Education at Liverpool Hope University between 2013 and 2015. The first was entitled 'Dangerous Ideas in Education' and the second 'Education in Challenging Times'. We would like to thank all those, from across our university and beyond, who contributed towards these seminars, including invited speakers, attendees and those who chaired what were often vigorous debates. In particular, we would like to thank Michelle Pryor who co-ordinated the organisation, publicity and dissemination of the seminars – some of which were streamed live to international partners. Fiona Michael should also be thanked for her patient and efficient support in the editorial process for this book.

We would like to thank Professor Kenneth Newport, Dean of Education and Pro-Vice Chancellor, for conceiving, encouraging and supporting this project to completion. He has been tireless in his advocacy for the continuing importance of teacher education at Liverpool Hope University, which enjoys such a long and distinguished history. We would also like to thank Associate Professors Alan Hodkinson and David Bolt for providing feedback on the original book proposal.

We owe a debt of gratitude to the many teachers in partner schools who work alongside us in generous partnership; and heartfelt thanks to our many hundreds of current 'beginning' and graduate teachers, from and with whom we have learned so much.

Jane Moore would like to thank her husband Stuart Moore and children Alex, Sophie and Jack for their unfailing love and support throughout.

Philip Bamber would like to dedicate this book to two great teachers: his mum and dad.

Abbreviations

ITE   Initial Teacher Education
LHU   Liverpool Hope University
Ofsted   Office of Standards in Education
SKE   Subject Knowledge Enhancement
UK   United Kingdom

Introduction

Philip M. Bamber and Jane C. Moore

Overview

Teacher education is experiencing a period of dramatic and seemingly irrevocable change within a wider context of turbulence in the English education system. This book joins the resulting debate that has engaged academics, politicians, teachers and others with considerable intensity over recent years. The scale and pace of change is intentional and determined. In 2013, for instance, the goal that 'half of all teacher training places [would] be led by schools by 2015' was announced by the then Secretary of State for Education (Gove, 2013), regardless of the operational system-wide challenges this created. The rationale for this policy was grounded in the rhetoric of choice and democratisation, with aspiring teachers given more options about the nature of their training, and schools given greater involvement and authority over the nature of the workforce they would be employing. Whilst others might question either the object or motive for change, there is also genuine appetite across the sector for review, innovation and re-imagining in how we prepare the teachers of the future. Ellis and McNicholl note that the rhetoric of 'reform' (2015, Preface) tends to characterise policy approaches and that this in turn prompts reactions of rejection and defence; they argue instead for 'a pedagogical agenda for the transformation of teacher education' (p.x). This book shares that purpose and spirit.

The policy drive to a school-led teacher 'training' system in England arguably threatens the very existence of university-based teacher education and, at least, fundamentally destabilises the well-established university teacher education programmes that have been at the centre of teacher preparation for some time. This volume represents a number of responses to this, at different levels. The contributions are drawn from a range of academics in the field, some of them practising teacher educators at Liverpool Hope University, one of the largest and longest established university teacher education providers in England. Some of these chapters highlight recent developments made at this particular institution though they are not thereby limited in scope and relevance; rather, the examples presented are intended to show what is possible in such times, as a counter-cultural response that might act as an encouragement and clarion call to others. The range of chapters from academics from other institutions demonstrates what

2 Philip M. Bamber and Jane C. Moore

we in the sector know and appreciate in our day-to-day work: that our collaborations and partnerships with others, in universities, schools and other organisations, are critical and essential and that they refute the characterisation of distance and introspection sometimes levelled at university academics in this field.

Our examination of teacher education in England is necessarily located within an international context. It includes important research from Wales, Scotland, Australia and New Zealand along with illustrations of policy and practice from numerous other countries. It evidences the impact of global policy discourse upon education at national, regional and local levels. For instance, individual contributions report on radical changes to teacher education in England and Wales, justified by relatively poor performance in international league tables. At the same time, it is shown how Learning for Sustainability has been embedded at all levels of Scottish Education as a response to the United Nations Decade of Education for Sustainable Development. Most importantly however, this book exposes the consequences of failing to disrupt the supraterritorial neo-liberal discourse that puts education in service to the knowledge economy. It seeks to provide an antidote to the passive instrumentalism that this generates. The contributors are fundamentally concerned with education as a means for transformation and growth, and we argue this is only meaningfully enacted through dialogue, often across diverse contexts, and a commitment to social justice.

Our approach in this volume is to take the overarching themes of professionalism, partnership and practice in turn, and explore how these are undergoing reconceptualisation and revision in different areas of the education sector. A number of chapters could have been located in any of the sections, and, indeed, many threads run across all three; this usefully highlights what we see as both pragmatic and profound issues relating to teacher education and the way in which it synthesises elements from diverse and overlapping areas. Cutting across each section are the implications for the nature of these elements in the context of a market-driven, rapidly changing, performance-focused and bureaucratic educational environment. Against this backdrop, the book brings together current and ongoing research in education, engaging with broader theoretical and policy perspectives, as well as providing focused studies that propose recommendations for professional practice.

The inescapable context of the political shift towards school-led routes into teaching has had significant implications for the status of teaching as a 'full' or true profession; as discussed in several chapters in this book, whilst professionalism is a contested and complex notion, it nevertheless has connotations of authority, autonomy and values which sit uneasily with more functional and competency-orientated definitions of teaching. We understand the notion of 'professional' as encompassing in-depth engagement with relevant fields of knowledge; the enhanced emphasis upon experiential knowledge of schooling within Initial Teacher Education (ITE) curricula in England has resulted in diminishing exposure of postgraduate ITE students to research-informed knowledge from the four traditional disciplines of education (history, philosophy, psychology and sociology) (Beauchamp et al., 2015) and new cognate fields deriving from these.

The breadth of the chapters contained in this publication reflect a counter-cultural vision for teacher education that sustains conversations, often across disciplines and subject areas, which highlight the important contribution of educational research and deepen our understanding of the relationship between theory and practice. We would argue that the development of research-rich cultures in schools (BERA, 2014) depends upon this. Meaningful academic engagement with theoretical perspectives and current research helps to provide robust and credible frameworks within which professional judgement can be exercised and professional identity formed; it is in this 'space' that the emerging/continuing professional discerns and articulates the values that sustain and ground his/her work.

There is a clear need for a detailed and considered discussion of the consequences, both actual and potential, that result from such rapid and wholesale change in the sector. These consequences are not just relevant to teacher educators and those directly associated with the profession but also to the wider population; the supply and quality of teachers and the health of the teaching profession are of direct interest and relevance to the whole of society. This book also takes into account some of the changes in the wider education system, such as the growth of academies and free schools, the marketisation of higher education and the need for multi-agency approaches in order to safe-guard children. Whilst of great social and political significance in their own right, these issues also overlap with the debate about teacher education, for example in terms of the freedoms schools may have to recruit those new to the profession, and how to ensure teachers are prepared to negotiate a professional environment that can be fragmented and fluid. Whilst focusing on the specific, the chapters in this volume also explore the general – ultimately, teachers are at the heart of any education system, and the manner in which they are prepared for their chosen profession is indicative of how a government or society views the purpose of education and the values it attaches to it.

This book takes a deliberately optimistic and proactive stance with regard to what Ellis and McNicholl call 'the amazing challenge' (2015, p.6) of teacher education. It covers a wide range of examples and perspectives, drawn from across the UK and internationally, and whilst the preoccupations of 2016 are reflected in their selection, there is commonality in the setting of the academic and other contexts within which these current issues are located. Philosophy and practice sit side by side and illuminate one another. This is a reflection of the unabashed complexity of teaching, and by extension, the complexity of educating teachers. An example might be useful here. Concerns about high levels of attrition in the sector have prompted questions about how to build resilience in the workforce. We take the view that resilience stems from formative preparation that builds on personal qualities and develops a secure sense of professional identity, rather than from mechanisms for coping with intense scrutiny and hectic timetables. Much of this is grounded in the centrality of the values that inform the way our professional lives are lived out – both as teachers and teacher educators. Values help us keep a necessary focus on the 'why' of how we act, from what is taught and how, to how schools are led, curricula designed and teachers educated.

4 *Philip M. Bamber and Jane C. Moore*

What follows introduces the 'Professionalism', 'Partnership' and 'Practice' sections into which the book is divided.

Professionalism

In their recent discussion of 'professional capital', Hargreaves and Fullan suggested that teacher education was at a 'crossroads' (2012, p.xii), though one from which the possible destinations seemed equally fraught with contention. They outlined what they saw as parallel misunderstandings about how to achieve 'better quality' teaching, including changes to pay (both punitive and performance-related) and increasingly prescriptive conditions to reduce the complexity and scope of teaching, and the autonomy of teachers by extension. Such measures are political responses to serious and complex issues – of inequality in educational outcomes for children, for example, at both national and international levels – but more tellingly indicate a conceptualisation of teaching and the teaching profession that many (including the contributors to this volume) view as limited and reductionist. Three or so years later, disagreement about 'destinations' (for example, the future of the teaching profession, how teachers should be prepared, how education should be 'delivered' and evaluated) has if anything intensified.

The term 'professional capital' denotes the broad range of shared attributes, responsibilities and esteem indicators that attach to a body of professional practitioners in a specific area or sector. A number of the writers in this volume identify a threat to the fundamental status of teaching as a profession at all, viewing the policy shift to a school-led, 'technician' teacher education system as a more or less overt dismantling of traditional, 'professionally-orientated' programmes which blend practice, theory, critical and reflective elements. In this section, Sue Cronin and David Berg et al. examine the impact of policy directives at national level, with recent experiences in England and New Zealand explored in Chapters 1 and 2 respectively. Here is a further example of different destinations from the same crossroads; in both countries, teacher education began in training colleges (with little or no standardised provision) and developed into a profession with established but disputed academic standing, resulting in similar and familiar tensions. However, whilst in England the policy direction is presently unequivocally committed to a school-led (and away from a university) system, Berg et al. explore New Zealand's continuing commitment to a more academically grounded preparation, nevertheless expressing some concern that this position might be threatened in the future. These writers robustly challenge the rhetorically convenient polarisation of school and university provision, however; here, as in other contributions to this volume, there is no desire to preserve or protect 'territories', or mount exclusive claims on the profession. A summary of the situation in Wales continues the themes addressed at the beginning of this section, neatly encapsulating the competing drivers in teacher education policy; the impetus to follow particular international models is constrained by accountability measures in familiar ways.

Introduction 5

In Chapters 3 and 4 of this section, the discussion broadens to focus on more philosophical aspects of professionalism. Both John Sullivan and John Shortt explore the importance of the relational aspects of teaching, shifting focus away from the ceaseless activity and 'busyness' of day-to-day school life to a proper regard for the 'other'. The learner is not a project, or set of data, or object to be acted upon; the learner is a distinct and separate being, whose education should be a matter of self-fulfilment and the realising of potential. Such a view runs counter to the prevailing culture of managerialism and accountability in education; prescribed objectives and targets at pupil, school and national levels sit uneasily with an approach that centres on freedom and becoming, on the patience and uncertainty that teaching and learning must entail. This discussion brings the work of Britzman and Green to mind (drawn on in Chapter 15 of this book), which explores the 'impossible' at the heart of teaching – having to act in complex situations without ever being sure of the outcome; of communicating with others who are always to some extent 'unknowable'. But these writers, and Sullivan and Shortt in their chapters, stress and embrace that 'otherness'; teachers should not mould or shape or make assumptions about their students, but should accept the essential uncertainty of these encounters as part of the privilege and responsibility of being an educator. This more sophisticated and nuanced conceptualisation of teaching accords with notions of professionalism that assert the centrality of values, purpose and reflection as underpinning foundations of practice. Both Sullivan and Shortt also look beyond the relationships of teachers and learners with one another to the relationship of the learner with what is learned and ultimately with the wider world; this 'outward' gaze properly locates each individual within larger communities, which might be geographical (from local to global, aligning with Chapter 10 in this volume), but which also extends across time. Nurturing this sense of 'connectedness' is, as Shortt asserts, at the centre of learning and teaching.

Ruth Pilkington's chapter concludes this section, bringing a number of these themes together. She also addresses the contested nature of teacher professionalism and proposes that the notion of 'critical professionalism' (Appleby and Pilkington, 2014) might offer a way to balance and align the conflicting and unsettling priorities discussed across these chapters. Pilkington's discussion of the nature of practice-based learning highlights the power of this model, whilst reminding us of the challenges to ensuring that such learning is properly accommodated and supported; highly demanding, closely scrutinised educational settings are often resistant to making the space (both in terms of time and philosophically) in which the critical dialogue and reflection required for learning can take place. The notion of 'critical professionalism' acknowledges the complexity of teaching and that the individual practitioner is responsible for ensuring her own commitment and engagement within its interwoven elements; essentially, though, the educational environments within which teachers work must enable their continuing learning and development through appropriate organisational structures. These include the opportunity to learn with and through others, to engage with and in research, and to have the space in which to do so. Whilst these

6   Philip M. Bamber and Jane C. Moore

activities do not seem new, it is the extent to which they are *genuinely* enabled that is key; it is a concern that some professional development provision can pay lip-service to these aims whilst being piecemeal and imposed. But true dialogue with and learning alongside others, in work that is informed by and located within relevant research and theoretical frameworks, is extraordinarily powerful. Engagement of this kind is at the heart of the notion of 'professional capital' that threads throughout this section and, indeed, the whole volume.

Partnership

The lessons for partnership in teacher education are elucidated on a range of levels in this book, including student-tutor partnership in Chapter 7, teacher-teacher partnership in Chapter 8, multi-agency partnership in chapter 9 and third-sector partnership in Chapter 10. In Chapter 6, Tina Cook provides the foundation for the second section of this book in her examination of the concept of partnership itself. She reiterates the importance of developing a relational pedagogy, as advocated by Shortt in Chapter 4, for what she terms a 'generative, participatory partnership approach'.

Cook begins by arguing that we must disrupt the 'illusory consensus' (Edelman, 1964) that has developed around the term 'partnership', through analysing the nature and purpose of the relationships underpinning partnership work. She helpfully exemplifies the negative consequences of failing to do so. This illustrates the urgency of nurturing a culture within teacher education which encourages all involved to ask questions, such as why are we doing this? What is the purpose? In a managerialist world of targets, avoidance of ultimate questions is all too common. Educators must resist the temptation to overlook challenging questions about purpose through focusing on organisational and practical aspects of curriculum and pedagogy. For instance, teacher educators can easily become consumed by the complex logistics required to establish partnership and facilitate placements. This evokes Boyer's plea for higher education itself to focus on purpose and process rather than action: 'what is needed is not just more programs, but a larger purpose, a larger sense of mission, a larger clarity of direction' (1996, A48). It is only through deliberation around the purpose and process of teacher education that we can guarantee congruence between means and ends.

Most importantly, Cook argues that 'challenge' is the pivotal characteristic of such effective partnership. Drawing upon examples from her own research and experience as a teacher, she identifies mutual critique within partnership as the catalyst for improved practice. This chapter demonstrates the difficult nature of this work, which requires partners to question their own perspective and practice in the light of others. It demands a readiness to 'let go' of their ideas about working practices and what are often deeply ingrained beliefs about what is good practice. These ideas are revisited in the concluding chapter of this book, in Keith Crawford's explication of the 'questioning, critical and pro-active' nature of genuine partnership.

The marketisation and commodification of education and notion of the student as consumer bring a range of challenges to teacher education as outlined in this book. In relation to the theme of 'partnership', the current preoccupation with student experience, student voice and student satisfaction in policy and practice can be seen to be antithetical to reciprocal partnerships that find a space for challenge, conflict and mutual critique as advocated by Dr Cook. Indeed, 'the paradox of real learning is that you don't get what you 'want' – and you certainly can't buy it' (Collini, 2011, p.12). Against this background, Morgan White sets out to challenge current notions of student partnership. Drawing upon the work of Hannah Arendt, he argues that it is in fact through attempts to assert the authority of students as partners with academics that students are ultimately denied the opportunity to acquire authority with respect to their own study. He concludes that student partnership, as it is presently understood, undermines the transfer of authority from the good teacher to the good student and robs higher education of its intrinsic value, resulting in what he describes as a 'university legitimation crisis'.

Geoff Baker, in Chapter 8, illustrates a successful model of collaborative professional development whereby teachers lead their own professional development in communities of practice. He provides evidence that when professionals are empowered in their own development and given space to share ideas and work collaboratively, authentic change in practice is likely to occur. While recognising the intensive nature of this work and the anxiety it can cause participants, Baker concludes that it is through such communities that teachers can transform practice and reflect upon what it means to be a professional. This theme echoes Pilkington's discussion in Chapter 5, which stresses the need for organisational structures to properly support and accommodate professional learning.

The importance and complexity of partnership work for education professionals at the start of the 21st century is nowhere more evident than in multi-agency work. In Chapter 9, Elizabeth Parr considers the social networks and relationships between schools and multiple agencies that ensure positive outcomes for the most disadvantaged families they serve. Drawing upon activity theory (Engestrom, 1987), she analyses how a school works in partnership with a Sure Start centre in an area of significant deprivation in England. Her work highlights the conflicting interests, aims and perspectives that these partners must navigate in multi-agency work. Echoing Cook's assertion that effective partnerships form the basis for disruption, she concludes that education professionals from both the school and Sure Start centre use their relationships with other agencies to challenge and develop their practices. Moreover, she argues that effective multi-agency work demands enhanced pre- and in-service professional development to support teachers in building an environment, language and ethos able to adapt to the practices of other agencies with differing professional and community agendas.

Chapter 10 revisits the ethical dimensions of learning to teach, elaborating further upon the responsibilities of teachers and teacher educators to look beyond the classroom and campus, in this instance to engage with issues of social justice in the global community. Philip Bamber and Andrea Bullivant illustrate how a

8 *Philip M. Bamber and Jane C. Moore*

collaborative process, involving teacher educators, a local Development Education Centre, schools and third-sector organisations, transformed student teacher perspectives on the broader purposes of education. Evidence is provided here that professional resilience is developed and sustained through nurturing a sense of vocation. If learning about global issues in this way is a significant factor in retaining teachers, this chapter provides a compelling incentive to incorporate global education for global social justice within teacher education, especially when the number of entrants to the profession in the UK is falling and those leaving is at an all-time high (Morrison, 2015).

As the Minister of State for Schools in England advocates accelerating the shift towards 'knowledge-based teaching' (Gibb, 2015, p.18), Bamber and Bullivant follow the recent work of the Jubilee Centre for Character and Virtues (see, for example, Arthur et al., 2015), and Sullivan, Shortt, Moore, Baker and Anderson in this publication, to argue instead for a renewed focus within ITE upon teacher formation and development of moral agency. Chapter 10 highlights the importance of whom the educator is becoming as a person, including their values, virtues and associated dispositions, and identifies collaboration and partnership as being critical to achieving these goals. The multi-agency development of an inventory measuring attitudes towards global learning also demonstrates that it remains possible to find spaces for innovative research within university-led teacher education in England.

A case study from Scotland concludes this section, outlining the pivotal role teacher education in a strategy to embed Learning for Sustainability across the education system. Here, the importance of partnership and collaboration to teacher education that promotes equity and sustainability is exemplified at the level of national policy.

Practice

This final section focuses upon practice in teacher education as it relates to the key areas of mathematics, literacy, special educational needs, behaviour management, science and technology. Addressing pressing challenges in their field, experts in these areas offer practical and relevant proposals for sustainable solutions which they argue must inform teacher education and other related spheres of education.

Mary Stevenson's starting point in Chapter 11 is the shortage in the supply of appropriately trained mathematics teachers, an issue for numerous countries around the world. She examines the effect of a major policy initiative in England involving the introduction and embedding of government-funded pre-ITE subject knowledge enhancement courses (SKEs), with a focus upon mathematics. Significantly, her research exposes deficits in the traditional degree route to pre-service teacher education. Furthermore, it argues that successful SKE programmes should serve to redefine our understandings of the nature of professional knowledge in relation to subject knowledge. Highlighting the importance of developing a 'profound understanding of fundamental mathematics' amongst

Introduction   9

future mathematics teachers, she outlines implications not only for the mathematics education community but also providers of undergraduate mathematics.

In the context of literacy and special educational needs provision, Owen Barden explores what he describes as the 'profoundly political and emotive' issue of dyslexia. He problematises the idea of identifying some learners as dyslexic, challenging the notion of using the homogenising label within a heterogeneous population. He argues that the models of literacy on which our conception of dyslexia rests are outdated because they neglect or dismiss many informal and emerging literacy practices, many of which have powerful implications for students' learning and agency. He concludes by recommending that professionals take into account new understandings of what counts as literacy in designing inclusive pedagogies and learning futures.

Babs Anderson brings into view an area of challenge that affects the well-being of too many children in school: bullying. She investigates the lack of awareness of the different forms of bullying amongst educators and the concomitant training required for them to feel secure in their ability to recognise this, to take active steps in preventing it and to deal with incidents, when they arise. The case studies she provides from within a primary school illustrate the proactive and reactive strategies that may usefully inform other levels of education (including pre-school and secondary) and diverse institutions and workplaces such as prisons. As a point of departure, Anderson follows others in this publication in warning against teacher education that reifies the development of cognitive aspects of the child rather than the promotion of social understanding. In particular, she highlights the difficulties of enhancing student teachers' understanding of the holistic well-being of the child, both cognitive and affective, when their own performance is measured against the competency based teaching standards, as is the case for all four nations of the United Kingdom and an increasing number of countries around the world.

The challenges of dealing with bullying, as explored in Chapter 13, are being amplified and intensified through the extensive use of social media and other mobile technology amongst young people. In the chapter that follows, Susan Rodrigues draws attention to other dangers of failing to recognise the 'silent revolution' of digital transformation: the technological developments that have triggered significant shifts in our students' ways of being and knowing. In contrast to the everyday experiences of our students, she argues that in formal educational settings how they come to know and be is stagnating. Drawing upon examples from Australia and the United States of America in the field of science education, Rodrigues outlines how we can make better use of technology by exploiting our students' cultural capital. It is argued that this ensures we provide relevant, authentic and purposeful experiences that support learner agency.

The final chapter in this section moves on from these discrete key areas of practice to broader considerations of how teacher educators work with school colleagues and other professionals across a range of curriculum areas and priorities. Jane Moore, Michelle Pearson and Sue Cronin present a discussion of the Hope Challenge, which is the name given to a new model of working with partners in

10 *Philip M. Bamber and Jane C. Moore*

the area of school improvement. Amongst the other seismic changes that have occurred in the English education system in recent years, the move to a self-improving system is one that has uprooted and destabilised existing mechanisms for support. Alongside the questions this raises about the capacity of schools to drive their own improvement strategies, and how school-to-school support might be accessed in a sector that is increasingly fragmented, there is also cause for unease in a school system that is driven by centrally determined, data-evidenced measures. The Hope Challenge offers some answers, both in terms of providing a framework for locally and collaboratively designed intervention projects (which are required to demonstrate effectiveness against all appropriate criteria), and in mobilising coordinated support from across university, HMI and local authorities in an unprecedented model of collaboration. The Hope Challenge offers a response to critics who question the continued relevance of university providers in teacher education, by demonstrating that, in fact, university teacher educators are ideally situated to bring others together, working as they do at 'a dynamic nexus of professional interaction, with huge opportunities for both knowledge and relationship brokering'.

Conclusion

These chapters illustrate how teacher education is subject to often dramatic and rapid change. They are an important and timely contribution to an international debate (see for example Arbaugh et al., 2015) about the future of the profession. This book purposefully explores and identifies sustainable, robust and informed responses to the challenges presented by the current turbulence in the sector. It is in no way a defence of the status quo. It demonstrates an openness to innovative ideas and approaches, founded upon a sense of both pluralism and fallibilism. Although Cook highlights the difficulties of letting go of long-held beliefs, the individual contributions described here illustrate the readiness of the teacher education community to be 'open reflectively to the new and loyal reflectively to the known' (Hansen, 2011, p.36). This demands a determination to envision possible and preferable futures of which this book is part.

References

Appleby, Y. and Pilkington, R. (2014). *Developing Critical Professional Practice in Education*. Leicester: NIACE.

Arbaugh, F., Ball, D., Grossman, P., Heller, D. and Monk, D. (2015). Deans' corner: views on the state of teacher education in 2015. *Journal of Teacher Education*, 66(5), 435–445.

Arthur, J., Kristjansson, K., Cooke, S., Brown, E. and Carr, D. (2015). *The Good Teacher: Understanding Virtues in Practice Research Report*. Birmingham: The Jubilee Centre for Character and Virtues, University of Birmingham.

Beauchamp, G., Clarke, L., Hulme, M. and Murray, J. (2015). Teacher education in the United Kingdom post devolution: convergences and divergences. *Oxford Review of Education*, 41(2), 154–170.

Boyer, E. (1996). The scholarship of engagement. *Journal of Public Service and Outreach*, 1(1), 11– 21.

British Educational Research Association (2014). *Research and the Teaching Profession: Building a Self-Improving Education System*. London: BERA. Available from: www.bera.ac.uk/wp-content/uploads/2013/12/BERA-RSA-Research-Teaching-Profession-FULL-REPORT-for-web.pdf?noredirect=1 (accessed 10 January 2016).

Collini, S. (2011). From Robbins to McKinsey. *London Review of Books*, 33(16), 9–14.

Edelman, M. (1964). *The Symbolic Use of Politics*. Urbana: University of Illinois Press.

Ellis, V. and McNicholl, J. (2015). *Transforming Teacher Education: Reconfiguring the Academic Work*. London and New York: Bloomsbury.

Engestrom, Y. (1987). *Learning by Expanding: An Activity-Theoretical Approach to Developmental Research*. Helsinki: Orienta-Konsultit.

Gibb, N. (2015). How E. D. Hirsch came to shape UK government policy. In: J. Simons and N. Porter (eds), *Knowledge and the Curriculum: A Collection of Essays to Accompany E.D. Hirsh's Lecture at Policy Exchange*, pp.12–20. London: Policy Exchange. Available from: http://policyexchange.org.uk/images/publications/knowledge%20and%20the%20curriculum.pdf (accessed 10 January 2016).

Gove, M. (2013). *Speech to Teachers and Headteachers at the National College for Teaching and Leadership*, 25 April. Available from: www.gov.uk/government/speeches/michael-gove-speech-to-teachers-and-headteachers-at-the-national-college-for-teaching-and-leadership (accessed 14 January 2016).

Hansen, D. (2011). *The Teacher and the World: A Study of Cosmopolitanism as Education*. London and New York: Routledge.

Hargreaves, A. and Fullan, M. (2012). *Professional Capital: Transforming Teaching in Every School*. London: Routledge.

Morrison, N. (2015). Number of teachers quitting the classroom reaches 10-year high. *TES*, 30 January. Available from: https://news.tes.co.uk/b/news/2015/01/29/number-of-teachers-quitting-the-classroom-reaches-10-year-high.aspx (accessed 15 October 2015).

Part I
Professionalism

1 Today's university challenge
Maintaining and strengthening professional jurisdiction for the preparation of teachers

Sue Cronin

Introduction: how have we ended up here?

Teacher educators in England are currently caught up in what James Noble Rogers called the 'perfect storm' which surrounds the future direction and position of university education departments' involvement in teacher education in England (Maddern, 2012). (It is important to emphasise the English context as the situation is different for university teacher educators in the rest of the UK.) England has become increasingly a significant outlier (Beauchamp et al., 2015), partly as a predictable outcome of political devolution facilitating greater divergence in education policy across the UK nations, but largely as a result of the political desire of the recent Coalition government to frame teacher education as craft-based training). The underlying conditions for the perfect storm in English teacher education are determined by this significant political and ideological push towards a privileging of practice in the form of a school-led model of teacher training combined with new allocation methodologies linked, in turn, to a new Ofsted inspection framework with associated increased demands (2015). The result is a greater uncertainty as to the viability of existing PGCE and mainstream provision offered by universities. As Ellis et al. in their research into the Work of Teacher Educators (WoTE) comment, 'the general direction of travel is clear: higher education's role in teacher education is under threat and, if not entirely extinguished, is in the process of minimalisation' (2013, p.278).

As an experienced teacher educator and manager in an English university, I am interested in the implications and consequences, both physical and philosophical, of this deliberate and unduly hasty repositioning of Initial Teacher Education (ITE) into a school-based setting. Why is it that our professional jurisdiction is singled out, over all other professions, for such attack? Although the positioning of teacher education has certainly been the constant subject of political debate and desire for reform over the last thirty years, the pace and drive of the current repositioning and the challenge to our professional authority are unprecedented.

The reality of this recent and radical repositioning forces a series of linked questions which university teacher educators must deliberate and address. Firstly, who has, and who should have, the right and professional jurisdiction to educate and work with beginning teachers – to what extent should it be university teacher

16 *Sue Cronin*

educators? Secondly, how much of the power to decide what, where and how best to educate beginning teachers should rest within the profession and how much with politicians? Lastly, does the teaching profession include the teacher educators? This final question raises a series of related questions about the nature of university teacher educators as boundary spanners. By nature working at the interface between school and university, are they accepted as part of the teaching profession or seen as part of a wider university academia?

The features of a teacher educator

These questions may indicate a slight degree of schizophrenia but reflect the common experience of many university teacher educators, who can feel uncertain where they are positioned and may to some extent feel undervalued by both university and school colleagues. As Reynolds et al. (2013, p.307) comment:

> [The teacher educators' role], with its multiple facets of practitioner inter-action, has the potential to collide with universities' traditional role of research and research exposition, which tends to ignore teaching and service, and also the school's role as the advocate of practice, which tends to ignore research.

Murray and Male (2005) collected data from a range of new teacher educators across their first years in universities and discovered that most struggled to establish their new professional identities and align what Southworth (1995) refers to as the 'situational self', formed through interactions with others, and the 'substantial self' which consists of a core of self-defining beliefs resistant to change. Indeed, Murray and Male concluded that the development of a new professional identity as a teacher educator often took at least three years. They noted that the move from what they defined as 'first-order' to 'second-order' practitioners caused the teacher educators to move from experts to novices as they shifted from the first-order setting of the school to the second-order setting of the university. Most teacher educators came with considerable expertise and a successful career in school behind them, but they entered the world of the university with little research experience and knowledge of how to work with adult learners or within the structures of the university. Their task was to come 'up to speed' quickly and develop pedagogies for working with adult beginning teachers whilst simultane-ously becoming research active. Both of these new aspects of the role of teacher educator bring challenges and require significant adaptations from any previous roles held in school. Thus, the role of the university teacher educator is an interesting one with inbuilt tensions resulting from this shift to second-order activity. As Taylor (1983, p.41) summarises:

> Teacher education is of its very nature Janus-faced. In the one direction it faces classroom and school, with their demands for relevance, practicality, competence, techniques. In the other it faces the university and the world of research, with their stress on scholarship, theoretical fruitfulness and disciplinary rigour.

It is interesting to speculate that perhaps this requirement to face in both directions and develop the aptitudes needed to successfully take on the mantle of boundary spanner may cause a degree of insecurity in teacher educators. Perhaps this is part of the reason why university teacher educators have not always been as robust as they could have been in their defence of why they should maintain a professional jurisdiction and the authority to play an intrinsic role in the education of future teachers.

The features of the professional

Pam Grossman (2008) has explored this threat to teacher educators in an interesting and challenging article entitled 'Responding to our critics: from crisis to opportunity in research on teacher education'. It is hard hitting in its findings, which are a clarion call to the profession:

> University-based teacher educators, and the profession of education more broadly, are facing a sharp attack on their ability and their right to control the preparation of teachers. . . . University-based teacher educators are dangerously close to losing their responsibility for overseeing the preparation of new teachers.
>
> (Grossman, 2008, p.10)

Grossman (2008) acknowledges that the challenges are not new but argues that what is new is the intensity of the challenge to our professional jurisdiction during the past two decades. Her article was written in 2008 and was based on her experiences in the field in the United States, but they are equally applicable and indeed more acutely relevant to the English context, where the pace of change and challenge since 2008 have exponentially intensified. Her analysis of professional jurisdiction is based on the work of Andrew Abbott (1988), who identified certain areas of effectiveness which a profession must demonstrate in order to retain its authority to train the next generation. There are three aspects Abbott identifies as key for professions, which he views as dynamic, interacting systems. Firstly is the requirement of effectiveness in the field, secondly the quality of the academic knowledge produced that supports the profession, and thirdly the responsibility for induction of newcomers to the profession. For the university teacher educator, this can be translated into a further set of key questions which must be attended to.

Key questions for the university teacher educator

A fundamental question for university teacher educators to address concerns the difference we make in preparing beginning professionals. What is the additionality of the university experience? What added value do we offer? If students are secure in their subject knowledge and enthusiastic to learn to teach, is this not sufficient? It is in the eyes of the former Secretary of State for Education Michael Gove and his schools' minister Nick Gibb, still in post in 2016. Nick Gibb was quoted in

18 *Sue Cronin*

The Guardian within three days of taking up his post in 2010 as saying: 'I would rather have a physics graduate from Oxbridge without a PGCE teaching in a school than a physics graduate from one of the rubbish universities with a PGCE' (Gibb, cited in Furlong, 2013). It is difficult to be certain who the insult is aimed at – is it the rubbish university degree or the subsequent PGCE from a rubbish university? – but on both fronts it is insulting and should be vigorously rebutted.

With the emergence of the School Direct route, universities have been involved in many conversations with schools that reflect a new power dynamic created and encouraged by the government. The discourse is that of the marketplace, schools are the customers and universities competing service providers. There is an increased requirement for universities to justify what they do that schools can't do – and can't do better. Even where schools recognise the advantage of the Masters' credits associated with a PGCE provided by the university, many appear to want this delivered in a minimalist way – in how few days can it be covered? Are written assignments a necessary requirement? The university accreditation of a PGCE is seen in terms of currency rather than perhaps its true value. Some of this is inevitable as schools are also forced into a business model and encouraged by the government to shop around for their provider. Value for money, with an emphasis on reducing costs, is the critical factor in decision-making for many teaching schools, who are tasked over time to become more sustainable with decreasing direct government funding. This creates a darker side for any university director involved with School Direct, where conversations can be focused on costs rather than on the value of the work. Fortunately, this is not the case with all schools; many teachers and school leaders do see the value in the contribution and greater involvement of a university working in partnership. But it still begs the question of where teacher educators have gone wrong as we cannot escape the reality that many schools do feel confident that they are better placed to deliver the professional training for the next generation of teachers. They do not appear to appreciate the significance of what universities can offer in educating beginning professionals and the potential of their work on the profession as a whole.

However, perhaps more disturbingly, there are some teachers and schools in the School Direct model who have taken on the new role of teacher educator not because of their confidence or belief that they can do the training better but rather because of the overt political pressures. Some school leaders have admitted that a school-dominated training route is not necessarily the best route, and certainly not in its early state of inception as School Direct, but have simply succumbed to the political directives and the DfE drive to develop a school-led model of initial teacher training. The pressures on teaching schools with the introduction of School Direct have been considerable, with both the NCTL and DfE representatives initially indicating to schools that there would be no university-based routes in a few years – only School Direct. This is coupled with a requirement for any school with teaching school status to focus on leading 'the development of school-led initial teacher training through School Direct or by gaining accreditation as an Initial Teacher Training provider' (and note it is ITT Initial Teacher Training rather than ITE Initial Teacher Education); this is the first of the six core areas of responsibility for teaching schools (National College for Teaching and Leadership, 2014).

The political thrust for school-led initial teacher training cannot be viewed as anything other than a direct challenge to the authority and expertise of university-based routes and one which teacher educators must address by articulating more clearly what additionality they bring in developing critical, resilient professionals. As university teacher educators, we need to argue the importance of engendering in our future teachers an ability to synthesise, critique and contest knowledge. The critical reflective spaces a university provide for a deeper engagement with big ideas, away from the busyness of the classroom and away from the rich but potentially narrow context of a particular school, are profoundly significant. The physical and psychological distancing from the site of practice is important in allowing beginning teachers to consider and reflect in a more objective way on what they are seeing and doing in schools. One of the concerns with School Direct must be its potential balkanisation of teacher education; it is marketed by the DfE as offering schools localised solutions for their workforce needs, and this, indeed, could be a positive. A school can select and train the person they feel will understand the needs of their community and 'fit in' with the ethos of the particular school. However, the negative side is an increasingly incestuous, potentially reductive model of training in which the vast majority of the programme is spent in one school, learning from trainers who work within the same school. Undoubtedly, some schools will see this as an advantage. Some are pleased that the trainees know and can replicate the 'xxxx' way (insert the name of many lead schools here), but this really does reflect an emphasis on training rather than educating. One School Direct trainer-teacher, based in a lead school, confided that she had some concerns she was training her student in how to be a 'mini-me': a replica version of herself. She had only ever taught in her school and her trainee was also a former pupil of the school; the trainee was doing very well and gaining good grades so the measurable outcomes were all good. But she wondered how this trainee would be prepared for the long term in their career as it was unlikely there would be a job in the school due to changing staffing requirements. This former pupil is not unusual; many School Direct schools have attracted ex-pupils and a far greater number of local applicants than the traditional university PGCE. Within a core PGCE, there may also be a large number of local students, but this is usually part of a healthy mix of students from further afield. This variety of backgrounds and prior schooling experiences adds to the richness that the students bring to the course; it ensures a breadth of perspectives that can be mined by the university tutor. There is a worry that some of this richness is in danger of being lost in this new model where schools become the sole centre of training, although this is not always the case, with many lead schools involving university-based training in their models.

Additional questions university educators must answer are: how relevant is the academic knowledge we generate? How does this knowledge support and

20 *Sue Cronin*

contribute to developments that have a positive impact on schools and pupils? Abbott (1988), cited by Grossman (2008), argued that the 'ability of a profession to sustain its jurisdiction lies partly in the power and prestige of its academic knowledge' (pp.53–54).

At present, there is insufficient academic knowledge about teacher education and for teacher education that can be used to defend against the critics. Educational research is criticised for its limitations from within and beyond the university sector. David Hargreaves argued as long ago as 1996 that educational research failed to provide a sound evidence base for teaching. It was not generating a cumulative body of knowledge and failed to resolve the complex problems faced by teachers in their classrooms. Interestingly, part of his solution was to adopt a more scientific approach, citing the example of evidence-based medicine. This argument has recently been revisited by Ben Goldacre (2013), commissioned by Michael Gove to look at how the use of evidence could be used to improve teaching. Goldacre has a strong belief in the power of random controlled trials to provide the solution to a more independent, evidence-based profession, resulting in a greater degree of freedom from central state control.

> Evidence based practice isn't about telling teachers what to do: in fact, quite the opposite. This is about empowering teachers, and setting a profession free from governments, ministers and civil servants who are often overly keen on sending out edicts, insisting that their new idea is the best in town. Nobody in government would tell a doctor what to prescribe, but we all expect doctors to be able to make informed decisions about which treatment is best, using the best currently available evidence. I think teachers could one day be in the same position.
>
> (Goldacre, 2013, p.7)

This is encouraging, suggesting a recognition of the need for teachers' professional jurisdiction over partisan politicians and, through the improved status of research-informed practice, implicitly a reinforcement of teacher educators' professional jurisdiction. Certainly recent Ofsted inspections also seem to be mentioning research, particularly in terms of outstanding providers of ITT. Michael Gove, as Secretary of State for Education, himself acknowledged the importance of research and evidence-informed teaching in his speech to head teachers:

> Indeed, I want to see more data generated by the profession to show what works, clearer information about teaching techniques that get results, more rigorous, scientifically-robust research about pedagogies which succeed and proper independent evaluations of interventions which have run their course. We need more evidence-based policy making, and for that to work we need more evidence.
>
> (Gove, 2010)

There are critics of the ethics of randomised control trials and Goldacre's assumption that it is the gold standard for research, and, indeed, Goldacre himself does include a small concession to some of the limitations of the use of it in an educational context. However, the foregrounding of evidence-based research and the emphasis on the need for research skills to be part of teacher training and CPD are something university teacher educators recognise and support. A recent joint BERA-RSA inquiry into Research and Teacher Education (2014) noted the importance of moving towards research and evidence-rich schools as opposed to simply data-rich schools. The findings indicate that creating research-literate teachers and schools can enable and maximise the capacity for system-wide self-evaluation and self-improvement. This is an area in which universities should naturally have some authority and additionality to offer. However, it is questionable if the then Secretary for State's vision for evidence-based research by the profession included university teacher educators; it is more likely he envisioned this to be a move away from university research to school-based teacher research. If this is the case, it again represents a lack of understanding of the nature of educational research and, in particular, how teacher educators' work ensures a weave of relevant research with practice. University teacher educators do not spend time in mystical ivory towers. By their very nature, they move fluidly between schools and university, acutely aware of the pressures and pragmatism needed in school settings but bringing a critical perspective of an informed outsider to existing and emerging practices.

Viv Ellis et al. (2013) carried out a project which followed a group of thirteen Higher Education teacher educators over the course of a year. The aim of their research was to gain a greater understanding of the academic work of the teacher educator in relation to their lived experiences. Their findings may explain why there is not already a substantive body of knowledge and research around teacher education. Ellis et al. (2013) found that all of those who participated were occupied largely with work which could be classified as 'relationship maintenance', involving partnership work with schools and pastoral work with students and in some cases with mentors. They concluded this 'relationship maintenance' was, in fact, the defining characteristic of these teacher educators rather than academic work typical of other university colleagues. Experienced teacher educators have noticed that maintenance work had intensified in recent years, with a greater burden of responsibility to be proactive in ensuring the quality of the partnerships and to provide a buffer between weaker students and the progressively regulated and managerialist cultures of some schools. The changing environment resonates for many university teacher educators as they face two increasingly pressured systems. The high stakes performativity culture within the school system is increasingly placing additional demands on teacher educators in terms of time and energy to shore up already stretched school mentors. These kinds of pressures are not unique to teacher educators; increasingly, all university lecturers have to balance the pressures of maintaining high student approval ratings against time needed to produce high-quality research. However, it may be argued this pressure is more acute for teacher educators as not only are student ratings a key trigger for an Ofsted inspection but schools will simply stop working with them if they do not look after them. These competing pressures are brought into sharp relief through

22   Sue Cronin

the School Direct model, which in theory allows schools to swap and change their partner provider annually. Ensuring this is not the case requires the establishment of a partnership built on a degree of trust and loyalty, which inevitably requires greater resourcing, time and energy. All of this work is critical work for university tutors who must support their school colleagues and students, but this is often at the expense of their own research and scholarly activity.

Teacher educators are between a rock and a hard place in terms of the work they prioritise. Ellis et al. (2013), however, conclude that this cannot continue to be the case; if they are to survive, university educators must reconceptualise their roles and their work. If they do not, they are in danger of becoming the new proletariat of the neoliberal marketplace where universities now find themselves situated. As Ellis et al. argue, lecturers are now forced to become 'capitalist entrepreneurs' and those who survive and thrive will be those who produce work of value and academic capital. Nothing else will be valued in the new 'political economy of Higher Education' (Ellis et al. 2013, p.268). This is a significant challenge for university teacher educators who wish to contribute to the research profile of a university. The introduction by the Conservative government of a Teaching Excellence Framework (TEF) (Department for Business, Innovation and Skills; Johnson, 2015) may bring a shift in the hierarchy in academic work from research to teaching which may favour more the expertise of teacher educators, but it is far too early in its political inception for teacher educators to have any degree of certainty about the likelihood of this as an outcome. Any benefit to the status of the academic work of the university educator may not be a directly intended outcome, but raising the status of excellence in teaching will surely offer opportunities for teacher educators to share their expertise and pedagogic knowledge.

A significant threat to professional jurisdiction comes from politicians and policy makers. Early indications of the recent Coalition government's challenge to the university's authority were articulated in the 2010 White Paper *The Importance of Teaching* (DfE, 2010). There is no indication of a change in direction under the subsequent Conservative government elected in 2015, and the White Paper remains the articulation of the ideological principle of a self-improving, school-led system. The latest guide to recruitment controls for PGCE routes states that 'Ministers are committed to the continued growth of school-led ITT provision' (NCTL, 2015, p.4). The White Paper states under the heading: 'We will reform Initial Teacher Training so that it focuses on what is really important':

> We will provide more opportunities for a larger proportion of trainees to learn on the job by improving and expanding the best of the current school-based routes into teaching – school-centred initial teaching training and the graduate teacher programme.
>
> (DfE, 2010, 2.21)

School Direct was initially, when first mooted by Michael Gove in 2010 as a new route, a small player in the field, but it quickly became a Coalition government priority for it to be the main route for teacher training. In a speech to schools at the National College for Teaching and Leadership Head Teachers' Conference in April 2013, Michael Gove set out the Coalition government's aim, which signalled the changes to come:

In total, last year, the first 100 teaching school alliances delivered over 10,000 ITT placements – and well over a third of all School Direct places are on track to be delivered by teaching school alliances next year. Our goal is for half of all teacher training places to be led by schools by 2015 – and we will welcome your help in making that happen.

(Gove, 2013)

Realisation of this goal of 'on the job' school-based routes is now becoming clear and centred around the School Direct model unveiled in 2012. Under the new Conservative government, the school-led system remains the overriding priority as the new recruitment information for 2016–2017 indicates: 59 per cent of numbers are allocated to school-led routes and only 41 per cent to traditional HEI routes.

The accompanying underlying business ontology of teacher training is writ large and articulated in early Coalition government speeches such as the keynote talk given by the new Chief Executive of the National Centre for Teaching and Leadership, Charlie Taylor, to head teachers at the North of England Education Conference.

School Direct is the new way of training teachers which puts schools, the employers, the customers, at the heart of the process. With School Direct, schools can bid directly for training places. Schools select the provider of teacher training they want to work with whether it is a university or a school based SCITT. They agree the content and focus of the course depending on their needs and they can negotiate directly with the provider on how the money for training should be divided. Most importantly they can choose and recruit the candidate they want – the candidate their school needs.

(Taylor, 2013)

The emotive use of language 'at the heart of the process' is a rhetoric designed to appeal to head teachers and subtly implying that they do not have the opportunities and voice to be at the centre of ITE at present. This would be refuted by many universities and, indeed, many head teachers, who would feel already involved in a strong university-school partnership. The idea of choice is also beguiling for schools; who would not wish to be able to get the right person for the job? Again, it is interesting to consider just how much choice is possible and how this is sustainable over a longer period of time. Anecdotally, schools are not experiencing the level of choice in terms of applicants expected. The implications of such a major shift in numbers and the rebalancing of time, space and funding from universities in favour of schools remain potentially severe (McNamara and Murray 2013).

24 *Sue Cronin*

The ability of universities to plan for the long term has been reduced from what was already a relatively precarious state, with changing allocations year-on-year.

Since the inception of School Direct and a school-led system for training, there have been two changes to the allocation and recruitment methodology employed by the government. The latest pilot for the 2016–2017 cohort is based on a no-limit approach to recruitment for HEI and School Direct until overall national targets are reached, but separate targets are applied to the HEI routes and to School Direct. A minimum target is applied to School Direct lead schools, and HEIs will not be allowed to take up any shortfall in this if schools fail to recruit. This potentially may lead to a shortage in recruitment and a further level of destabilisation for the sector as the country's supply needs become increasingly dependent on large numbers of potentially short-term and small-scale School Direct and school-based initial teacher training (SCITT) partnerships.

Wider repercussions for the closure of university education departments in terms of the professional knowledge and research generated and their role in contributing to future improvements within the teaching profession seem not to be acknowledged or understood. Ian Mentor (2013a) noted the vulnerability of education departments as many are reliant on the funding brought in by teacher education. Mentor, in his role as Vice President of BERA, stated that universities had now moved beyond an interesting time for teacher education into a critical time. The previous Coalition government's obsession with reducing universities' contribution to teacher education is not only a threat to initial teacher education departments but the resultant knock-on effect causes a wider threat to education departments as a whole. As John Furlong notes, the implications for the future of research-led universities in professional education could be 'dramatically changed and dramatically weakened' (Furlong, 2013). His pessimistic predication is already becoming a reality; as part of evidence to a select committee in November 2015, UCET noted that three universities have pulled out of teacher education, shifting resources to more stable and reliable funding streams (UCET, 2015, p.1). For institutions where initial teacher education is a core element of overall provision, there is an increasing vulnerability.

Is it hard not to speculate if part of this concerted push towards school-based initial teacher education is linked to a belief that it is easier to influence and manage school teachers than university academics – is this part of the rationale for removing the site of learning and transformation from the university to the more compliant school sector? This would be an over-simplistic and false binary as a traditional university-based PGCE is itself located for two-thirds of the time in school and that site of learning is a key and influential component. All universities work in partnership with schools, and they play an important and increasingly strategic role in the planning and delivery of programmes. It was slightly ironic that Michael Gove as Secretary of State for Education felt threatened by the influence of what he terms 'The Blob':

> But who is responsible for this failure? Who are the guilty men and women who have deprived a generation of the knowledge they need? Who are the

modern Enemies Of Promise? Well, helpfully, 100 of them put their name to a letter to The Independent newspaper this week. They are all academics who have helped run the university departments of education responsible for developing curricula and teacher training courses.

(Gove, 2013)

Certainly many such academics may argue that they feel their effect is far less influential, as Allen (2009) articulated in her paper based on a research project investigating 'How beginning teachers re-orient their practice in the transition from the university to the workplace'.

[P]rospective teachers during pre-service training value both the theory that they learn on campus and the practice that they observe in schools. However, once they become practitioners, they privilege the latter. Upon entry to the workplace, graduates come to associate good practice with that of the veteran teacher, whose practice and cache of resources they seek to emulate.

(Allen, 2009, p.647)

Previously, Zeichner and Tabachnick (1981) had reported the 'washing out' of the impact of preservice teacher education, concluding that 'the only debate seems to be over which socialising agents or mechanisms play the greatest role in reversing the impact of [university]' (1981, p.7).

This concurs with Lortie (1975) who had previously proposed that the greatest influence on student teachers was not the university but the seven-year apprenticeship already undertaken as pupils in schools themselves. The students have already, Lortie argued, developed entrenched beliefs about good and bad teaching through an apprenticeship of observation resulting in a replication of practice with teachers teaching how they were taught. This metaphor of apprenticeship was qualified by Lortie (1975), who recognised it was not a traditional notion of an apprentice who is privy to the inner thoughts and reasoning of the master, learning at their side listening to their reflections in action. This, he recognised, was not the case with teaching, where these reflective thoughts are not shared and the apprenticeship is based on what is garnered through noticing and interpreting and extrapolating from these observations. Britzman (1986, p.443) has also argued that:

[student teachers] bring to their teacher education more than their desire to teach. They bring their implicit institutional biographies – the cumulative experience of school lives – which, in turn, inform their knowledge of the student's world, of school structure, and of curriculum.

This biography, Britzman would argue, is not taken sufficiently into account by teacher educators, who should do far more to explicitly address the cultural and social capital that their students possess at the start of their programmes. Britzman finishes on a positive note for teacher educators as she does not see the

26 *Sue Cronin*

effect of the prior life experiences as an inevitable permanent influence. She argues it is possible for the university teacher educator to play an important role by allowing space for a consideration of the beginning teachers' own histories and by providing the opportunity to theorise critically on what the impact of these experiences has been on their development as a professional. This is a strong argument for the important role of the university in the development of a transformative professional rather than a technician replicating the status quo.

The Coalition government embarked on an ideologically driven agenda to ensure schools are the lead partner in initial teacher education; it has been continued under the following Conservative government. The status quo, until this point, could be viewed as a largely reciprocal arrangement of partnership between many schools and universities working together but, in the main, with universities exercising the overriding decision-making in terms of selection and programme organisation and assessment procedures. It could be argued, however, that schools involved in ITE hold more influence practically as the site of professional learning and as already occupying the majority of the time given to the PGCE programme. It is somewhat ironic that many influential politicians have not recognised the strength of existing partnerships, giving possibly too much credence to the belief that the universities exert the most powerful influence on beginning teachers. The reality is that many university teacher educators (Reynolds et al., 2013) have to work hard to embed theoretical perspectives which are not in conflict with the school voice but provide a framework for reflection and contestation. This tension is one acknowledged by many in the field of teacher education (Zeichner, 2010). Many students may assert this to be an unhelpful tension between the ideas and theories suggested by the university and those propounded at the workplace. However, the tension is a necessary one, with the university environment offering alternative perspectives and challenging the potential for the status quo in terms of practice and replication. The knowledge for learning to teach should be contested and troublesome (Perkins, 1999). It is not a case of 'top tips' for how to survive; it must be a deeper engagement with difficult issues and the complexities of learning to teach.

Conclusion

The scene is set for a period of great uncertainty for university educators (Mentor, 2013b; Burgess, 2013; Furlong, 2013; Winch, 2013), but it is also an opportunity to reassess, re-evaluate and re-articulate the value and additionally offered by the university in the professional development of beginning teachers. The period of unprecedented disturbance may be an important and significant point in the history and future of university education departments. It is a call to arms; university educators need to galvanise into action and take a far more confident stance on why they should have professional jurisdiction in the field of initial teacher education. They should have a clearly articulated and shared understanding within their own university as well as externally as to the additionality and value they bring to the field. They need to reimagine the possibilities for the centrality of university involvement in the preparation of teachers. To do this, they need to have an understanding of what is of value to the field: what do those at the front edge of education, teachers and head teachers as well as those in positions of political influence, value and require? And what is it that, as university educators and public intellectuals (Giroux, 2012), we believe to be the essential knowledge, understanding and the associated pedagogies for initial teacher education? That is the university challenge.

References

Abbott, A. (1988). *A System of Professions*. Chicago: University of Chicago Press.

Allen, J. (2009). Valuing practice over theory: how beginning teachers re-orient their practice in the transition from the university to the workplace. *Teaching and Teacher Education*, 25(5), 647–654.

Beauchamp, G., Clarke, L., Hulme, M. and Murray, J. (2015). Teacher education in the United Kingdom post devolution: convergences and divergences. *Oxford Review of Education*, 41(2), 154–170.

BERA-RSA (2014). *Research and Teacher Education: Building the Capacity for a Self-improving Education System. Final Report*. London: British Educational Research Association.

Britzman, D. (1986). Cultural myths in the making of a teacher: biography and social structure in teacher education. *Harvard Educational Review*, 56(4), 442–457.

Burgess, H. (2013). *Challenge and Change in Teacher Research Intelligence Education*. London: British Educational Research Association.

Department for Education (DfE) (2010). *The Importance of Teaching: The Schools White Paper 2010*. London: HMSO.

Ellis, V., Glackin, M., Heighes, D., Norman, M., Nicol, S., Norris, K., Spencer, I. and McNicholl, J. (2013). A difficult realisation: the proletarianisation of higher education-based teacher educators. *Journal of Education for Teaching*, 39(3), 266–280.

Furlong, J. (2013). Globalisation, neoliberalism and the reform of teacher education in England. *The Education Forum*, 77(1), 28–50.

Giroux, H. (2012). The war against teachers as public intellectuals in dark times. *Truthout*, Op-Ed, 17 December. Available from: www.truth-out.org/opinion/item/13367-the-corporate-war-against-teachers-as-public-intellectuals-in-dark-times (accessed 21 March 2016).

Goldacre, B. (2013). *Building Evidence into Education*. Department for Education. Available from: www.gov.uk/government/news/building-evidence-into-education (accessed 21 March 2016).

Gove, M. (2010). *Speech to the National College Annual Conference, Birmingham*. DfE publication. Available from: www.gov.uk/government/speeches/michael-gove-to-the-national-college-annual-conference-birmingham (accessed 21 March 2016).

Gove, M. (2013). *Speech to Teachers and Headteachers at the National College for Teaching and Leadership*, 25 April. Available from: www.gov.uk/government/speeches/michael-gove-speech-to-teachers-and-headteachers-at-the-national-college-for-teaching-and-leadership (accessed 14 January 2016).

Grossman, P. (2008). Responding to our critics: from crisis to opportunity in research on teacher education. *Journal of Teacher Education*, 59(1), 10–23.

28 *Sue Cronin*

Hargreaves, D.H. (1996). *Teaching as a Research based Profession: Possibilities and Prospects*. Annual Lecture 1996 (London Teacher Training Agency). London, Teacher Training Agency.

Johnson, J. (2015). *Teaching at the Heart of the System*. Speech to Universities UK (UUK). Available from: www.gov.uk/government/speeches/teaching-at-the-heart-of-the-system (accessed 21 March 2016).

Lortie, D. (1975). *Schoolteacher: A Sociological Study*. Chicago: University of Chicago Press.

Maddern, K. (2012). Report issues warning over drop in teacher training applications. *TES*, 31 August. Available from: www.tes.com/article.aspx?storycode=6287758 (accessed 22 March 2016).

McNamara, O. and Murray, J. (2013). Research-informed teacher education for a new era? *Research Intelligence*, 121 (Summer), 22–23.

Mentor, I. (2013a). From interesting times to critical times? Teacher education and educational research in England. *Research in Teacher Education*, 3(1), 38–40.

Mentor, I. (2013b). What is going on? Critical times in teacher education and educational research. *Research Intelligence*. British Educational Research Association.

Murray, J. and Male, T. (2005). Becoming a teacher educator: evidence from the field. *Teaching and Teacher Education*, 21(2), 125–142.

NCTL (2014). *Teaching Schools: A Guide for Potential Applicants*. Available from: www.gov.uk/guidance/teaching-schools-a-guide-for-potential-applicants (accessed 20 March 2016).

NCTL (2015). *Postgraduate ITT Recruitment Controls. A Guide for the 2016 to 2017 Academic Year*. Available from: www.gov.uk/government/uploads/system/uploads/attachment_data/file/468099/ITT_recruitment_control_guidance_2016-17_v1.1.pdf (accessed 21 March 2016).

Ofsted (2015). *Initial Teacher Education Inspection Handbook*. Available from: www.gov.uk/government/uploads/system/uploads/attachment_data/file/459282/Initial_Teacher_Eduction_handbook_from_September_2015.pdf (accessed 22 March 2016).

Perkins, D. (1999). The many faces of constructivism. *Educational Leadership*, 57 (3).

Reynolds, R., Ferguson-Patrick, K. and McCormack, A. (2013). Dancing in the ditches: reflecting on the capacity of a university/school partnership to clarify the role of a teacher educator. *European Journal of Teacher Education*, 36(3), 307–319.

Southworth, G. (1995). *Looking into Primary Headship:A Research Based Interpretation*. London: Falmer Press.

Taylor, C. (2013). Keynote speech to the North of England Education Conference, NCTL Publication. Available from: www.gov.uk/government/speeches/charlie-taylors-keynote-speech-to-the-north-of-england-education-conference (accessed 21 March 2016).

Taylor, W. (1983). *Teacher Education: Achievements, Shortcomings and Perspectives*. Paper presented at The John Adams Memorial Lecture, The Institute of Education, London.

UCET (2015). *Evidence to the Education Select Committee: Supply of Teachers*. 30 November. Available from: www.ucet.ac.uk/7097 (accessed 21 March 2016).

Winch, C. (2013). What kind of occupation is teaching? *Research Intelligence Education*. British Educational Research Association.

Zeichner, K. (2010). Rethinking the connections between campus courses and field experiences in college- and university based teacher education. *Journal of Teacher Education*, 61, 61–89.

Zeichner, K. and Tabachnick, B. (1981). Are the effects of the university teacher education washed out by school experiences? *Journal of Teacher Education*, 32(3), 7–11.

2 Building professionals and elevating the profession?

The work of university-based initial teacher educators in Aotearoa New Zealand

David A.G. Berg, Alexandra C. Gunn, Mary F. Hill and Mavis Haigh

Introduction

In this chapter we ask how institutional constructions of university-based teacher educators in Aotearoa New Zealand may support the development of preservice teachers as emerging professionals, thus contributing to aspirational and elevated understandings of teaching as a profession. Currently the majority of New Zealand's primary and secondary initial teacher education (ITE) is situated in universities; however, this is not yet the case for early childhood education (ECE). In our discussion, we offer a short history of ITE in New Zealand, a brief analysis of how policy has shaped provision, a summary of the way teacher educators work is constructed from the Work of Teacher Educators–NZ research project (WoTE-NZ) and a discussion of the significance of our findings in regard to supporting the development of professional teachers and enhancing teaching as a profession.

We are a small grant-funded research team representing two major New Zealand universities. Prior to serving as university-based teacher educators we practised as teachers. Our shared experience comprises early childhood, primary and secondary teaching.

Zeichner (2006, p.326) has challenged US universities to 'take teacher education seriously as an institutional responsibility or do not do it'. We suggest in order to take ITE seriously, the leaders of New Zealand's universities must recognise that the work of teacher educators is often different from that of academic staff in other departments. Indeed, universities' abilities to provide ITE rests in part on the nature of teacher educators that are employed and those teacher educators' abilities to remain engaged with the teaching profession, while making a distinct contribution from that of school-based colleagues. Our research suggests that for some teacher educators, engagement with the profession is becoming increasingly difficult, while for others, opportunities to build upon practice knowledge by engaging in research and scholarship are limited. Furthermore, we argue that leaders of New Zealand universities would be wise to recognise that their dominance in ITE may be contested as it is elsewhere.

30   *David A. G. Berg* et al.

The ideologies that pose a 'very real and sustained threat to "traditional" "university-based" routes . . . [and the] deliberate undermining of richer conceptualisations of the teacher as informed and empowered professional' in England, highlighted in the introductory chapter of this volume by Moore and Bamber, are also evident in New Zealand. For example, our nation's new partnership schools (a form of charter school) are permitted to 'negotiate the number of registered teachers they employ' (Ministry of Education, 2015, para.9), perhaps implying that neither ITE nor professional registration are considered by government as necessary (within teacher-led early childhood education, teacher registration is not compulsory and only 50 per cent of that teacher workforce are currently required to be qualified). Given these circumstances and ideologies, it is increasingly important therefore that university-based teacher educators and their leaders offer a clear vision of teaching as a profession and teachers as professionals, and furthermore provide coherent arguments about why the important work of teacher education should be entrusted to them.

Our research has explored institutional constructions of university-based teacher educators and examined the work engaged in by people in these roles. As part of this study, our investigation into university recruitment practices produced multiple constructions of the university-based teacher educator role. We named these: professional expert, traditional academic and dually qualified. Having identified these constructions, we are able to ask how they serve the object of building the profession of teaching. In so doing, we acknowledge that the terms 'professional' and 'profession' are contested and lack consensus of usage (Evans, 2008). However, while we recognise this, we leave it to others to discuss and suffice to suggest that the major constructions of the teaching profession in New Zealand are evolving and evident in the work of its teaching unions, Education Council of Aotearoa New Zealand and Ministry of Education.

A brief history of initial teacher education in New Zealand

The story of ITE in New Zealand tells of an evolving and emerging profession and illustrates the influence of 'travelling reforms' (Seddon, 2014) and their application in a unique cultural historical context. Indeed, Ell and Grudnoff (2013, p.74) have argued that 'Despite its physical isolation, networks of influence (Granovetter, 1973) and a colonial past ensure that New Zealand is very much in the thrall of international discourses'. Here we outline the history of ITE in New Zealand. We believe that the evolution of teaching from humble beginnings to complex and aspirational notions of a profession are likely to resonate with international readers, and an understanding of this is necessary to make sense of ITE in the nation today.

Prior to 1875, the establishment and provision of schools was the responsibility of provincial governments in New Zealand, which, according to King (2003, p.233), 'had fulfilled (their charge) with varying degrees of conscientiousness'. At that time the majority of teachers in schools had immigrated to New Zealand from England and Scotland (Morton-Johnson and Morton, 1976) and the increasing population of home grown teachers were prepared for their role by serving apprenticeships as pupil-teachers in schools (Kean, 2001). The selection criteria were liberal: regulations in the province of Otago merely stipulated that apprentice teachers 'must be at least 13 years old and healthy' (Morton-Johnson and Morton, 1976, p.4). At this point conceptions of teaching as a profession were remote. McClean (2009, p.57) argued 'The notion that anyone with a little learning could become a teacher, if there was nothing better offering, was familiar to colonial settlers'. However, the nature of teacher preparation began to change in 1876 when the nation's first teacher-training school opened: the Dunedin Normal School. From the outset, training at the school was offered in conjunction with the opportunity to study academic subjects at the fledgling University of Otago (Morton-Johnson and Morton, 1976), thus introducing theory into ITE and challenging simplistic conceptions of learning the 'craft' of teaching through observation. Nevertheless, this separation of roles is perhaps an early example of the embodiment of the so-called theory-practice gap that is a longstanding issue in ITE (Loughran, 2011). Over time, the relationships between colleges and universities waxed and waned: by the 1920s, students' attendance at university had become optional and colleges offered education courses in addition to training. Half a century later, in the 1970s, many training colleges delivered joint education degrees in collaboration with universities. Two inter-related themes seem to offer some explanation for this, both of which are familiar to those currently interested in ITE. The first theme focused on aspirations to improve the 'quality' and the status of teachers, as evident in the discussion of raising the standard of their preparation to the same level as doctors and lawyers (McClean, 2009). The second theme comprised the practical issues of financing ITE and recruiting sufficiently well-qualified student teachers into the profession.

As of 2015, the Education Council of Aotearoa New Zealand (successor to the now defunct New Zealand Teachers Council) is the professional body that sets and maintains the professional standards demanded of those entering the profession. These standards, the Graduating Teacher Standards (GTS) (New Zealand Teachers Council, 2007), were drawn up after consultation with the educational community. They go beyond demanding essential pedagogical and content knowledge, as is perhaps more evident in England's Teachers' Standards (Department for Education, 2011), to describe graduating students from ITE as emerging professionals with knowledge of theories (standards 2a, 2b), who have reflected on and explored 'the complex influences that personal, social and cultural factors may have on teachers and learners' (standard 3a) and 'have an understanding of education within the bicultural, multicultural, social, political, economic and historical contexts of Aotearoa New Zealand' (standard 3c) (New Zealand Teachers Council, 2007). We contend that universities in partnership with schools and early childhood centres are well equipped to support preservice teachers from ITE programmes to meet these standards by bridging the so-called theory-practice gap (Loughran, 2011) and facilitating opportunities to engage with important ideas and critique, reflect, examine, theorise, research and grapple with the work and identity of professional teachers.

32 *David A. G. Berg et al.*

Policy and ITE provision

It is perhaps not surprising that some of the major changes to ITE over the last 30 years have come about through the economic policy reforms of neo-liberalism rather than explicit educational reform. Indeed, in 1987, New Zealand's Treasury published a two-volume brief for the re-elected Labour government, the second volume of which focused on education and reflected the language and arguments of the right wing economic politics of that time (Ray, 2009). Indeed, the brief's authors argued that 'Education shares the characteristics of other commodities traded in the market place' (Treasury, 1987, p.33). New Zealand's government embraced 'market values', and, as a result, competition was encouraged across the tertiary sector. This led to the deregulation of ITE, bringing fierce competition and variable standards (Alcorn, 2014; Rivers, 2006). In response to these challenges, in 2004, the then Minister of Education announced a moratorium for new ITE programmes (Mallard, 2004). Kane (2005) estimated that at that time over 90 per cent of New Zealand's primary and secondary student teachers and 45 per cent of its early childhood teachers were being educated, at least in part, by universities. The culture of competition also resulted in mergers between tertiary institutions, notably colleges of education and universities. Starting in the 1990s, Waikato and then Massey Universities merged with their local colleges of education, and by 2007 all of New Zealand's colleges of education had merged with universities, bringing the vast majority of ITE into the university sector. Nevertheless, an aspiring preservice teacher in New Zealand in 2012 could choose between 26 providers, comprising seven universities, six polytechnics, eight private training institutions and three wānanga (providers of tertiary education in a Māori context) (Ministry of Education, 2012). To date, 'market values' continue to shape the tertiary environment and ITE provision in New Zealand. Thus, it could be argued that the movement of ITE into universities in New Zealand has not resulted from the desire to raise the quality of teachers, but rather in response to economic policy.

In addition to the changes in the economic landscape, concerns about the quality of New Zealand's teachers led to government agencies commissioning 20 or more reviews and reports from 1990 to 2010 that have led to policy changes for teacher education (Ell and Grudnoff, 2013, p.76). Of particular significance to ITE, the Education Standards Act (2001) resulted in the New Zealand Teachers Council (subsequently replaced by the Education Council of Aotearoa New Zealand in 2015) gaining responsibility for the approval and monitoring of ITE qualifications.

Just over a hundred years after the end of provincial control of education in New Zealand, processes of globalization began to more obviously shape the nation's education policies. Furlong (2013, p.29) noted that during this time teacher education globally moved from 'a relative backwater' to an 'essential concern for every education system that wants to come out on top'. The interest in the Programme for International Student Assessment (PISA) from both politicians and media in New Zealand and the drive to emulate the top-performing nations lends support to this claim. This interest was fuelled during the first decade of the new millennia by the internationally influential reports published by McKinsey and Company and the Organisation for Economic Development (OECD) that brought increased attention to the work of ITE, as teachers were identified as a highly significant factor for the success and competitiveness of education systems (Barber and Mourshed, 2007; Mourshed, Chijioke and Barber, 2010; OECD, 2005). In his discussion of the influence of these reports, Coffield (2012, p.131) has argued that these conclusions 'quickly hardened into new articles of faith for politicians, policy makers, educational agencies, and many researchers and practitioners'. Evidence of the adoption of this faith in New Zealand can be found in the Minister of Education's report *A Vision for the Teaching Profession* (Ministry of Education, 2010). This report made recommendations on strategies aimed at bringing about 'changes needed to support a more professional teaching profession' (p.12). These included a recommendation that ITE, 'move toward being provided only at postgraduate level (so that entry into teaching is dependent on holding a postgraduate qualification rather than one of the graduate level qualifications that is currently the norm)' (p.4). Echoing historical themes in New Zealand ITE, the report argued that, 'To ensure that the teaching profession can attract and retain high quality individuals, broad changes are needed in the way that the profession is perceived' (p.2). It is of note that New Zealand's strategy 'to come out on top' is in stark contrast to that of England, where funding for the short-lived Masters in Teaching and Learning Award ended with the arrival of the Conservative-Liberal Coalition government in 2010: new programmes of ITE at the Masters level have commenced (during 2014 and 2015) in seven of New Zealand's eight universities.

Higher education in New Zealand has also been the subject of education policy. Indeed, an additional 'travelling reform' (Seddon, 2014) has had considerable impact on university-based ITE: the research evaluation exercises that have shaped institutions internationally (Middleton, 2009) have been enacted in New Zealand as the Performance Based Research Fund (PBRF). The PBRF has resulted in significant pressure on university departments and individual academics to publish research. This is important to universities as it not only attracts funding, but also impacts on their status as research institutions. In contrast to an individual academic's quality of teaching and service to the institution and the community, research outputs are much more quantifiable and as such have become an increasingly significant measure of success, important for employment and promotion.

Thus, at this moment in the story of ITE in New Zealand, universities are presented with an enviable opportunity to make a unique contribution to the development of the teaching profession, while also facing challenges of their own. In this context we have sought to understand how universities are responding to the current policy environment by investigating constructions of the category of academic worker: the university-based teacher educator.

Work of Teacher Educators–New Zealand Research (WoTE-NZ)

Our research project, the Work of Teacher Educators –NZ (WoTE-NZ), set out to understand the work of teacher educators in New Zealand universities and to

34 *David A. G. Berg* et al.

consider how university-based ITE can contribute to the development of emerging professionals. Our study was underpinned by the following research questions:

- How is 'teacher educator' constructed and maintained as a category of academic work?
- What do university-based teacher educators do? What are they working on?
- How do the pedagogical activities of teacher educators shape opportunities for student teachers' learning?
- What are student teachers' interpretations of and motives towards artefacts and activities within ITE?

We acknowledge that teacher educators are a heterogeneous group and can be difficult to define (Murray, Swennen and Shagrir, 2009); however, our work focused exclusively on university-based teacher educators as a consequence of the current dominance of universities in ITE provision in New Zealand. We have sought to use this study to contribute to a growing body of research that considers the Work of Teacher Educators (WoTE) internationally. Most significantly, we have built on research from the UK and Australia that explored the discursive construction and material conditions of teacher educators' work (Ellis et al., 2011; Ellis, McNicholl and Pendry, 2012; Ellis et al., 2013; Nuttall et al., 2013).

Our study was conducted in two phases: the first phase explored the cultural historical production and maintenance of 'teacher educator' as a category of worker within universities (Gunn et al., 2015), whereas the second phase examined teacher educators' accounts of their own work. Combining an analysis of constructions of teacher educator with an analysis of the practices of teacher educators we have been able to explore the implications for ITE in New Zealand. Following Ellis et al. (2011), we used Engestrom's (1987, 2001) cultural historical activity theory as a lens to view conceptions of teacher educators' work and understand the activity systems in which that work is done.

In the first phase of our study we monitored a national university recruitment website and institutional websites over a period of six months spanning October 2013 to March 2014. This allowed us to collect advertisements and job descriptions for 37 posts in seven institutions. After careful consideration 11 of these were identified as being related closely to the work of ITE. To supplement the collected materials, we contacted the named personnel responsible for the job advertisements to request their participation in a telephone interview. Seven interviews were conducted with the use of a structured interview guide. Participants were asked to explain how decisions were made about: the content of the job advertisements; the processes involved in constructing the job and person descriptions; who was involved in the recruitment processes; and how teacher education was organised within their institution. We also asked the interviewees to share their views on teacher education as academic work.

In the second phase, we recruited a purposive sample of 15 teacher educators from two universities. This sample included teacher educators representing early childhood, primary and secondary education sectors. These participants engaged in five activities: initial telephone interviews; work diaries; work shadowing observations; follow up interviews; and a participatory data analysis workshop where they were invited to work with the research team to understand the data using the tools of cultural historical activity theory. In addition to these, and extending the WoTE work conducted in the UK and Australia, preservice teachers who participated in the ITE activities that we observed, when work shadowing the teacher educators, were also invited to share their perspectives about the purposes of the activities in which they were engaged.

Three clear categories of teacher educator were evident from the findings both of a discourse analysis and a membership category analysis that were conducted independently of each other. The first type of teacher educator identified we named a 'professional expert'; the second, 'dually qualified'; and the third, 'traditional academic'. A 'professional expert' is a teacher educator who is qualified to teach in schools or early childhood centres and has teacher registration and a practising certificate from the Education Council. The work of this type of teacher educator consisted of teaching and supervision of students in schools, with the added responsibility of building and maintaining relationships with colleagues in practice settings. The academic work of research was not a required feature of their work. Teaching work was described in recruitment materials as 'delivery' and these teacher educators as 'needing to be supervised'. In sharp contrast, the 'traditional academic' construction of teacher educator was much more aligned to work that is common across university departments. The work of research was a strong feature of this category. There was no expectation that the teacher educators in this category have experience in schools or teacher registration. Thus, neither of these categories can engage in the full scope of the work of university-based teacher education. One category is excluded from the work of research and the other excluded from school and early childhood centre-based work. In contrast, the third category of teacher educator, 'dually qualified', comprised the work of both of these other constructions and thus would be able to engage in the full scope of this work. Dually qualified teacher educators are expected to have current teacher registration and school experience, together with research capability. Thus, they are qualified and able to teach in schools and to engage in educational research. However, in the first phase of this study we were only able to identify one position featuring the full scope of teacher educator work among the 11 advertised teacher educator positions (with the remaining ten positions comprising five in each of the other two categories). The phase two findings bolstered those in phase one, demonstrating that professional experts' and traditional academics' work differed, as did their status within the university. This notwithstanding, a further significant finding was that all of the teacher educators who participated in our study were engaged in the work of scholarship and research. However, for some this was completed outside of their formal work time and included private doctoral study. In summary, the most significant finding from the first phase of our research has been that current employment practices are favouring two of three identified constructions of teacher educator in New Zealand.

36 *David A. G. Berg* et al.

Consequences of the bifurcation of teacher educator work

New Zealand's teacher educators work within a dual policy environment. This can be challenging, as responding to the policy environment of higher education and the policy environment of the school sector, including requirements from the Ministry of Education and the Education Council, may appear to be a double bind. These overlapping activity systems have unique objects of activity, rules and communities of practice. However, we maintain that the tension and challenge of working in partnership across these systems offers rich opportunities to enhance the profession of teaching in schools and early childhood settings by supporting the development of research-savvy, critically reflective and pedagogically proficient teachers – if approached thoughtfully. Furthermore, research active teacher educators who are able to work in genuine partnership with teachers in schools to research practice and build applied knowledge can serve the teaching profession by building collaborative scholarship.

The Ministry of Education in New Zealand funds ITE. Prior to funding, the Education Council must approve programmes. One condition of approval is that those teacher educators involved in the work of visiting, mentoring and assessing preservice teachers in schools and early childhood centres hold current Education Council practising certificates, are registered teachers and have school or early childhood teaching qualifications. A teacher or teacher educator must renew his/her practising certificate every three years to remain eligible to teach. This process is rigorous, involving holders providing evidence that they 'have been meaningfully assessed against and have met the Practising Teacher Criteria', are 'fit to teach' and 'have completed satisfactory personal development' (Education Council New Zealand, 2015). We support this requirement, despite the significant personal and institutional challenges it brings, as it ensures that those who are part of the community of professional teachers are involved in the process of inducting newcomers to the profession and suggest it has potential to bring theory to practice and practice to theory.

A major feature of the higher education policy environment in New Zealand is the Performance Based Research Fund (PBRF). As New Zealand's research evaluation, it has been initiated to increase the quality of research and research informed teaching (Smart, 2013). Consequently, universities compete for funding and status. For reasons explored elsewhere (see Hill and Haigh, 2012), university-based teacher educators may find it more of a challenge to produce research outputs than colleagues in other university departments. One seemingly pragmatic way universities appear to be responding to PBRF is to bifurcate the workforce into what we have termed 'traditional academics' and 'professional experts'. Traditional academics can engage in the work of scholarship alongside their teaching, while their professional expert colleagues can do the busy and lower status work within the academy associated with practice (Spencer, 2013). It is important to note that we recognise the value of both these categories of teacher educator and are mindful of the outstanding work done by colleagues in these categories. Rather than diminishing their work, our purpose is to argue that current employment practices that seem to almost exclusively employ these categories are deeply problematic. In contrast, we suggest that if universities support all teacher educators to research, thus work on the dual objects of 'research productivity' and 'quality ITE', universities and ITE will benefit. Furthermore, we argue that research is integral to 'a profession' as new knowledge is generated for practice. Consequently, university-based teacher educators can be ideally placed to support the development of research-savvy and researching professionals. However, this is subject to them also being included in the work of research.

We believe that the dually qualified category of teacher educator is ideally placed to challenge the so-called 'theory-practice' gap that Loughran (2011, p.280) argues is 'an abiding issue in education'. An example of this from our own teaching and research is found in work around assessment in primary schools. The Education Council expects graduating teachers as they enter the profession to 'have knowledge of a range of relevant theories, principles and purposes of assessment and evaluation' (Graduating Teacher Standard 2b) and to 'systematically and critically engage with evidence to reflect on and refine their practice', 'gather, analyse and use assessment information to improve learning and inform planning' and 'know how to communicate assessment information appropriately to learners, their parents/caregivers and staff' (Graduating Teacher Standard 5 a, b, c). Traditional academics who work in the field of assessment can, and do, in our experience, teach the theory of assessment very effectively. Equally, our professional expert colleagues offer rich insight into the realities of assessment practices in classrooms. However, a comprehensive understanding of assessment theory and ongoing scholarly work married with practical experience of using assessment in primary classrooms allows us to show the importance of theory and how it informs practice. We support the argument made by Korthagen, Loughran and Russell (2006, p.1027) that 'Teacher education practices that support the search for "the recipe" for how to teach or make it appear as though teaching is simple and unproblematic reduce the impact of the conflicting demands associated with learning to teach'. However, we are aware that helping preservice teachers apply and appreciate theory in the messy and complex world of practice demands teacher educators have expertise in both. Consequently, we argue that the recruitment practices that we observed that largely ignored the third category of teacher educator, the dually qualified, are short-sighted and are excluding would-be teacher educators who are best placed to synthesise theory and practice. These practices have implications for the profession of teaching as those entering it are less likely to encounter teacher educators that can bridge the worlds of research and practice and use both scholarship and professional experience to scaffold their development. Furthermore, this situation has implications for universities, who may find themselves ill-prepared should New Zealand's ITE move to the postgraduate level as this would require teacher educators with both professional accreditation and higher degrees.

Conclusion

In this chapter we have charted the journey of the teaching profession from 19th century pupil-teachers to 21st century university-prepared professionals.

38 *David A. G. Berg et al.*

Linda Darling-Hammond (2010) has noted that teaching (in the USA) is in a similar position to where medicine was in 1910. She explains that the time in preparation programmes for physicians ranged enormously in both length and quality. For contemporary readers, it may be hard to imagine that arguments were made against the professionalisation of medicine that suggested 'medicine could best be learned following a doctor around in a buggy' (p.39). Few in our societies would be prepared to trust ill-prepared physicians with responsibility for our medical care. Rather, we are likely to expect a rigorous professional preparation for their work. At this time, wealthy nations, such as New Zealand, have the opportunity to accord similar status to the teaching profession and support the development of richly prepared professional teachers.

We are encouraged that New Zealand's Ministry of Education, rather than looking to school-based models of teacher preparation, is trialling Master's level ITE which incorporates theory with practice following celebrated successes overseas, most notably in Finland. At the time of writing we are approaching the end of the second year of the trial and questions remain to be answered as to how best to proceed. However, we believe this rich conceptualisation of university-based teacher preparation has potential to serve the profession of teaching in Aotearoa New Zealand by supporting the development of highly skilled, thoughtful teachers able to cope with complex and changing learning environments with diverse students. Such a model enacted in New Zealand would support calls to give greater collective agency to the professional community and thus elevate the profession, as is currently the case in Finland (Toom et al., 2010). Consequently, we call on those responsible for the recruitment and development of teacher educators in New Zealand's universities to flex to ensure their practices support these richer conceptions of ITE and in so doing serve emerging professional teachers, the teaching profession and their own long-term needs.

References

Alcorn, N. (2014). Teacher education in New Zealand 1974–2014. *Journal of Education for Teaching*, 40(5), 447–460.

Barber, M. and Mourshed, M. (2007). *How the World's Best-Performing School Systems Come out on Top*. Dubai: McKinsey.

Coffield, F. (2012). Why the McKinsey reports will not improve school systems. *Journal of Education Policy*, 27(1), 131–149.

Darling-Hammond, L. (2010). Teacher education and the American future. *Journal of Teacher Education*, 61(1–2), 35–47.

Department for Education (2011). *Teachers' Standards*. London: Department for Education. Available from: www.gov.uk/government/uploads/system/uploads/attachment_data/file/301107/Teachers__Standards.pdf (accessed 28 October 2015).

Education Council New Zealand. (2015). *Renewing a Full Practising Certificate*. Available from: www.educationcouncil.org.nz/content/renewing-full-practising-certificate (accessed 28 October 2015).

Ell, F. and Grudnoff, L. (2013). The politics of responsibility: teacher education and 'persistent underachievement' in New Zealand. *The Educational Forum*, 77(1), 73–86.

Ellis, V., Blake, A., McNicholl, J. and McNally, J. (2011). *The Work of Teacher Education, Final Research Report*. WOTE phase 2. Oxford: Department of Education, University of Oxford.

Ellis, V., McNicholl, J. and Pendry, A. (2012). Institutional conceptualisations of teacher education as academic work in England. *Teaching and Teacher Education*, 28(5), 685–693.

Ellis, V., Glackin, M., Heighes, D., Norman, M., Nicol, S., Norris, K., Spencer, I. and McNicholl, J. (2013). A difficult realisation: the proletarianisation of higher education-based teacher educators. *Journal of Education for Teaching*, 39(3), 266–280.

Engstrom, Y. (1987). *Learning by Expanding: An Activity-theoretical Approach to Developmental Research*. Helsinki: Orienta-Konsultit.

Engestrom, Y. (2001). Expansive learning at work: toward an activity theoretical reconceptualization. *Journal of Education and Work*, 14(1), 133–156.

Evans, L. (2008). Professionalism, professionality and the development of education professionals. *British Journal of Educational Studies*, 56(1), 20–38.

Furlong, J. (2013). Globalisation, neoliberalism, and the reform of teacher education in England. *The Educational Forum*, 77(1), 28–50.

Granovetter, M. (1973). The strength of weak ties. *American Journal of Sociology*, 78(6), 1360–1380.

Gunn, A. C., Berg, D., Hill, M.F. and Haigh, M. (2015). Constructing the academic category of teacher educator in universities' recruitment processes in Aotearoa, New Zealand. *Journal of Education for Teaching*, 41(3), 1–14.

Hill, M. and Haigh, M. (2012). Creating a culture of research in teacher education: learning research within communities of practice. *Studies in Higher Education* 37(8), 971–988. doi:10.1080/03075079.2011.559222

Kane, R. (2005). *Initial Teacher Education Policy and Practice. Final Report*. Wellington: Ministry of Education.

Kean, D. (2001). *In a Class of its Own*. Dunedin: Dunedin College of Education.

King, M. (2003). *Penguin History of New Zealand*. London: Penguin.

Korthagen, F., Loughran, J. and Russell, T. (2006). Developing fundamental principles for teacher education programs and practices. *Teaching and Teacher Education*, 22(8), 1020–1041.

Loughran, J. (2011). On becoming a teacher educator. *Journal of Education for Teaching: International Research and Pedagogy*, 37(3), 279–291. doi:10.1080/02 607476.2011.588016

Mallard, T. (2004). *Focus on Quality Teaching*. Speech to the Biennial Conference for Teacher Education Forum of Aotearoa New Zealand, 6 July, Auckland.

McClean, M. (2009). New Zealand teachers. In: E. Rata and K.Sullivan (eds), *Introduction to the History of New Zealand Education*, pp.57–69. North Shore: Pearson.

Middleton, S. (2009). Becoming PBRF-able: research assessment and education in New Zealand. In: T. Besley (ed.), *Assessing the Quality of Educational Research in Higher Education: International Perspectives*, pp.193–208. Rotterdam: Sense.

Ministry of Education (2010). *A Vision for the Teaching Profession: Education Workforce Advisory Group Report to the Minister of Education*. Wellington: Ministry of Education. Available from: www.beehive.govt.nz/sites/all/files/10.pdf (accessed 28 October 2015).

Ministry of Education (2012). *Review of the New Zealand Teachers Council: A Teaching Profession for the 21st Century*. Report to Hon. Hekia Parata, Minister

40 *David A. G. Berg* et al.

of Education. Available from: www.educationcouncil.org.nz/sites/default/files/
Review%20of%20the%20NZ%20Teachers%20Council%202012%20-%20report
%20to%20Minister%20of%20Education.pdf (accessed 28 October 2015).

Ministry of Education (2015). *Key Features of Partnership Schools/Kura hourua.* Wellington: Ministry of Education. Available from: www.education.govt.nz/ministry-of-education/specific-initiatives/partnership-schools-kura-hourua/key-features-of-partnership-schools-kura-hourua/ (accessed 28 October 2015).

Morton Johnston, C. and Morton, H. (1976). *Dunedin Teachers College: The First Hundred Years.* Dunedin: Dunedin Teachers College Publication Committee.

Mourshed, M., Chijioke, C. and Barber, M. (2010). *How the World's Most Improved School Systems Keep Getting Better.* Dubai: McKinsey.

Murray, J., Swennen, A. and Shagrir, L. (2009). Understanding teacher educators' work and identities. In A. Swennen and M. van der Klink (eds), *Becoming a Teacher Educator*, pp.29–43. The Netherlands: Springer Science+Business Media B.V.

New Zealand Teachers Council (2007). *Graduating Teacher Standards Poster (English): Aotearoa New Zealand.* Wellington: Ministry of Education. Available from: www.educationcouncil.org.nz/sites/default/files/gts-poster.pdf (accessed 28 October 2015).

Nuttall, J., Brennan, M., Zipin, L., Tuinamuana, K. and Cameron, L. (2013). Lost in production: the erasure of the teacher educator in Australian university job advertisements. *Journal of Education for Teaching: International Research and Pedagogy*, 39(3), 329–343. doi: 10.1080/02607476.2013.799849

Organisation for Economic Co-operation and Development (2005). *Teachers Matter: Attracting, Developing and Retaining Effective Teachers.* Paris: OECD.

Ray, S. (2009). New Zealand education in the twentieth century. In: E. Rata and K. Sullivan (eds), *Introduction to the History of New Zealand Education*, pp.16–30. North Shore, New Zealand: Pearson.

Rivers, J. (2006). *Initial Teacher Education Research Programme: A Summary of Four Studies.* Wellington: Ministry of Education.

Seddon, T. (2014). Making educational spaces through boundary work: territorialisation and 'boundarying'. *Globalisation, Societies and Education*, 12(1), 10–31.

Smart, W. (2013). *In Pursuit of Excellence: Analysing the Results of New Zealand's PBRF Quality Evaluations.* Wellington: Ministry of Education.

Spencer, I. (2013). Doing the 'second shift': gendered labour and the symbolic annihilation of teacher educators' work. *Journal of Education for Teaching*, 39(3), 301–313.

Toom, A., Kynäslahti, H., Krokfors, L., Jyrhämä, R., Byman, R., Stenberg, K., Maaranen, K. and Kansanen, P. (2010). Education: suggestions for future policies. *European Journal of Education*, 45(2), 331–344.

Treasury (1987). *Government Management: Brief to Incoming Government 1987 (Vol. 2).* Wellington: Government Printer.

Zeichner, K. (2006). Reflections of a university-based teacher educator on the future of college- and university-based teacher education. *Journal of Teacher Education*, 57(3), 326–340.

International vignette 1
Teacher education in Wales

Susan Wyn Jones and John Lewis

Background

Ever since education was devolved to the Welsh government in 1997, the curriculum and related educational matters have diverged from that of England. This makes Wales an interesting context in which to view initial teacher education and training (ITET) and professional partnerships associated with the sector.

In Wales, at present, ITET is provided by three centres. These centres were created following Furlong's first review into initial teacher training in Wales, in 2006 (Furlong et al., 2006). The centres work in professional partnership with schools across the principality, with universities (some in collaboration) managing ITET at a strategic level.

Since 2006, when the centres were first created, Wales (like other parts of the United Kingdom) has taken part in two further Programmes for International Student Assessments (PISA). Wales' poor standing in these assessments (OECD 2009; OECD 2012) has led to successive government education ministers commissioning a plethora of reviews and reports into the state of Welsh education in an attempt to pinpoint the issues and drive up standards across the sector (Tabberer's *Review of Initial Teacher Training*, 2013; OECD's *Improving Schools in Wales*, 2014; Donaldson's review of the Welsh National Curriculum, 2015). This has naturally shone a spotlight on ITET provision in Wales.

The current position of ITET in Wales

On the basis of recommendations in the most recent Furlong report (2015) into ITET in Wales (published in conjunction with the Donaldson review of the Welsh national curriculum), initial teacher training is now on the brink of entering a new phase. The number of ITET centres in Wales could shortly change. New alliances may be forged; old partnerships could be strengthened or abandoned as universities bid to gain accreditation to train teachers in Wales.

The way forward may depend to some extent on the government in power in 2016 and its vision for excellence in teaching. Currently, the Labour government in Wales is keen to pursue its own ideals. For example, in comparison with that of England, ITET provision in Wales is not as diversified. Wales offers an

42 Susan Wyn Jones and John Lewis

employment-based graduate teacher programme (as well as the traditional university-led-provision). However, compared to the School Direct programme in England, which trains a high percentage of trainee teachers directly in schools, this is at present only a small part of ITET in Wales. Although one centre offers the Teach First programme, at present Wales does not advocate the School Centred Initial Teacher Training (SCITT) programme found in England.

Regardless of the government in power, come 2016 the current aims to raise standards are likely to be the tenets of any future policy reform. The current education minister wishes to align the Welsh education system more closely with that seen in Germany and Finland (rather than a Singapore/China model). Any new government may have a different vision but the basic premise will be the same – standards must rise, and ITET must play its part in attaining that goal.

The future

Teacher training in Wales was deemed 'adequate and no better' by Tabberer in his review of ITT in 2013. The new Furlong report into ITET for the Welsh government (2015) outlines why reform is necessary, noting that Wales must produce a 'new generation of capable, professional teachers equipped with the qualifications, skills and resilience needed to deliver [Wales's] reform agenda and build a sustainable self-improving education system fit for the future'. Furlong's recommendations for reform have all been endorsed by the Welsh Education Minister (Welsh Government, 2015). The sector will not only have new centres but 'revised professional standards to develop and support practice for the future', and accreditation, financial incentives and 'alternative routes into teaching' will all be reviewed.

Across the sector and beyond, there is broad agreement that excellent teachers make a difference to children's progress and prospects. The new ITET centres in Wales, in whatever guise, must ensure they produce the best teachers for the profession. Furlong (2015) could not have put it better when he said:

> Wales does still have a large number of individuals and institutions that remain highly committed to the provision of good quality initial teacher education . . . I am sure that the sector will seize the opportunities to give Wales the quality of teacher education that it needs for the future.

References

Donaldson, G. (2015). *The Donaldson Review of Curriculum and Assessment.* Cardiff: Welsh Government.

Furlong, J. (2015). *Teaching Tomorrow's Teachers: Options for the Future of Initial Teacher Education in Wales.* Cardiff: Welsh Government.

Furlong, J., Hagger, H., Butcher, C. and Howson, J. (2006). *Review of Initial Teacher Training Provision in Wales: A Report to the Welsh Assembly Government (the Furlong Report).* Oxford: University of Oxford Department of Education.

International vignette 1: Wales   43

OECD (2009). *PISA 2006 Technical Report.* Paris: OECD Publishing.
OECD (2012). *PISA 2009 Technical Report.* Paris: OECD Publishing.
OECD (2014). *Improving Schools in Wales: An OECD Perspective.* Available from: www.oecd.org/edu/Improving-schools-in-Wales.pdf (accessed 16 November 2015).
Tabberer, R. (2013). *A Review of Initial Teacher Training in Wales.* Cardiff: Welsh Government.
Welsh Government (2015). Minister endorses 'radical plan' to transform teacher training. Available from: http://gov.wales/newsroom/educationandskills/2015/10292704/?lang=en. (accessed 16 November 2015).

3 Teaching as contemplative

John Sullivan

Introduction

Teachers in many societies have been expected to be agents of the nation state, local powers, ruling class or to work on behalf of the church (or other religious authorities). Education is often treated as in service to the economy, with teachers equipping the future workforce with the skills to maintain and extend competitiveness in the market. Such emphases often privilege doing over being, and performativity over personhood; they can end up by manipulating and colonising teachers and students rather than enhancing their lives. In this chapter I propose a re-appropriation of contemplation as a central and necessary feature of teaching (and of education more generally). There are four parts to the chapter. First, I acknowledge the active dimension of teaching, often requiring immediate decisions, unpremeditated and rapid responses, practical competence and necessary compromises in the midst of complex pressures and competing expectations within and beyond the classroom. Second, various connotations of contemplation (within the context of teaching) are identified and commented upon. Third, I explore how seeing education in the light of Buber and Freire opens the door to a contemplative dimension to teaching. Fourth, I indicate some of the ways that a contemplative approach to teaching can offer a valuable counter-weight to some contemporary cultural assumptions about education and teaching.

Acknowledging the active dimension of teaching

First, some caveats. Teachers often have to work at a level lower than the contemplative because of the pressures of numbers of students to be taught, a shortage of time, intrusive requirements from government and its agencies (for example, inspectors and examination boards) or institutional expectations and ethos – as well as facing often recalcitrant learners who are rebelling against their experience of being colonised by other 'voices'. But awareness of the good that can be received by adopting a more contemplative approach to teaching can serve as a goad and as an attraction to aim for more than the limited horizons that seem envisaged in current educational policies. A contemplative approach to teaching holds open a space for the possibility of transcendence, beyond the concerns of the moment. It can safeguard teachers from the temptation of perceiving the classroom merely as an arena of conflict and therefore prevent them from behaving in it without due reverence. It can protect them from abusing their power in the ways so powerfully described by George Steiner in *Lessons of the Masters* (Steiner, 2005).

I am not saying that teaching is only contemplative. There is a tension between the openness essential to contemplation and the systematic and structured organization required of teachers; and there is also a dialectic between receptivity on the part of students to what is being conveyed and the active reconstruction of experience by learners. The great thirteenth century thinker Thomas Aquinas argued that teaching is both active and contemplative (Boland, 2007); the Dominican order, of which he was such an illustrious member, has as its task the handing on (in preaching and teaching) of what has been contemplated. In the preparation for and the daily work of teachers, there is a necessary focus on the diverse range of activities in which they must engage, and on the development of many technical skills, as key elements contributing to the quality of their performance. This emphasis, however, can be carried too far. Nigel Tubbs poses a striking challenge when he asks:

> We have to ask: how is it that, in England at least, within four years of embarking on training for this career, something between a third and a quarter of new teachers leave, or are seeking to leave, the profession? How is it that the experience of being a teacher so quickly and effectively undermines the desire to be a teacher?
>
> (Tubbs, 2005, pp.61–62)

In response to these questions, he suggests that

> Whilst salary, status, conditions, health, paperwork and compliance all play their part in demoralising teachers, of much greater significance in the long run is that teaching has lost its sense of nobility as an activity in the world. Bluntly, teaching has lost all meaning about its contribution to humanity.
>
> (Tubbs, 2005, p.62)

To address this situation, two counter-weights are needed in aid of a healthier climate for teaching. First, it is necessary to restore, as part of teachers' intellectual and professional repertoire, the capacity for and confidence in critical questioning; Neil Postman, himself borrowing from Ernest Hemingway, once devoted the first chapter of a book to the proposal that education should equip learners with a built-in crap detector (Postman and Weingartner, 1969). Critical thinking and questioning, by themselves, will not be enough to create a healthy professional environment for teachers. However, they provide essential equipment that enables teachers to penetrate and expose the poverty of prevailing political policies for education. They also help in casting light on the colonisation and downgrading of the vocabulary of education that occurs when metaphors drawn from business and the curse of managerialism are deployed. Second, what is also needed is the

46   *John Sullivan*

counter-balancing and healing role of a contemplative approach to teaching. This chapter has as its focus the promise of teaching as contemplative.

These two features, critical questioning and contemplation, are rarely held together sufficiently as complementary and mutually reinforcing forces. Usually teachers and educational theorists tend to stress one of these much more than the other, with contemplation receiving much less attention in modern times as an integral aspect of teaching. The great Brazilian educator Paulo Freire seems to me to have got near to combining them, while still giving priority to the critical questioning in service of liberation. In summarising Freire on the kinds of knowledge that teachers should have, Donald Macedo, in his foreword to *Pedagogy of Freedom*, mentions the following prerequisites: 'recognition that teaching is ideological, always involves ethics, a capacity to be critical, recognition of our conditioning, humility, critical reflection' (Freire, 1998, p.xiii). In the same work, in a chapter entitled 'Teaching is a Human Act', Freire (1998, p.108) lists the following qualities or virtues needed by teachers: 'a generous loving heart, respect for others, tolerance, humility, a joyful disposition, love of life, openness to what is new, a disposition to welcome change, perseverance in the struggle, a refusal of determinism, a spirit of hope, and openness to justice'. Some of these qualities depend on the political sensitivity aroused by critical questioning, while others are the fruit of a capacity for appreciation made possible by a contemplative approach to teaching.

Connotations of contemplation

The term contemplation brings to the fore a number of considerations. If teaching is the handing on of what one has contemplated, this immediately suggests that the teacher has devoted time to coming to know well what she is going to teach. Prior to the teaching, the teacher has reflected on the topic to be taught, become familiar with it and internalised it, to some degree at least. Contemplation evokes the sense of there being an inner landscape from which the teacher works, beyond being merely the possessor of a tool-kit of knowledge and skills which has no purchase on her life. The contemplative teacher depends on and promotes self-awareness and self-knowledge. She sees the whole, and the parts in relation to the whole, of what is being taught; she facilitates interconnectedness in students' learning. Contemplative teachers are more concerned about the growth of wisdom than about short-term success. Associated features or virtues that are jointly conducive to a contemplative outlook include attentiveness, receptivity, hospitality, appreciation, waiting and patience, silence and stillness, sensitivity and tact or restraint, reflection, an invitational rather than an impositional or intrusive tone. The contemplative is good at letting be, ready to remain still before what is given rather than too quickly assessing what one has won by one's own actions. She is appreciative, even loving, and ready to enjoy what life presents; her seeing goes beneath the surface and into the life of what is contemplated, capable of taking this into herself as a gift from the other. This makes possible knowledge as union instead of as possession. Contemplation can be a highly charged (in the sense of keenly alert) passivity, reached in a state of calm restfulness. It is unaggressive and non-judgemental. Contemplation enables – but cannot guarantee – attunement to the object studied, instead of being alienated from it.

Contemplation suggests stillness, silence, waiting, reverence, being present, relationship, receptivity, deep listening and attentiveness, pondering and integrating what is contemplated into who one is and the rest of what one holds onto. In order to note how challenging and counter-cultural this is, compare these features of contemplation with the prevailing pressures in education of promotion, packaging, delivery, accumulation, measurement and accountancy, productivity, performativity and the notion of learners as customers who are purchasing (either directly or via whoever sponsors them) a commodity. In contrast to the constantly distracted self-in-competition-with-others that results from these pressures in education and society, the Augustinian friar Martin Laird points out that 'There are two dynamics of contemplation: deepening concentration and expanding awareness . . . These give birth to twins: inner solitude and a loving solidarity with all' (Laird, 2011, p.19). For teachers and students, a contemplative approach stabilises the self and fosters communion with the other; and communion with one person is a small step on the long pathway to solidarity with all.

Hannah Arendt notes how Aquinas defines contemplation as *quies ab exterioribus motibus* – being undisturbed by external movement and concerns. 'Truth . . . can reveal itself only in complete human stillness . . . Traditionally, the term vita activa receives its meaning from the vita contemplativa' (Arendt, 1958, p.16). Contemplation meant beholding the truth (p.264) and, in the medieval perspective which Aquinas shared, 'all activities of the vita activa had been judged and justified to the extent that they made the vita contemplativa possible' (p.265). Arendt shows that a reversal of this priority gradually took place, such that the active life took precedence over the contemplative (pp.262–268). Instead of human works being modelled on (and participating in) what they had received as gift from creation, the focus shifted away from the relatively passive nature of contemplation to the human processes of active fabrication and knowledge-making; this is partly a shift from metaphysics or ontology to epistemology, partly a move from beholding and receiving to agency and the fruits of our own labours.

John Henry Newman's comparison between poetry and science has a bearing on this shift.

> Reason investigates, analyses, numbers, weighs, measures, ascertains, locates, the objects of its contemplation, and thus gains a scientific knowledge of them. Science results in system, which is complex unity; poetry delights in the indefinite and various as contrasted with unity, and in the simple as contrasted with system. The aim of science is to get a hold of things, to grasp them, to handle them, to comprehend them; that is, to master them. Its success lies in being able to draw a line round them, and to tell where each of them is to be found within that circumference, and how each lies relatively

48   *John Sullivan*

to all the rest. Its mission is to destroy ignorance, doubt, surmise, suspense, illusions, fears, deceits ... But as to the poetical ... It demands, as its primary condition, that we should not put ourselves above the objects in which it resides, but at their feet; that we should feel them to be above and beyond us, that we should look up to them, and that, instead of fancying that we can comprehend them, we should take for granted that we are surrounded and comprehended by them ourselves. It implies that we understand them to be vast, immeasurable, impenetrable, inscrutable, mysterious ... Poetry does not address the reason, but the imagination and affections; it leads to admiration, enthusiasm, devotion, love.

(Newman, 2001, pp.386–387)

Newman's description of the poetic here gets close to what I mean by the contemplative. The poetic way of seeing, as with the contemplative, is partly a matter of the relationship between the knower and the known, and also of the purpose of that relationship. It may be thought that the poetic is purely subjective, but here James Taylor, in a book on the importance of poetic knowledge in education, makes a useful distinction between subjectivism and subjectivity when he quotes Andrew Louth:

Science is concerned with objective truth ... independent of whoever observes it ... Objective truth ... seeks to be detached from the subjectivity of the observer. In contrast to such objective truth, subjective truth is a truth which cannot be detached from the observer and his situation ... When Kierkegaard claimed that all truth lay in subjectivity, he meant that truth which could be expressed objectively (so that it was the same for everyone) was mere information that concerned everyone and no one. Real truth that a man would lay down his life for, was essentially subjective: a truth passionately apprehended by the subject. To say, then, that truth is subjective is to say that its significance lies in the subject's engagement with it.

(Taylor, 1998, pp.72–73)

Taylor then says: 'In other words, truth that is subjective is truth that one has made one's own ... Poetic experience leading to poetic knowledge is concerned "with bringing men into engagement with what is true"' (quoting Louth).

Maria Lichtmann, in her book on teaching and the contemplative life, reminds us that so much of what teachers do has its focus on content and skills, on what people know and can do. Even the word 'curriculum' has its origins in the Latin 'cursus' meaning 'running in rapid motion'. She says 'by definition, curriculum is not contemplative; it does not take the time to see into the temple that is in our midst' (Lichtmann, 2005, p.7). So often, under the pressures of examinations, inspection, league tables, competing priorities among our colleagues and alternative calls on the attention of pupils, teachers feel impelled to 'cover the material', with little time to engage with or to relate to this material in ways that are revelatory, that yield treasures for us to behold and cherish. This militates against the goods that contemplation promotes and opens the door to distractions and temptations that threaten to undermine or corrupt educational encounters. Lichtmann (p.10) quotes a famous passage from St Bernard of Clairvaux, exposing different motivations for studying; these motivations also apply to teaching:

> For there are some who desire to know only for the sake of knowing; and this is disgraceful curiosity. And there are some who desire to know, that they may become known themselves; and this is disgraceful vanity . . . There are also some who desire to know in order to sell their knowledge, as for money, or for degrees; and this is disgraceful commercialism. But there are also some who desire to know in order to edify; and this is love.

It seems clear to me that a contemplative approach to teaching helps in the process of purifying our motives and cleansing our vision, reducing the risk that our attempts to know and to teach will be muddied by inner drives that are self-seeking, grasping, manipulative or unworthy. If we want to promote, to enrich, even to transform the inner life of our students, then our teaching must transcend a concern for marketable skills and testable knowledge; it must, to some degree at least, be contemplative. It must be recognized, however, that, as Lichtmann (p.117) points out: 'transformation cannot be controlled or verified; it does not show up on tests . . . does not have a lesson plan . . . [and] cannot be forced'.

Contemplation, through its receptivity and reflectiveness, can at least help us in the right direction. Lichtmann observes: 'If reflection establishes our freedom from the herd mentality, then receptivity uses that freedom positively – for communion' (Lichtmann, 2005, p.90). If the teacher is to create the right conditions for learning, he must embrace a contemplative capacity. After all, Lichtmann (p.93) shrewdly notes, 'Someone needs to be at home for our students to feel welcome'. It seems to me that only the contemplative teacher is still enough, sufficiently at rest within herself, and adequately rooted to be appropriately open and warmly welcoming to her students.

To emphasise the importance of teaching as contemplative is to underline the key role of the teacher's gaze and vision, with regard first, to each of her or his students, second, to the material which is the focus of learning at the time and third, with regard to the purposes and possibilities of the educational endeavour as a whole. The gaze in fact is central, not only by the teacher, at each student and at the object of study, but also a gaze at the teacher, from both the student and the object of study. A teacher has to be alert to what the object of study is saying to her or to him, as well as attentive to what the student has to say to him or to her. Integral to the teacher's role is a quality of openness, of letting be, of hearing into speech. For this to occur, there must be an unthreatening atmosphere of communication for all participants (teachers and students). There need to be opportunities for depth of penetration into what is being studied; here the relentless pressure for greater coverage of topics undermines the transformative possibilities that emerge when depth of appreciation, reflection and response is facilitated. The priority so often given in education to grasping control, mastery,

50   *John Sullivan*

accumulation of credits and the instrumental deployment of knowledge undermines, corrodes and suffocates what a more contemplative approach to teaching promises to open up for students and their teachers. Contemplation is a form of observation radically different in nature and purpose from the kinds of surveillance so integral to the panopticon into which so many universities and other public services have degenerated in recent years.

Education in light of Buber and Freire

Two contrasting emphases have struggled for dominance in education. One treats education as a matter of leading out. Its focus is on what is within the learner. It depends on sensitivity and responsiveness to individual potential. It requires a degree of freedom from coercion for learners. It adopts an invitational mode or tone. It stresses the needs of individuals. The other emphasis that jostles for position treats education as a way of forming others. Its focus is on moulding the type of person desired by society. It depends on prior agreement on and confidence about ideals, purposes, values, knowledge and skills to be developed. It assumes authority and relies on a mandate. It adopts an interventionist mode. It stresses the requirements and expectations of the sponsoring community. Tubbs (2005, p.114) summarises and comments on how Martin Buber compared the first emphasis to teaching as a form of gardening, assisting the natural growth of students and then likened the second emphasis to the work of the sculptor. According to Tubbs, Buber concludes that the sculptor has too much confidence in his relation with the student. He, the master, knows too much. The gardener, on the other hand, has too little confidence in his relation with the student. He does too little. Buber criticizes both for one-sidedness. 'The gardener merely "releases" the unique force of each child [while] the sculptor nurtures by copying history into the child' (Tubbs, p.114).

The Irish educator and monk Mark Patrick Hederman (2012) has recently offered an inspiringly humane vision of education, one which clearly benefits from his own contemplative sensitivities, as well as his experience as a teacher and his reading of Buber and Freire. For Hederman education is 'a contact rather than a content' (p.59). Relationship is at the heart of the educational endeavour and crucial to its efficacy. He embraces Buber's insight that the whole of the teacher affects the whole being of the pupil (Hederman, p.62, referring to Buber, 1974, p.134). It seems more than plausible to claim that a contemplative approach to teaching helps to preserve the awareness of this holistic influence. Hederman (p.77) draws attention to how Buber distinguishes education from propaganda: 'Education lifts the people up. It opens their hearts and develops their minds, so that they can discover the truth and make it their own. Propaganda, on the other hand, closes their hearts and stunts their minds.' Again, I believe it can justly be expected that a contemplative approach to teaching is more likely to avoid slipping into propaganda, because it is less possessive of students, seeing them less as objects and more as subjects in their own right. After all, as Hederman reminds his readers, 'Cherishing and challenging have always been the two poles between which education has had to make its tightrope walk' (p.139). Cherishing is at the very heart of a contemplative orientation. Such cherishing does not mean turning a blind eye to shortcomings, nor does it entail the teacher being sentimental about or ready to ignore these. Instead, the teacher should confirm the potentiality rather than the present state of a person (Hederman, p.144).

Hederman draws on Paulo Freire to complement and fill out his educational philosophy. He is aware that Freire's *Pedagogy of the Oppressed* 'stresses that education can never be neutral; it either promotes freedom or conformity' (Hederman, 2012, 73). As summarised by Richard Shaull in his foreword to Freire's landmark book, education

> either functions as an instrument which is used to facilitate the integration of the younger generation into the logic of the present system and being about conformity to it, or it becomes 'the practice of freedom', the means by which men and women deal critically and creatively with reality and discover how to participate in the transformation of their world.
>
> (Freire, 1972, p.14)

Many years after *Pedagogy of the Oppressed*, Freire, in one of his last books, revealed a contemplative dimension as a constitutive element of the teacher's work in facilitating freedom:

> The importance of silence in the context of communication is fundamental. On the one hand, it affords me space while listening to the verbal communication of another person and allows me to enter into the internal rhythm of the speaker's thought and experience that rhythm as language. On the other hand, silence makes it possible for the speaker who is really committed to the experience of communication rather than to the simple transmission of information to hear the question, the doubt, the creativity of the person who is listening. Without this, communication withers.
>
> (Freire, 1998, p.104)

The contemplative as counter-weight to some cultural assumptions about teaching

Like other public services, education has been infiltrated and infected by various features of the disease of managerialism. Rastier (2013) exposes many of the damaging consequences for education of the emphasis on markets, commodities, competition, performativity, utilitarianism and consumerism. Other features of managerialism include measurement, surveillance, the demand for predictability of outcomes and the increasing stranglehold of associated bureaucracies. Among the consequences of these developments, in the midst of enhanced productivity and efficiency (and greater profits for the few), one finds dehumanisation, exploitation, loss of a sense of the common good, the promotion of insistent and radical individualism, the reduction of all values to some economic calculus.

52 *John Sullivan*

The strong and the successful are rewarded, while the weaker members of society are penalised as parasites. As distractions from long-term and deep commitment to truths, values and relationships that require discipline and restraint, as well as self-giving, we find the promotion of a culture that has become banal, the attenuation of social life and the undermining of communities and institutions that mediate between the state and the individual. In order to serve more closely the needs of the economy and to satisfy students-as-customers, who are swindled into believing they are purchasing a private and positional good through their education, recent curriculum and pedagogical trends have contributed to the erosion of critical thinking, short-termism, a loss of historical perspective and the fragmentation of knowledge into packages that can be accumulated in a personal credit-bank. Over-reliance on technology as an educational panacea frequently functions as a distraction from the development of deep, disciplined, comprehensive and coherent approaches to knowledge. Sound-bites titillate our attention momentarily, immediately to be replaced by new attractions for superficially spending our time and expending our energy while the search for significance and meaning becomes a chimaera or fantasy not worth pursuing with persistence, patience and rigour. I have written elsewhere (Sullivan, 2000; 2003) on the necessity for educators to wrestle with managerialism and to counter its stress on certain competencies (conducive to economic productivity) by re-vitalising a concern for character and for enduring purposes.

How might a contemplative dimension in teaching offer a counter-weight to some of these developments? It reminds us that teaching is not merely a matter of mastering a set of techniques. It points the way beyond being driven by utility. Coleridge lamented a situation he could see was already being promoted as early as 1830: 'Education . . . [is] defined as synonymous with Instruction', 'where the population [is] mechanized into engines for the manufactory of new rich men' (Coleridge, quoted in Pfau, 2013, p.424). A contemplative approach prompts teachers and students to pause in the midst of their frenetic transactions of delivery and consumption, leaving space for questioning ends as well as means. It permits teachers (and by implication, if to a lesser extent, students) to be guided by internally owned purposes and principles, rather than by externally driven targets. It is person-centred, not competency- or skill-oriented. It fosters deliberation rather than calculation and meaning rather than measurement. By undermining the tendency to which mass education is prone – because of high student-teacher ratios and intensification of time pressures – to slip into practices of 'batch-delivery' that envisage students-in-general, rather than the diversity, complexity, vulnerability and mystery of real people, a contemplative dimension gives emphasis to particularity, personhood and presence, along with a poetic and philosophic perspective. In an unpublished lecture given by my colleague at Liverpool Hope University, Laura Waite, she spoke of disrupting notions of normalcy. In the context of special educational needs, she was referring to how important it is for teachers to avoid pigeon-holing people and to transcend preconceived categories as to what they are capable of; this is not only a matter of justice to them, but also an enriching of the capacity of teachers – indeed of us all – to be open to receive from others the precious gifts that they can offer because of their experience and perspective. A contemplative approach to teaching enhances the kind of awareness and sensitivity advocated so powerfully by Waite.

Let me briefly draw upon three writers who, while not explicitly focusing on contemplation, draw attention to features of the educational landscape that would benefit from a contemplative approach by teachers. First, in a book with the splendidly provocative title *Why Education is Useless* Daniel Cottom laments the 'corporatized rhetoric of evaluation increasingly brought to bear upon higher education in recent decades' (2003, p.165). Here he is referring to the inexorable demand for accountability, justifying any outlay by teachers of time and resources, as well as the expectation that learning outcomes can be specified in advance; he also has in view student satisfaction surveys which can have undesirable (even if unintended) side-effects. Cottom (p.166) rightly claims that there is a difference between the market for goods and the market for ideas. To mistake the goods at stake by failing to advert to this difference leads to the distortion of relationships in education. For example, one of the legitimate purposes of education is, rather than to provide satisfaction, to provoke dissatisfaction with the way the world is; such a sense of dissatisfaction is a necessary preliminary step to prompting the desire to contribute to improving the way things are done in the world. And while clarity in communication is a virtue, judging a teacher via student's assessment that 'the course was easy to understand' might be entirely inappropriate. Cottom makes a striking and pertinent observation: 'One can easily predict what would be the fate of an educator today if his peer reviewers boasted, as Plato often did of Socrates, that this individual generally left his listeners in a state of greater perplexity than that in which he had found them' (Cottom, p.167). The teacher's responsibility is a much richer and more multi-faceted concept than the notion of accountability which predominates in educational policy, a point recognized by Cottom (p.199) and which I have developed further elsewhere (Sullivan, 2004, pp.268–271). Finally from Cottom, he opens the way to contemplation when he says

> we cannot dispense with useless metaphysical questions, which pragmatists quite correctly see as a waste of time that will never pay off, for the same reason that we cannot have done with art: because it is through such profitless agencies that we live and move and have our being.
>
> (Cottom, 2003, p.201)

The second writer whose work I want to refer to, in aid of my case for teaching as contemplative, is Ellen Rose, who makes a plea for slowing down, for silence and for reflection 'in our digital-cellular-online-robotic-information-saturated-hyper society' (2013, pp.4–5). She says that 'Increasingly, our day-to-day activities entail navigating a high-speed, perpetually changing, interactive, hyperactive, electric media-sphere in which the value accorded to reflection – the inclination to stop and think – is rapidly diminishing' (Rose, p.76). In trying to keep up with our devices on which we have become over-reliant, we run the danger of thinking

54 *John Sullivan*

about ourselves as machines. As one student commented 'You need to unplug yourself in order to make any serious progress' (Rose, p.88). To which Rose responds: 'only within the uncharted space of silence is it possible to fully synthesize the daily onslaught of information, and perhaps generate from it new questions and new possibilities' (p.32). It follows from this observation that teachers must so structure their classroom environment that they open up spaces for silence, brief though these might have to be. Rose also alerts teachers to the messages they might unwittingly be conveying if they allow themselves to be caught up in the maelstrom of frenetic and endless activism demanded in their work.

> Teachers are not alone in having to contend with a host of responsibilities during the course of a single workday, but one of their important roles is to serve as exemplars, to model ways of being in the world. Children learn something when they see their role model rushing around, filling fleeting moments during the day with day-plans, report cards, and other busy work. They learn something quite different when they see their teacher sitting quietly with a book, relishing an opportunity for silence and reverie.
>
> (Rose, 2013, p.73)

When I was a headteacher, I felt guilty if I happened to be reading in my office when someone knocked on the door; was I doing real work at that moment? I think I was a prisoner of excessive activism and needed to bring to my work a contemplative counter-balance. It might well be asked: are we, as teachers, living from the ideas and values that we profess? Have we appropriated and internalised the truths we seek to convey? Students have an uncanny radar that picks up inauthenticity in us; they detect any lack of congruence between our prescriptions and our practice.

The third writer to be drawn upon is Chris Higgins. I take two points he makes as having particular relevance to my argument here. The first – and this is an extension and implication of his words, not something he states explicitly – is that reflectiveness, self-cultivation and contemplation cannot be 'front-loaded' to a professional life; that is it cannot be confined to pre-service preparation. As he points out 'Past insights and growth quickly spoil if self-cultivation is not ongoing' (Higgins, 2011, p.6). We can say much the same about contemplation: a contemplative approach to teaching depends for its authenticity, fertility and health on repeated and ongoing acts of contemplation; it cannot function with fresh insight, sustained receptivity and an enduring capacity to appreciate what and who is before us if it is drawing only upon some past period when contemplation was operative but which is now a distant memory. The learning that contemplation makes possible must be renewed constantly; it cannot be 'banked' and then withdrawn occasionally while the capital accumulated lasts. The second point is about perceiving classroom activities, experiences and relationships as not merely arenas for applying what teachers have learned in the past, but as ongoing sources for knowledge. Higgins builds from Alasdair MacIntyre an understanding of how

Teaching as contemplative 55

practices, of which teaching is one, 'should be thought of as ethical sources rather than as targets of application' (Higgins, p.11). In other words, it is not that we first (and as a separate act) develop our understanding of ethical principles and only then see how they should be implemented 'on the ground'. Rather, it is only in the midst of the practices that the goods at stake are disclosed, clothed as they inevitably are with the particularities, ambiguities and complexities of context, situation, agents, influences, tensions, dilemmas and decisions.

Teachers constantly have to face the pressing question; what is to be done next? This is inescapable. However, behind this question, motivating and guiding the answer given, there should always be an awareness of two other underlying questions: what is this task, this exercise, this activity, in aid of? And, what sort of person do I want to become (as teacher and as student)?

Teachers who carry out their work for the sake of and to honour themselves – to boost their income, self-esteem, reputation, their sense of power or influence or achievement – are doomed to defeat and disappointment; students will not be interested in boosting their teachers' income, self-esteem or reputation. A teacher must be detached enough from the fruits of her labour not to depend upon clear or immediate results, approval, affection or recognition. Outcomes and goals recede into the future and can be elusive, but meaning and significance in the work for the teacher can be found in the here and now if they can bring to it a contemplative dimension.

If teachers carry out their work for the sake of and to honour their students, this is certainly an improvement on the self-centred teachers; it is noble to want to serve students, to help them grow in knowledge, skill, awareness and confidence. However, such service and reaching out in this way by teachers can be experienced by students as an embrace that stifles and smothers. The teacher's pedagogical provision can come across as colonisation of the life-world of students; the conviction that the teacher is doing them some good, filling some gap, making up for some deficiency in their lives can demean what students bring to the classroom, by-pass their natural gifts, ignore their perspective and unwarrantably assume what their needs are. As the French philosopher Louis Lavelle pointed out, 'the greatest good we can do for others is not to communicate to them our riches, but to reveal to them their own' (quoted in Dufour, 2006, p.63, from Lavelle, 1993, p.167).

Even better is to teach for the sake of and to honour the subject entrusted to teachers and for which they are stewards (and this subject is some aspect of truth, beauty, goodness). In the long run, what matters is not the relationship the teacher has with the student (though that does matter in the short run, in establishing an ambience that is conducive to learning), but the relationship the student has with the content of the lesson. As Freire (1998, p.106) says about his role as teacher, '[this is] essentially one of inciting the student to produce his or her own comprehension of the object, using the materials I have offered'. However, the relationship the teacher has with that content will be the prompt for the student to embark on that relationship, the spark that will ignite real engagement, the model of how such a relationship might be transformative.

56 *John Sullivan*

There is a double attendance or waiting needed by the teacher: attending to and waiting upon the student (the person to be awakened and empowered) and attending to and waiting on the subject of the lesson (the aspect of truth to be conveyed).

Conclusion

The moments of contemplation in the practice of teaching may often have to be snatched, rather than experienced as a secure possession, but they rest upon a basic orientation to life in which a contemplative outlook is integral. Here a contemplative approach to teaching could be considered a matter of ecological concern, of caring for the pedagogical environment so that this arouses, facilitates and reinforces learning. If so many acts of the teacher inevitably demand and display self-giving, preserving a contemplative approach – even one that ebbs back and forth, like the tides, to the fore at one moment and withdrawing at another – ensures that such self-giving remains life-giving for teachers as well as pupils and prevents it from becoming a slow process of suicide. If there is any validity to my proposal that teaching should be a contemplative activity, there are implications for the initial education, formation and training of teachers, for their continuing professional development, for those responsible for their working conditions and for the way their work is managed, evaluated and supported, and, most important of all, for how they envisage and conduct their own lives. But that, as they say, is another story.

References

Arendt, H. (1958). *The Human Condition*. New York: Doubleday.
Boland, V. (2007). *Thomas Aquinas*. London: Continuum.
Buber, M. (1974). *Between Man and Man*. Translated by Ronald Gregor Smith. London: Fontana.
Cottom, D. (2003). *Why Education is Useless*. Philadelphia: University of Pennsylvania Press.
Dufour, X. (2006). *Enseigner Une Oeuvre Spirituelle*. Paris: Parole et Silence.
Freire, P. (1972). *Pedagogy of the Oppressed*. London: Penguin.
Freire, P. (1998). *Pedagogy of Freedom*. Lanham, Maryland: Rowman & Littlefield.
Hederman, M.P. (2012). *The Boy in the Bubble*. Dublin: Veritas.
Higgins, C. (2011). *The Good Life of Teaching*. Oxford: Wiley-Blackwell.
Laird, M. (2011). *A Sunlit Absence*. Oxford: Oxford University Press.
Lavelle, L. (1993). *The Dilemma of Narcissus*. New York: Larson Publications.
Lichtmann, M. (2005). *The Teacher's Way*. New York: Paulist Press.
Newman, J.H. (2001). *Rise and Progress of Universities and Benedictine Essays With an Introduction and Notes by Mary Katherine Tillman*. Leominster: Gracewing/ Notre Dame: University of Notre Dame Press.
Pfau, T. (2013). *Minding the Modern*. Notre Dame, IN: University of Notre Dame Press.
Postman, N. and Weingartner, C. (1969). *Teaching as a Subversive Activity*. New York: Doubleday.

Teaching as contemplative   57

Rastier, F. (2013). *Apprendre Pour Transmettre L'Education Contre l'ideologie Manageriale*. Paris: Presses universitaires de France.

Rose, E. (2013). *Reflection*. Toronto: Canadian Scholars Press.

Steiner, G. (2005). *Lessons of the Masters*. Cambridge, MA: Harvard University Press.

Sullivan, J. (2000). Wrestling with managerialism. In: M. Eaton, J. Longmore and A. Naylor (eds), *Commitment to Diversity*, pp.240–259. London: Cassell.

Sullivan, J. (2003). Skills-based models of leadership. In: W.K. Kay, L.J. Francis and K. Watson (eds), *Religion in Education*, Vol. 4, pp.205–232. Leominster: Gracewing.

Sullivan, J. (2004). Responsibility, vocation and critique: teacher education in a Christian context. In: J. Astley, L. Francis, J. Sullivan and A. Walker (eds), *The Idea of a Christian University*, pp.263–278. Milton Keynes: Paternoster.

Taylor, J. (1998). *Poetic Knowledge*. New York: State University of New York Press.

Tubbs, N. (2005). *Philosophy of the Teacher*. Oxford: Blackwell.

4 Education for shalom

Dimensions of a relational pedagogy

John Shortt

Introduction: the need to reconnect with purpose

Katya is a thoughtful 13-year-old student in a large school in Kiev. Her older brother, Vanya, is in the Ukrainian army and there has been no word from him now for over a week. She tries to forget her worries about him and the ongoing war by focusing on her studies. The subject for the first lesson of the day is Mathematics, and this is one of Katya's favourite subjects. The teacher is enthusiastic for the subject but strict in her approach to classroom life and distant in her relationships with her students. Katya wants to talk with others, not about the war, but about the mathematical topic before them. However, talking to others is not allowed in this class. English Language comes next. Katya finds languages difficult, but she enjoys the opportunities this teacher gives everyone to practise their English with one another. The teacher is relaxed and fun-loving, and he relates easily with all the students as he moves around the room. History comes next, and this takes the form of a lecture, delivered with little expression by a teacher who seems to be disconnected from what he is saying and disconnected from the students before him, who are all scribbling their lecture notes in complete silence.

With school finished for the day, Katya walks home to her mother's apartment at the end of the morning, still trying not to think about Vanya and the war, still attempting to focus on her studies. She wonders what it is all for. How does it all connect together? How does Mathematics relate to History or to Language or the other subjects of the school curriculum? It all leads to a good job when you leave school, or so her mother and teachers seem to be saying. It all helps the national economy, they say, and the government and media seem to agree. But the nation is divided and people are killing each other; somehow, to Katya's mind, job prospects and economic issues seem trivial in the face of such suffering. Why can't people get on with one another? What have classes in Mathematics, English and History got to do with learning to live together in peace, with or without prosperity? Can her teachers help? Is the way they teach something to do with it?

With her own family's and nation's problems such a concern to her, Katya does not ask whether it might be different elsewhere in the world. Doubtless, the experiences of Mary in Dublin or Mahmoud in Doha, Banji in Lusaka or Raquel in Lima would differ significantly from that of Katya in Kiev and from one another. In more peaceful contexts than that of Ukraine, they may be more concerned about environmental issues than civil war. However, if they share her questions about connectedness, both within the curriculum and among people, and about connection with the overall purpose of the education they are experiencing, it is not likely that these questions will be receiving much attention in discussions of education in their schools or their national contexts. Policy-makers and educationalists in general are more likely to be preoccupied with their country's position in international comparison studies such as PISA (Programme for International Student Assessment) than with the overall purposes of education. School leaders and teachers are more likely to focus on their school's performance in relation to other schools.

Katya's questions are lost sight of in what Gert Biesta (2009) has called 'an age of measurement', an age not limited to the Western world but one that is having global impact through PISA and similar studies. Biesta (2009, p.34) argues that preoccupation with the measurement of educational outcomes is having a profound influence on research that seeks to provide an evidence-base for educational practice and also on practice itself, 'from the highest levels of educational policy at national and supra-national level down to the practices of local schools and teachers'. He questions 'whether we are indeed measuring what we value, or whether we are just measuring what we can easily measure and thus end up valuing what we (can) measure' (Biesta, 2009, p.35).

This loss of sight of issues of ultimate value and overall purpose is partly due, Biesta (2009, p.36) says, to what he terms 'the "learnification" of education: the transformation of educational vocabulary into a language of learning'. He highlights two problematic aspects of this:

> One is that 'learning' is basically an individualistic concept. It refers to what people, as individuals do – even if it is couched in such notions as collaborative or cooperative learning. This stands in stark contrast to the concept of 'education' which always implies a relationship: someone educating someone else and the person educating thus having a certain sense of what the purpose of his or her activities is. The second problem is that 'learning' is basically a process term. It denotes processes and activities but is open – if not empty – with regard to content and direction. This helps to explain why the rise of the new language of learning has made it more difficult to ask questions about content, purpose and direction of education.
>
> (Biesta, 2009, pp.38–39)

When there is an absence of explicit attention to questions of value and purpose, there can be implicit acceptance of a 'common sense' view of the aims of education. Biesta comments:

> We have to bear in mind, however, that what appears as 'common sense' often serves the interests of some groups (much) better than those of others.

60   *John Shortt*

> The prime example of a common sense view about the purpose of education is the idea that what matters most is academic achievement in a small number of curricular domains, particularly language, science and mathematics – and it is this common sense view which has given so much credibility to studies such as TIMMS, PIRLS and PISA.
>
> (Biesta, 2009, p.37)

In this chapter, I seek to respond to the need to reconnect with the purpose of education by proposing that in the idea of shalom we can find an aim that answers Katya's questions and is not beset by the problems of learnification, individualism and exclusive focus on measurable outcomes identified by Gert Biesta.

My proposal has its source within a particular worldview, one that is by no means universally accepted in our plural world, but it is offered as a contribution to ongoing discussion of the ends of education in the hope that it may contain insights of general interest, including to those who may not share the set of basic values and beliefs that characterise that worldview. This is not to suggest that the differences in ultimate commitment themselves are beyond rational discussion: indeed, I have argued at length elsewhere to the contrary (Shortt, 1991), but that is not the focus of this chapter.

Shalom and knowing of the third kind

'Shalom' is a Hebrew word that is often translated as 'peace'. However, if we understand 'peace' as it is generally understood in our current English language usage as freedom from or cessation of war or violence or, alternatively, as an inner emotional or mental tranquillity, we fall very far short of the full and positive meaning of shalom.

Old Testament scholar Walter Brueggemann (1976, p.185) says that shalom 'conveys a sense of personal wholeness in a community of justice and caring that addresses itself to the needs of all humanity and all creation'. Cornelius Plantinga writes of shalom as:

> the webbing together of God, humans, and all creation in justice, fulfilment, and delight . . . Shalom means universal flourishing, wholeness and delight – a rich state of affairs in which natural needs are satisfied and natural gifts fruitfully employed, a state of affairs that inspires joyful wonder as its Creator and Savior opens doors and welcomes the creatures in whom he delights. Shalom, in other words, is the way things ought to be.
>
> (Plantinga, 1995, p.10)

Nicholas Wolterstorff defines shalom in terms of relationships of four kinds and writes:

> Shalom is present when a person dwells at peace in all his or her relationships: with God, with self, with fellows, with nature . . . To dwell in shalom is to

Education for shalom 61

enjoy living before God, to enjoy living in one's physical surroundings, to enjoy living with one's fellows, to enjoy life with oneself.

(Wolterstorff, 2002, p.101)

These and other accounts show that the meaning of shalom as used in the Old Testament is wide-ranging and includes wholeness, community, justice, caring, flourishing, delight, well-being, soundness and integrity. Shalom is relational and is therefore a matter of what could be termed 'knowing of the third kind'. Whereas Gilbert Ryle (1949, pp.28–32) distinguished between 'knowing that' and 'knowing how', this is knowing with a direct object, knowing a person, place or thing.

The three kinds of knowing are related. Some 'knowing that' is necessary for relational knowing for it would be strange to claim to know a person and not be able to state some facts about her or him even though the facts that we state may not be exactly the same as those stated by somebody else who also knows that person. At the same time, it is possible to make an in-depth study of facts about a person and still not be justified in claiming to know that person. In a similar way, some interpersonal skills may also be necessary for relational knowing but they cannot be sufficient for it because we may know to some extent how to relate appropriately to a person without actually knowing that person. Relational knowing cannot be reduced to either 'knowing that' or 'knowing how' or even to a combination of the two. Something more is required by way of a direct acquaintance with or immediate awareness of the person, place or thing that is known.

These distinctions among kinds of knowing are reflected in many languages. In French, for example, relational knowing is 'connaître' while 'savoir' is used for both 'knowing that' and 'knowing how'. German distinguishes usages even further for it has different words for all three kinds of knowing – 'wissen' (know that), 'können' (know how) and 'kennen' (know a person or place). In contrast with the distinctions made in contemporary languages, the Hebrew conception of knowledge was strongly relational. The word used almost always in the Old Testament for knowing of any kind is 'yada'. This is the word used when intimate sexual relations are written about in terms of 'knowing' a man or a woman. The same word is used for knowledge of God. Knowing God is not merely an awareness of his existence but a recognition of who he is and of his demands upon the obedience of those who know him. The opposite of knowing God is not ignorance of him but a turning away from him in sinful rebellion.

Persons in relation

As we have seen above, Wolterstorff defines shalom in terms of relational knowing of other people, of the physical world, of God and of oneself. In similar but less explicitly religious terms, John Fisher gives an account of what he terms the four 'domains of human existence: relation with self, in the Personal domain; relation

62   John Shortt

with others, in the Communal domain; relation with the environment, in the Environmental domain; and relation with Transcendent Other, in the Transcendental domain'. He goes on to say of the Transcendental domain that it is to do with: 'relationship of self with some-thing or some-One beyond the human level, i.e. ultimate concern, cosmic force, transcendent reality, or God . . . involves faith toward, adoration and worship of, the source of Mystery of the universe' (Fisher, 2000, p.43).

In the remainder of this chapter, I will focus mainly on education for shalom in the communal and environmental domains with some brief comments on shalom as relation with God/Transcendent Other. For the sake of space, I will leave shalom-ful relation with self to one side, except to suggest that it may be, to a large extent, a result of getting the other three kinds of relation right.

I turn first to the communal domain, that of relation with other human beings, as a domain that is of central and obvious significance for teaching and learning. In their joint contribution in the opening pages of a book entitled *No Education Without Relation*, the authors say this:

> [E]ducation is not mainly about the facts that students stuff into their heads . . . education is not mainly about developing thinking skills . . . education is primarily about human beings who need to meet together, as a group of people, if learning is to take place . . . learning is primarily about human beings who meet. Meeting and learning are inseparable.
>
> (Bingham et al., 2004, p.5)

In similar vein, Parker Palmer (1998, p.16) quotes Martin Buber's statement that 'all real living is meeting', and he relates this immediately to education by adding that 'teaching is endless meeting'. Again, also in similar vein, Brueggemann (1976, p.167) says that 'learning is meeting' and goes on to point out that this poses problems for our usual way of thinking that education is for competence: 'We are learning slowly and late that education for competence without education as meeting promises us deadly values and scary options'.

All of this is based in a particular view of human being and nature which finds expression, for example, in poet John Donne's talk of no person being an island or, more positively, in the usual English translation of the word 'Ubuntu' as used by the Xhosa people of southern Africa: I am because we are.

Rowan Williams, drawing upon the small but very significant body of work of Russian writer Vladimir Lossky, writes of 'an essential mysteriousness' about the notion of the person in the human world which is about the place the person occupies in terms of being 'the point where the lines of relationship intersect'. He continues:

> To be the point where lines of a relationship intersect means that we can't simply lift some abstract thing called 'the person' out of it all. We're talking about a reality in which people enter into the experience, the aspiration, the sense of self, of others. And that capacity to live in the life of another – to

Education for shalom   63

have a life in someone else's life – is part of the implication of this profound mysteriousness about personal reality.

(Williams, 2013, pp.12–13)

This view of the human being and human nature is quite far removed from the Cartesian rationalist view that was dominant in philosophy of education in the mid to late 1900s and is still quite influential in spite of the postmodern shift that has taken place since. In those days, the development of the individual student's rational autonomy was widely accepted as the central aim of education and a 552-page volume appeared with the title of *Education and the Development of Reason* (Dearden, Hirst and Peters, 1972). In a paper published just a few years after that book, Paul Hirst (1979, pp.101–102) discusses propositional knowledge (knowing-that), procedural knowledge (knowing-how) and what I have termed knowledge of the third kind, and he concludes that knowledge of people, places or things is always reducible to knowing-how and knowing-that plus 'another non-knowledge element' that he does not define any further.

Relatively unknown at that time was the personalist philosophy of John Macmurray whose work was mostly written in the 1930s, 1940s and 1950s and who now, nearly 40 years after his death, is coming to be seen as a philosopher for the twenty-first century. Macmurray argued that we should move from the isolated self of rationalist philosophy to see the self in relation to the Other:

I exist as an individual only in a personal relation to other individuals. Formally stated, 'I' am one term in the relation 'You and I' which constitutes both the 'I' and the 'You'. But within this relation, which constitutes my existence, I can isolate myself from you in intention, so that my relation to you becomes impersonal. In this event, I treat you as object, refusing the personal relationship.

(Macmurray, 1961, p.28)

This is very similar to Martin Buber's talk of 'I and Thou' (Buber, 1970) but seems to have been arrived at independently by the less widely-known Macmurray. According to Macmurray's biographer, John E. Costello, they knew each other, and Buber was an admirer of Macmurray's work and is quoted as saying to him, 'I see no difference between us . . . it is simply that you are the metaphysician and I am the poet' (Costello, 2002, p.322). Buber and Macmurray said very similar things about persons in relation with other persons but there is, I think, a significant difference between them: Buber gave attention to our relationship with the physical environment in a way that Macmurray with his focus on relations between persons does not seem to have done. It is to this relationship I turn in the next section.

Partnership with the otherness of the world

The title of this section is a phrase used by Parker Palmer that shows the influence of Buber upon his thinking. Buber (1970) famously distinguished

64 *John Shortt*

between I-You (Thou) and I-It relationships. At first sight, it might seem that I-You relationships are relationships with other people and I-It relationships are relationships with things in the physical world, but this is far from what Buber intends by the distinction. Our relationships with both our fellow human beings and with things in the world can be both I-You and I-It and, indeed, should be both provided, always that the I-You relationship remains the primary one. We can experience a person or thing as an object or we can relate to the person or thing as anOther subject. It is not that we are not to be objective but to be exclusively objective and detached, i.e., always in I-It mode, is to be objectivist.

Buber gives an example of observing a tree in a range of I-It modes and encountering it in an I-You relation:

> I can accept it as a picture . . . I can feel it as movement . . . I can assign it to a species and observe it as an instance . . . I can overcome its uniqueness and form so rigorously that I recognize it only as an expression of the law . . . I can dissolve it into a number, into a pure relation between numbers, and eternalize it. Throughout all of this the tree remains my object and has its place and its time span, its kind and condition. But it can also happen, if will and grace are joined, that as I contemplate the tree I am drawn into a relation, and the tree ceases to be an It . . . This does not require me to forego any of the modes of contemplation. There is nothing that I must not see in order to see, and there is no knowledge that I must forget. Rather is everything, picture and movement, species and instance, law and number included and inseparably fused.
>
> (Buber, 1970, pp.57–58)

Esther Meek (2011, p.262) likens the movement between I-It and I-You to the rhythm of breathing. She also makes a distinction between what she terms the 'looking' of the I-It relation and the 'seeing' of the I-You relation (2011, p.463): '*Looking* is passive, across a space, non-interactive . . . By contrast, seeing is active and interactive, a kind of interpenetration . . . embodied . . . a phenomenon of love, or reveling. It attends, gazes, and soaks in.'

Buber (1970, pp.56–57) says that we may 'encounter the You in all spheres of life' including our relationships with nature as well as with one another and with God: 'In every You we address the eternal You, in every sphere according to its manner'. This is not a pantheism that identifies God with the world. Meek (2011, p.381) says that reality is gift and is therefore 'metonymously personal . . . fraught with the personal, imbued with the dynamic interpersonal relationship which contexts it, yet freely distinct from Giver and recipient'.

The I-You relationship with the world should be characterised by love and care rather than a desire for mastery and control. Palmer urges us to practise knowing as a form of love so that we may enter this 'partnership with the otherness of the world', and he continues:

> By finding our place in the ecosystem of reality, we might see more clearly which actions are life-giving and which are not – and in the process participate

Education for shalom 65

more fully in our own destinies, and the destiny of the world, then we do in our drive for control.

(Palmer 1998, p.56)

We are indeed placed in 'the ecosystem of reality'. If Ubuntu's 'I am because we are' is a way of saying that we are persons in relation, then perhaps we can express something of this partnership with the physical world as 'I am (and we are) because the physical world is'. We are embodied beings, made of the dust of the earth or, as some put it, made of stardust.

Buber, Meek, Macmurray and Palmer all share a belief in a God who is personal and who is the Transcendental Other encountered in relation with nature. They could add a third Ubuntu-like 'I am . . .': 'I am (and we are) because God is'. This is the relation that they believe makes all other relationships meaningful. They relate to the world as being, as Gerard Manley Hopkins put it, 'charged with the grandeur of God'.

However, many people in our plural world do not believe in a personal God, so does this talk of partnership with otherness contain any insights for them? I think it can. In spiritual but less explicitly religious terms, this encounter with the You in nature can perhaps be described as being with the 'moreness' that Dwayne Huebner (1991, p.15) writes about: 'There is more than we know, can know, will ever know. It is a "moreness" that takes us by surprise when we are at the edge and end of our knowing'.

Conclusion: teaching for shalom

The questions running around in Katya's mind about her school studies raise the need to reconnect with purpose in education. I have suggested that the Hebrew idea of shalom can help us in our search for ultimate values and overall purpose. Shalom is about community, connectedness and flourishing and resonates with the common good, an idea that has a long history as far back as Aristotle. What the even older idea of shalom has that is absent in the common good as usually defined are the interests of the natural world. Partnership with the otherness of the world is rather more than care for the environment because it promotes human flourishing: shalom involves relationship with it for its own sake.

What could all this mean for the teachers and students in Katya's school in Kiev, Mary's in Dublin, Mahmoud's in Dubai, Banji's in Lusaka or Raquel's in Lima? What might a relational pedagogy look like if rooted in shalom?

Connectedness is, I think, a key characteristic. One of Katya's teachers is connected with her subject but not, apparently, with her students. Another appears to really enjoy being with his students and is probably also enthusiastic about his subject. A third is clearly disconnected from both subject and students. Palmer (1998, p.115) says that 'connectedness is the principle behind good teaching'. Not only is it the case that, as he puts it (1998, p.1), 'we teach who we

66   *John Shortt*

are' as we relate to those among whom we teach and learn, but we also need to be connected with what we are teaching. He (1998, p.107) writes:

> [O]ur conventional images of educational community ignore our relationships with the great things that call us together – the things that call us to know, to teach, to learn . . . By 'great things' I mean the subjects around which the circle of seekers has always gathered – not the disciplines that study these subjects, not the texts that talk about them, not the theories that explain them, but the things themselves. I mean the genes and ecosystems of biology, the symbols and referents of philosophy and theology, the archetypes of betrayal and forgiveness and loving and loss that are the stuff of literature . . . the artifacts and lineages of anthropology, the materials of engineering with their limits and potentials, the logic of systems in management, the shapes and colors of music and art, the novelties and patterns of history, the elusive idea of justice under law.

Connectedness is not only between and among teachers and students and between them and the great things of the subjects they are teaching and studying, it is also across the curriculum. Katya is puzzled about the wholeness and interrelatedness of her studies. Teaching for shalom-ful wholeness requires teachers to work together to provide an integrated curriculum in their schools, colleges and universities. Individual teachers can take their students across subject-area boundaries in their teaching of their own specialism. Take Francis Su for example. He is a mathematics professor in California (and also a song-writer and currently President of the Mathematical Association of America) who seeks to cultivate in his students 'a mathematical yawp . . . that expression of surprise or delight at discovering the beauty of a mathematical idea or argument' and help them to transform it into poetry (Su, 2010, p.760). Another example is a unit entitled 'Art meets Science' in Charis Science, one of the products of the Charis Project, in which teachers are encouraged to help their students to explore Joseph Wright's 18th century paintings *The Alchymist* and *An Experiment on a Bird in the Air Pump* as part of their study of the nature of science (Shortt, 2000, pp.21–28).

Humility is another characteristic of teaching for shalom. In his book *Exiles from Eden*, Mark Schwehn (1993, p.49) says, 'Some degree of humility is a precondition for learning'. I would add that it is also a precondition of good teaching. Teaching for shalom-ful I-You relationships with one another and with our physical environment calls for humility before the Otherness of our fellow human beings and the Otherness of the natural world, the 'moreness' that leads us to acknowledge that there is always more to know, more than we can ever know. Knowing is always coming to know. As Palmer (1998, p.108) puts it, 'humility is the only lens through which great things can be seen – and once we have seen them, humility is the only posture possible'.

Love and care are also important characteristics. If, as Palmer argues, knowing is a form of love and if learning is coming to know then learning is falling in love.

Education for shalom   67

The relational teacher is therefore not so much, as Plato said Socrates saw himself to be, a midwife in the service of ideas as she is a matchmaker who introduces the to-be-lover to the to-be-loved in the hope that the falling in love of learning takes place. Wittgensteinian philosopher D.Z. Phillips (1970, p.163) said that the teaching of religious beliefs is a matter of 'elucidation . . . displaying a thing of beauty'. Teaching that something is beautiful involves talking about it and drawing attention to its features in the hope that learners will come to see for themselves. I would suggest that this is true right across the curriculum and not only in religious education.

There is much more that could be said about relational pedagogy that promotes shalom e.g., the importance of listening in dialogue with the Other and the place of silence, but I hope that I have covered some of the key characteristics here.

References

Bingham, C., Sidorkin, A.M., Biesta, G., Margonis, F., Hutchinson, J.N., McDaniel, B.L., Pijanowski, C.M., Mayo, C., Tengel, B.S., Romano, R.M. and Thayer-Bacon, B.J. (2004). Manifesto of relational pedagogy: meeting to learn, learning to meet. In: C. Bingham and A. M. Sidorkin (eds), *No Education Without Relation*, pp.5–7. New York: Peter Lang Publishing.

Biesta, G.J.J. (2009). Good education in an age of measurement: on the need to reconnect with the question of purpose in education. *Educational Assessment, Evaluation and Accountability*, 21(1), 33–46.

Brueggemann, W. (1976). *Living Toward a Vision: Biblical Reflections on Shalom*. Philadelphia: United Church Press.

Buber, M. (1970). *I and Thou*. Trans. W. Kauffman. New York: Charles Scribner's Sons.

Costello, J.E. (2002). *John Macmurray: A Biography*. Edinburgh: Floris Books.

Dearden, R.F., Hirst, P.H. and Peters, R.S. (eds) (1972). *Education and the Development of Reason*. London: Routledge & Kegan Paul.

Fisher, J. (2000). Being human, becoming whole: understanding spiritual health and well-being. *Journal of Christian Education*, 43(3), 37–52.

Hirst, P.H. (1979). Human movement, knowledge and education. *Journal of Philosophy of Education*, 13(1), 101–108.

Huebner, D. (1991). Education and spirituality. *Journal of Curriculum Theorizing*, 11(2), 13–34.

Macmurray, J. (1961). *Persons in Relation*. London: Faber and Faber.

Meek, E.L. (2011). *Loving to Know: Covenant Epistemology*. Eugene, OR: Cascade Books.

Palmer, P.J. (1998). *The Courage to Teach: Exploring the Inner Landscape of a Teacher's Life*. San Francisco: Jossey-Bass.

Phillips, D.Z. (1970). *Faith and Philosophical Enquiry*. London: Routledge & Kegan Paul.

Plantinga, C. (1995). *Not the Way It's Supposed to Be*. Grand Rapids, MI: Eerdmans.

Ryle, G. (1949). *The Concept of Mind*. Chicago, IL: University of Chicago Press.

Schwehn, M. (1993). *Exiles from Eden: Religion and the Academic Vocation in America*. New York: Oxford University Press.

68 *John Shortt*

Shortt, J. (1991). *Towards a Reformed Epistemology and its Educational Significance.* PhD diss., University of London Institute of Education. Available from: www.johnshortt.org/Pages/MyPhDThesis.aspx (accessed 19 August 2015).

Shortt, J. (ed.) (2000). *Charis Science: Units A1 – A9.* Nottingham: The Stapleford Centre.

Su, F.E. (2010). Teaching research: encouraging discoveries. *American Mathematical Monthly,* 117(9), 759–769.

Williams, R. (2013). *The Person and the Individual: Human Dignity, Human Relationships and Human Limits.* London: Theos.

Wolterstorff, N.P. (2002). *Educating for Life: Reflections on Christian Teaching and Learning.* Grand Rapids, MI: Baker Academic.

5 Is being critical enough?

Ruth Pilkington

Introduction

The issue of professionalism within education has been a hotly contested subject for several decades, if not longer. While traditional views of professionalism based upon ideas of subject specialist knowledge, accountability and autonomy, and service still predominate for educators (Bourner, Katz and Watson, 2000), increasingly many of these notions are subject to debate and reconceptualisation as the environment for UK education (and indeed that in most western anglophone nations) has shifted to an increasingly market-led, competitive and accountability-driven system (Barnett, 2008). This is valid across the sectors, both compulsory and non-compulsory. This has changed how education operates, impacting upon the work and perceived status of teaching in particular. Learners experience these shifts as a series of developments, for example:

- a focus on service and quality leading to increased use of surveys in order to elicit and establish quality and gain feedback;
- changes in resourcing: larger group sizes and classes, for example;
- increased emphasis on choice, league tables and indicators of quality around education, institutions and subject;
- inspections and peer review and observation resulting in a growth of external presence in the classroom;
- perceived changes to teaching with absence for training, illness (stress-related) and other work calling away regular core staff, leading to a growth in part-time and cover teachers.

On the other hand, institutions and the staff who teach and interact with learners experience greater pressures in the new environment. These emerge as the following:

- an emphasis on audit for outcomes, work and performance;
- requirements for visibly evidencing effectiveness, excellence and performance for marketing and promotional purposes;
- increased pressures on individuals' performativity and providing measures of effective teaching and excellence;

70   *Ruth Pilkington*

- rapid changes to teaching, assessment and learning as a result of policy nationally and within institutions themselves;
- constant change and accommodation to new initiatives and agendas – a requirement for ongoing and agile responses by individual and organisation structures and systems.

Several chapters within the current book have explored some of the issues mentioned above for teachers suggesting a range of solutions. Berg et al. in Chapter 2, for example, investigated this from the perspective of initial teacher education. It bridged challenges facing both novice teachers and those working in various roles to support those teachers, and suggested the crucial need for experienced teacher educators and mentors to gain a clear professional identity supported by reflection and scholarship. Shortt (Chapter 4) introduced the concept of relational pedagogy in his discussion of how professionalism might be addressed. He discussed the importance of values and the situated, relational nature of teaching, something that emerges again in this chapter from a more practical and applied perspective. Finally, in Chapter 3, Sullivan discussed a number of solutions that reside in contemplative approaches to practitioner development. Potential approaches included acknowledging the need for reflective space and perspective by teachers to develop as professionals and as enablers of others' learning. The notions of space, dialogue and identity emerge here in this chapter in the discussion of how teachers across all sectors can be enabled and supported in their development. Looking across the various sectors, however, the situation with respect to teachers' sense of professionalism and identity remains largely unresolved in the face of these changes, although the volatility of the situation can be seen in the following illustrations from the various UK sectors:

1   For HE in the UK, there is a current and lively debate around professional standards and a Teaching Excellence Framework, with this debate being replicated in Australia and the US. At the time of writing, the growth in professional recognitions in the sector is at 24 per cent per annum; many institutions have invested in CPD frameworks enabling them to award professional status for those involved in teaching and learning, some setting targets of 100% participation; and the HE Academy, as gatekeeper for professional recognition using the UK Professional Standards Framework (UK PSF), is actively pursuing ways and means of tracking good standing for the sector.

2   Over the past two decades several national initiatives took control of the professionalisation of staff. In 2001 regulations came into play for FE teachers to have qualifications. Reinforced in the 2006 White Paper, this resulted in a qualifications framework under FENTO being reviewed and transferred to LLUK and requirements for both a licence to practise and for ongoing CPD. This resulted in an extremely rapid professionalisation of that particular

Is being critical enough? 71

sector; however, the fact that the requirements for qualifications and CPD have been deregulated and now reside with the FE institutions indicates how politically vulnerable the professionalism of teaching can be.

3   Within compulsory education and training, there has long been a require-ment for secondary teachers to qualify in order to teach, but this is currently challenged by initiatives allowing practitioners to acquire their qualifi-cations whilst teaching/in the workplace, an issue which may suggest de-professionalising the workforce.

4   The nursery sector has also explored professional qualifications for staff, but costs in the sector make this even more vulnerable to shifting political interests and funding.

These examples all indicate a lack of clarity on professionalism in education. They set the backdrop for a chapter which interrogates how practitioners might respond to the challenges of policy and government agenda setting within environments which are competitive, marketised, consumer-orientated and resource-poor, and where the organisations themselves are in flux, spanning business-orientations and public accountability.

This chapter argues the rationale for organisations to take a more constructive approach to enabling learning for teachers alongside a need for a pro-active and critical stance by practitioners towards directing and engaging with professional learning and development. In doing so, it moves beyond an individually framed notion of critical professionalism (Appleby and Pilkington, 2014) to suggest an organisationally relevant solution.

Rather than engage directly with the concept of 'professionalism', which is a term that has been amply discussed by others (Robson, 2006; Sachs, 2001; Cunningham, 2008), this chapter builds on two models, one by Barnett, Parry and Coate (2001) using a curricular framework, and a second which targets organisational space and support for teaching (Appleby and Pilkington, 2014). The broadly accepted conclusion on professionalism suggests that it is contested, contingent, situated and relational, and changes over time (Evans, 2008). I would add that it is something that is ongoing and emergent for the practitioner: constructed within a discourse between policy and national directives (frameworks, agendas, political interests) in the first instance; translated by the organisation itself (framed by local policy, mission and priorities, and environment) to inform local agendas; and, finally, experienced and enacted by the individual (interpreted in the light of values, perceptions and assumptions, goals and position). This extends beyond philosophy and suggests an organisation-led and applied solution. Given that the environment for education is also in a dynamic state of flux and supercomplexity (Barnett, 2008), and career paths are diverse and often uncertain, the meaning of professionalism for an individual has to be locally defined, and becomes liquid and impermanent. As a consequence, when considering professionalism in education, I propose we should address how professionals learn, and how an organisation should support this.

72   Ruth Pilkington

The solution can be founded on a consideration of three ideas informed by the two models:

1   Professional learning structured around Barnett, Parry and Coate's model (2001) of curriculum founded on a tripartite relational representation of three circles, knowledge, action and self. This allows a deconstruction of the nature of professional learning.
2   A discussion of professional capital as a real and crucial element in organisational success. This shifts the responsibility for professional learning.
3   An organisational solution using constructed space around systems and process of educational work.

Professional learning

Within the Barnett et al. (2001) model three circles represent three factors in a professional learning curriculum for teachers. These are labelled knowledge or knowing; self, identity or being; doing, action or acting. The size and positioning of the circles in relation to each other indicate the significance and emphasis on the three factors when learning any particular subject curriculum: in this case 'teaching'. The three circles can be presented relationally by degrees of overlap and distance between them, showing how the three factors influence each other, and can also vary over time in terms of their respective size and relationship. A novice learner, for example, may find the curriculum places more emphasis on the acquisition of a discrete knowledge base (knowing) and learning the appropriate skills to apply to the doing of the subject, whereas the circle of self and being may grow in importance as mastery is achieved. The model is useful for exploring and conceptualising what is required within professional learning and how the visually represented components may alter over time. It communicates the dynamic, complex, contextualised nature of professional educational learning, and this is discussed further below.

For professional learning as teachers, we might envision the first circle as representing the necessary knowledge base: what a teacher needs to know. As can be imagined, this exposes complexity, especially where in teaching at post-compulsory levels there is an accepted duality of knowledge, requiring the teacher to have both knowledge of the subject and knowledge of teaching. This is often unpacked in debates on dual professionalism (Peel, 2005; Robson, 2006) within the FE sector and is a significance aspect of how the UK PSF for HE is structured. The recent shift to workplace education of secondary teachers in the UK is altering what used to be a system of postgraduate teacher education founded on a pre-requisite generic pedagogic knowledge base allied to subject knowledge at degree level. Pedagogic knowledge would be developed in the academic setting and subsequently applied to practice. As compulsory teacher training is increasingly being situated in the workplace from an early stage, the format for initial professional education is changing. Workplace learning (Eraut, 1994, 2004) is far more reliant upon the individual, and his/her perspectives, motivations, aims and previous experience, so it is arguably less standardised and more subjective. Moreover, when we consider the professional knowledge base of teachers, there is the added complexity facing practitioners and practice educators and their curricula illustrated by Shulman's deconstruction of teacher knowledge. He describes seven significant areas of knowledge for teaching (1987) in which pedagogic knowing and subject knowledge are just the start. Teachers, Shulman argues, also need knowledge of systems and processes within teaching, generic knowledge of learners, educational purposes and educational contexts. Some of these admittedly lie beyond a discrete knowledge base that is taught; rather, their knowing must be acquired within the organisation and the workplace and involves a shifting set of concepts dependent upon role and career phase. This suggests progression in knowledge acquisition: a transfer between learning in an academic setting and learning in the organisation.

Teacher education is further complicated by the notion of evidence-based practice and the concept of a teacher as practitioner-researcher responsible for creating and constructing knowledge on the basis of ongoing and scholarly inquiry. This privileges work-based, practice-relevant learning and emphasises criticality of perspective and rigour with respect to how professional learning is designed, informed and interpreted. Scholarship of teaching and learning (SoTL) has acquired considerable importance within HE globally, and increasingly lecturers are expected to participate actively not only in the construction of their specialist subject knowledge base, but also in actively contributing to the pedagogic knowledge base of the community of practice (Vloet, Jacobs and Veugelers, 2013). This form of practice-centred, critical learning implies maturity and expertise on the part of the practitioner, a research orientation, and places a responsibility on the teacher to both teach a subject and research their practice. At the same time, whilst this may be expected and desirable, it is rarely facilitated within a teaching workload. Professional teacher knowledge is extremely complex and demanding, therefore, and is strongly structured and motivated by workplace interests.

The circle on 'doing and acting' in Barnett et al.'s model opens up a range of challenges and tensions for teachers allied to the discussion above on the professional knowledge base because, whilst some generic skills can be acquired and taught outside the practising of teaching, teachers are more often than not characterized as learning through the 'doing of practice' (Guile and Lucas, 1999; Grossman, Hammermas and McDonald, 2009). This reflects the thesis of professional learning within communities of practice disseminated by Lave and Wenger (Wenger, 1998) and notions of apprenticeship where the practitioner learns by doing. It recognises the highly experiential nature of professional learning and mastery acquisition (Dreyfus and Dreyfus, 1986). It is the basis and focus for much of the literature built up around reflection and reflective practice (Schön, 1983; Van Manen, 1995; Boud, Keogh and Walker; Larrivee, 2008), which, for example, positions learning firmly within experience-based activity. Whilst this circle may be a relatively lesser one for the practitioner within sectors requiring qualifications as a license to practice, it can swallow the knowledge circle

74   *Ruth Pilkington*

for those sectors where pedagogic knowledge is entirely positioned in work-based, experiential, reflective learning. And what's more, the location for learning about teaching challenges the quality and standardisation of such knowledge, as well as challenging organisations in its management and direction.

There are implications for learning that occurs through the doing of practice, however. Because professional learning occurs in its practising, it is very strongly influenced by the community of peers, and by how we talk about practice, by the discourse of a group and of an organisation. It is culturally framed (Becher and Trowler, 2001), in other words. It takes place within significant networks (Roxå and Mårtensson, 2009) and is reliant upon 'professional talk' (Cunningham, 2008). It will be influenced by an individual's assumptions and prior knowledge, by his or her taken-for-granteds (Ghaye and Ghaye, 1998), unless subjected to critical interrogation through scholarly engagement with wider bodies of knowledge and perspectives, or by the questioning input of peers (Reynolds and Vince, 2004). In other words, professional learning becomes an outcome of social construction within and around practice, making it personalised and difficult to generalise. On the other hand, space for engaging in professional talk, deconstruction and reconstruction through dialogue and facilitated and/or critical reflection becomes an essential precondition for learning by teachers and I suggest is both necessary and desirable. Unfortunately, it is an aspect of practice that is often squeezed by workload pressure. For example, curriculum design and review by educators, which should be a team-based activity and opportunity for learning, is increasingly left to individuals to do alone and under time pressure. Professional learning through talk is regarded as being of low value because it is too nebulous for measurement. On the other hand, as the literature on peer observation suggests (Gosling and Mason O'Connor, 2009), it is effective and can support professional learning where it is part of a genuine peer-led dialogue. Social knowledge construction and its embedding within work is also strongly benefitted by formal mentoring approaches (Tynjälä et al., 2012; Brockbank and McGill, 1998), and can consequently be positioned as a crucial leadership function within educational and organisational structures.

The final circle in the model addresses identity, the sense of being a teacher and its purpose. Shulman recognises this importance within his seven areas of knowledge (1987), and I suggest that this circle is a crucial one for teachers within a discourse of social justice and the social purpose of education (Freire, 1970). According to Barnett, Parry and Coate (2001), this circle can be neglected in some disciplines and highly prioritised in others such as counselling and health professions. It relates to stance, positionality, motivation, and can be profoundly influenced by the organisation, by career stage and by work-life tensions. It is an aspect of teaching that influences our agency as decision makers and as actors within the setting, and in enacting educational decisions for and with our learners. It is a central component within critical and reflective learning, especially if we are to gain a sense of self-awareness, meta-reflection and to be able to interrogate and evaluate our actions (van Manen, 1995; Ghaye and Ghaye, 1998; Larrivee, 2008). Further, it informs our practice and learning as practitioner-researchers where an ethical stance is crucial to how we use and interpret the evidence base (Cousin, 2009). It is specifically identified as a field within professional practice with a history that goes back to Aristotle's discussion of phronesis and praxis. In sum, the third circle encompasses attributes and dispositions as well as identity, and the 'self' circle is therefore both a complex individual construct as well as being influenced by the wider professional body, organisational and societal values.

Use of Barnett, Parry and Coate's (2001) model positions the professional teacher in the centre of constructing and developing his/her knowledge, but it also exposes the importance of setting, context and the locus of learning. The discussion so far has highlighted the contribution of learning in practice and in doing to practitioner education, as well as interrogating the locus for teacher learning in relation to career stage and expertise. It also emphasises the role of peers and dialogue and reflective space and structure for practising experienced professionals. It has allowed me to identify some of the capabilities and capacities necessary to enable professional knowledge construction by individuals. In Appleby and Pilkington (2014), this capacity was conveyed as the characteristics for critical professionalism (p.31), where the individual is required to develop three characteristics. S/he must appreciate the complex nature of the teacher's knowledge base; be able to operate within the discourses and learning of diverse communities; and engage in critical reflection on practice as prerequisites to effective professional practice. The practitioner may need to be a critical professional, but I argue the onus for learning should not rest solely with an individual given the supercomplex and dynamic environment of education. It is necessary to add a further component to our discussion of professional learning that enables practitioners to negotiate and engage with employers on the subject of professional learning and the use value of teachers within the educational process. This is achieved using the concept of 'professional capital', and I argue this can shift how organisations and teachers can and should structure and frame professionalism.

Professional capital in teaching

Professional capital relates to 'use value' in that it is about recognising one's worth, potential and contribution in achieving the educational purpose of the institution and the sector. Teachers are essential to the educational purposes of the organisation in respect of serving the learner-as-client and society-as-client, and they mediate this process for the educational organisation. As the tools for delivering and also influencing and designing effective education processes, teachers form the primary means of production within educational organisations. This position can be overwhelmed by a sense of powerlessness and vulnerability on the part of the individual in the face of rapid changes and managerialist agendas, however. I would argue, therefore, that by engaging more proactively and purposefully with the concept of professional capital, and recognising what it implies, the individual teacher can start to influence his/her own change and development and that of practice. Further, both employers and practitioners benefit from having greater awareness of the teachers' role and their value.

76 *Ruth Pilkington*

Professional capital can influence employability and perceived value to the employer, provide a sense of self-worth, refreshing and motivating the individual where s/he is able to develop his or her professional capital and value. This does not require that a practitioner focus solely on career and position within an organisation, but rather that s/he directs and influences accumulation of 'capital' by developing as a critical professional and by deliberate reflection upon, and consideration of, opportunities and goals. Whilst the teacher must recognise potential and manage individual capacity in achieving this, the organisation must also recognise and accommodate how the professional learns within the workplace. Organisations need in turn to provide opportunities for individuals to engage with networks and in collaboration, enabling critical application and enhancement of knowledge and skills aligned to personal, professional, organisational and/or career needs.

By raising the profile of the teacher as an agent for change, for achieving educational purposes and for educational enhancement, teachers can actually begin to negotiate differently with employers. By reframing professionalism around professional capital, it is possible for arguments to be made for appropriate and relevant development of teachers that is also responsive to their work-based, reflective, collegially framed learning preferences. In other words, employers should acknowledge how professional teachers learn so that as primary means of production they are not wasted as tools, but used sustainably and effectively. I argue that by using professional capital to talk differently about teachers' contributions within educational processes and outcomes, it is possible to renegotiate the professional contract between employers and employee, with the consequence that both sides reframe professional learning and the costs attached to ensuring an effective and sustainable means of production. Practitioners and employers can then begin to consider how to embed learning within the doing of teaching, within the practice systems and processes of education, and by constructing space for professional learning into organisational structures.

The chapter has so far argued that practitioners in education learn in the 'doing of teaching' through critical reflection that is informed by values, wider understandings, scholarship, reflection on practice and interrogation of assumptions and prior learning. Practitioners need to operate effectively in multiple discourses to enable learning across multiple communities of practice and organisations, and they need to appreciate the complex nature of professional knowledge and its relationship with practice as well as how professional learning can be undertaken effectively. Alongside this, educational practitioners need to direct their own learning by being able to identify and use opportunities for learning selectively to enhance self and practice. They should also be able to apply agency in an organisational context and make judgments and initiate actions on their own and others' behalf, reflecting the demands of practice, position and career. A final and essential requirement of success in this is for teachers themselves to recognise their professional capital and how to develop and apply it. On the other hand, by acknowledging that professional educators learn by 'doing teaching', through professional talk with peers, and through critical, scholarly and informed reflection, employers can structure organisational space to enable professional learning and practice enhancement to take place in the workplace in ways that complement teaching rather than constraining it. The crucial question is how this can be achieved by organisations whose priorities are being transformed by the new educational marketplace.

An organisational solution

Much of what has been said thus far about learning for teachers in the workplace has been about accepting the conditions and parameters for learning. In the final section of the chapter, I explore how this can be enabled sustainably and cost effectively.

There are in essence three dimensions for an organisational response that can structure professional learning for teachers. Whatever is adopted must:

1 be embedded within educational processes and organisational systems and purposes;
2 accommodate the scholarly, dialogic and reflective requirements for professional learning outlined above;
3 respond to the diverse needs of career stage, functions and roles of staff.

These requirements can be met by adopting approaches of learning organisations for example (Senge, 1990; Pedler, Bourgoyne and Boydell, 1996). An alternative is to rethink how the individual professional learning needs of dialogue, reflection and scholarship can be incorporated more strongly into traditional development practices, and to build these into the processes surrounding teaching. This means incorporating them into curriculum design, delivery, evaluation, review and enhancement practices. Learning becomes less about costly formalised development programmes and more about rethinking processes. It is about building in space for learning and reflection into work-based activity. I acknowledge that there will always be a place for formal frameworks for learning: workshops and courses, for example, and I would add to this list formally constituted communities and forums as learning space, and even the recognised and purposeful use of projects to promote learning. Alongside this, however, the value of incorporating mechanisms that encourage reflective time and space, collaboration and enhancement within curriculum processes actually outweighs those formal systems because these practitioner-centred mechanisms are responsive to primary drivers for teachers. These primary drivers are about teaching. They encompass the learner, the subject and creating a positive and effective learning environment.

This reframing of professional learning as an organisational objective generates an approach constructed around the concepts of learning space and enabling structures, the SCORED model. This can be broken down as:

Space allowing reflection on practice by practitioners built around the design, delivery and review of curriculum. These emerge by expanding work-based processes.

78   *Ruth Pilkington*

Communities of practice where teachers learn from others. These can emerge around initiatives and interests, events and subject enhancement, be practitioner or organisationally led.

Opportunities for learning that are structured to foster discussion and sharing of good practice. For example, conferences, review, validation processes, forums and meetings can become spaces constructed around practice activity through which professional talk is encouraged.

Research and scholarship around learning and teaching. This raises the profile of teaching to an equivalent one for subject research, and ensures that teaching becomes an evidence-based profession where the gathering of qualitative and quantitative data fulfils a genuine purpose of informing enhancement rather than quality assurance and accountability.

Education using formal courses. These have a place in initial education and should target professional and organisational needs. They benefit from using mentoring and reflection to enhance transfer into the workplace (Tynjälä, Stenström and Saarnivaara, 2012).

Development of critical professional perspectives. These crucial factors underpin the individual's professional capital and influence as central to the educational purpose and outcomes of the organisation.

The sort of mechanisms that might be constructed to achieve the aims listed above include construction of learning space and enabling structures using peer observation, team-led course development and review, peer discussion, team learning and reflection built in throughout the annual work and practice cycle. Communities of practice should be encouraged at local, team and department level, and also across organisations and subjects, using forums, groups and networks. The creation of communities of champions to share practice and to support change agents emerges as a leadership activity within teaching. It also supports peer-led communities for wider exchange and sharing. The organisational culture should facilitate practitioner-based conversations that privilege the teacher as an autonomous and trusted agent for enhancement and change who is also committed to educational excellence. Teachers should be given time within practice to explore, reflect on and advance practice rather than being required to accumulate and report visible objectives as is increasingly the case in some sectors of education. Other mechanisms involve using mentoring, buddy pairings, learning sets and enhanced peer review. Formal opportunities for learning can additionally be constructed around project activity, scholarship and research using action research and by adopting SoTL approaches to enhancement, especially if they are supported through community events and journals, conferences and workshops (Mårtensson, Roxå and Olssen, 2011).

The proposals listed above are unlikely to flourish if they are dependent on the practitioner for their introduction and maintenance. In such conditions, the 'champion' will burn out or become disenfranchised and frustrated. The success of these initiatives depends upon an organisation acknowledging and daring to accommodate professional requirements for space, time, reflection and scholarship as mechanisms for securing a primary means of production. In the short term, this may require a radical reconfiguration of educational work and workplaces: fewer isolated offices and more space in the day for collegial discussion; physical spaces for staff to meet in and explore practice; repositioning of evidence and data gathering away from accountability and audit and towards teaching enhancement and development of learning; and a reworking of the psychological contract to one based on trust and mutual recognition of how educational purposes can be fulfilled effectively and sustainably. In the longer term, the focus on developing the professional capital of teachers using methods that complement effective professional learning needs will, I suggest, actually result in educational institutions becoming more agile and capable of accommodating to the shifting demands of the educational marketplace because the workforce will have the power and capacity to horizon scan, predict and proactively develop the curriculum (Argyris and Schön, 1974) for educational futures rather than crisis managing imposed demands as a reactive and defensive process to the detriment of the learner and learning experience. In conclusion, although I accept this solution to how we promote and support teaching may involve rethinking aspects of work processes and systems, in the end the advantages and benefits for teaching practitioners and employers, learners and education are considerable and worth the investment in the longer term, especially if education is to be globally competitive and equipped for a supercomplex future. In the end, it may be about employers reconceptualising their (teaching) employees' contribution to the organisation's goals and work and reprioritising teacher support and professional development accordingly.

References

Appleby, Y. and Pilkington, R. (2014). *Developing Critical Professional Practice in Education*. Leicester: NIACE.

Argyris, M. and Schön, D. (1974). *Theory in Practice. Increasing Professional Effectiveness*. San Francisco: Jossey-Bass.

Barnett, R., Parry, G. and Coate, K. (2001). Conceptualising curriculum change. *Teaching in Higher Education*, 6(4), 435–449.

Barnett, R. (2008). Critical professionalism in an age of supercomplexity. In: B. Cunningham (ed.), *Exploring Professionalism*, pp.190–207. London: Bedford Way Papers.

Becher, T. and Trowler, P.R. (2001). *Academic Tribes and Territories*. Buckingham: SRHE and Open University Press.

Bourner T, Katz, T. and Watson, D. (2000). *New Directions in Professional Higher Education*. Buckingham: SRHE and Open University Press.

Brockbank, A. and McGill, I. (1998). *Facilitating Reflective Learning in Higher Education*. Buckingham: SRHE and Open University Press.

Cousin, G. (2009). *Researching Learning in Higher Education: an Introduction to Contemporary Methods and Approaches*. Abingdon: Routledge.

Cunningham, B. (ed.) (2008). *Exploring Professionalism*. London: Bedford Way Papers.

Dreyfus, H.L. and Dreyfus, S.E. (1986). *Mind over Machine: The Power of Human Intuition and Expertise in the Era of The Computer*. Oxford: Blackwell.

80   *Ruth Pilkington*

Eraut, M. (1994). *Developing Professional Knowledge and Competence*. London: Routledge.

Eraut, M. (2004). Informal learning in the workplace. *Studies in Continuing Education*, 26(2), 247–273.

Evans, L. (2008). Professionalism, professionality and the development of education professionals. *British Journal of Educational Studies*, 56(1), 28–38.

Freire, P. (1970). *Pedagogy of the Oppressed*. Harmondsworth: Penguin.

Ghaye, A. and Ghaye, T. (1998). *Teaching and Learning through Critical Reflective Practice*. London: David Fulton Press

Gosling, D. and Mason O'Connor, K. (2009). *Beyond the Peer Observation of Teaching*. SEDA, Paper 124. London: SEDA.

Guile, D. and Lucas, N. (1999). Rethinking initial teacher education and professional development in FE: towards the learning professional. In: A. Green and N. Lucas (eds), *Further Education and Lifelong Learning: Realigning the Sector for the Twenty-First Century*. London: Bedford Way Papers.

Grossman, P., Hammerness, K. and McDonald, M. (2009). Redefining teaching, re-imagining teacher education. *Teachers and Teaching: Theory and Practice*, 15(2), 273–289.

Larrivee, B. (2008). Development of a tool to assess teachers' level of reflective practice. *Reflective Practice*, 9(3), 341–360.

Mårtensson, K., Roxå, T. and Olssen, T. (2011). Developing a quality culture through the scholarship of teaching and learning. *Higher Education Research & Development*, 30(1), 51–62.

Pedler, M., Burgoyne, J. and Boydell, T. (1996). *The Learning Company: A Strategy for Sustainable Development*. London: McGraw Hill

Peel, D. (2005). Dual professionalism: facing the challenges of continuing professional development in the workplace? *Reflective Practice*, 6(1), 123–140.

Reynolds, M. and Vince, R. (2004). *Organizing Reflection*. Aldershot: Gower.

Robson, J. (2006). *Teacher Professionalism in Further and Higher Education: Challenges to Culture and Practice*. London: Routledge

Sachs, J. (2001). Teacher professional identity: competing discourses, competing outcomes. *Journal of Educational Policy*, 16(2), 149–161.

Schön, D. (1983). *The Reflective Practitioner*. New York: Basic Books. Reprinted 2009, Aldershot: Ashgate.

Senge, P. (1990). *The Fifth Discipline: The Art and Practice of the Learning Organisation*. New York: Doubleday

Shulman, L.S. (1987). Knowledge and teaching: foundations of the new reform. *Harvard Education Review*, 57(1), 1–22.

Roxå, T and Mårtensson, K (2009). Significant conversations and significant networks – exploring the backstage of the teaching arena. *Studies in Higher Education*, 34(5), 547–559.

Tynjälä, P., Stenström, M. and Saarnivaara, M. (eds) (2012). *Transitions and Transformations in Learning and Education*. London: Springer.

Van Manen, M. (1995). On the epistemology of reflective practice. *Teachers and Teaching: Theory and Practice*, 1(1), 33–50.

Vloet, K., Jacobs, G. and Veugeler, W. (2013). Dialogic learning in teachers' professional identities. In: M. Ligorio and M. Cesar (eds), *Interplays between Dialogic Learning and Dialogical Self*, pp.419–457. Charlotte, NC: IAP.

Wenger, E. (1998). *Communities of Practice: Learning, Meaning and Identity*. Cambridge, UK: Cambridge University Press.

Part II

Partnership

6 Working at the intersection

Partnerships as participatory mechanisms for disruption

Tina Cook

Introduction: intersection – a place where two or more roads meet

'Intersection' is a common term in America for what we in the UK might call 'crossroads', the place where roads cross, and we wait in turn for each other to pass by without engagement (hopefully). It is not, however, this understanding of intersection as the place where we successfully negotiate around each other that I am alluding to here. My use of intersection denotes a space where people do come together and, rather than avoid each other in that middle space, actively engage with each other. In mathematics, as I understand it, the intersection is a set that contains elements shared by two or more given sets. This is a more appropriate way for conceptualising the type of intersection discussed in this chapter.

It is important to understand what is meant mean by the words we use as they shape our perceptions of what and how things are and how processes might function. Without a clear definition, there is the likelihood of commonly used terms or phrases becoming commonly understood without shared meaning. Naming is merely a shorthand identification of a general practice; it does not define the properties of the practice being named. A name can 'easily be used to substitute concept for precept, the name of the thing for the thing itself . . . Once assigned and classification has occurred, exploration ceases' (Eisner, 1988, p.17).

The sharing of common terminology can build what Easen (2000, quoting Edelman, 1964) termed 'illusory consensus'. This has the potential to fall apart when the naming words begin to be endowed with specific and different meaning and actions by the various parties involved (Easen, 2000). To avoid masking the differences between the agreed name and the tacitly understood practice those involved need to engage in a more critical form of dialogue to clarify understandings of the concept (Cook, 2004).

Illusory consensus is evident in the use of the term 'partnership'. Partnerships are generally seen as a 'good thing' with partnership working widely cited as key to effective provision. The call to work in partnership can be found in most educational policies; for instance, Education Scotland states that there is a need for local authorities and schools to 'to create strong partnerships with a range of

84 *Tina Cook*

organisations to deliver a personalised learning experience for every child and young person' (n.d). In such policies, the form partnership might take is generally not made explicit. It could be argued that the label 'partnership working' has been applied as a way of encouraging work across agency boundaries and across stakeholders long before understandings about how the process of working together has been developed. More often used than clarified, 'partnership' tends to be used as an umbrella term embracing different relationships based on different organisational structures and processes. Partnerships are generally conceptualised, however, as striving for a supportive place, where shared understandings are aired. People engage in partnerships with the hope of being in a comfortable place, a place where agreement can take place and overarching common interests between different players are assumed. Such assumptions can, however, as Ballock and Taylor (2001, p.2) state:

> underplay the difficulties in bringing together different interests and different cultures. For this reason, it is important to bring a critical perspective to bear, to understand the expectations and assumptions that lie behind a term that commands such widespread support across the political spectrum and to be clear about its implications.

Defining partnership

Notions of partnership working do not have a ready framework or defined model to draw on. Partnerships exist along a broad continuum of practice with different interpretations enabling them to mean different things to different people, even when those people are engaged in the same partnership. Definitions of partnerships working are as varied as the practice. Le Riche and Taylor (2008, p.11) suggest there is

> a pervasive conceptual confusion about the meaning of 'partnership' . . . partnership work is more often implicit than explicit and simultaneously contested and taken for granted . . . The danger is that this lack of clarity will lead to an uncritical approach to partnership.

In general, partnerships tend to be conceptualised as a means of facilitating a democratic and inclusive process, one that provides opportunities for expressing opinions and building shared understandings. The nature of the partnership relationship is generally presumed as a genial way of bringing different agencies or groups of people together. Defining the characteristics of partnership, Mayo and Taylor (2001) identified equality and reciprocity as key elements within that relationship, and Rummery (2002) states that two defining characteristics are a degree of interdependence and of trust. Bidmead and Cowley (2005) framed partnership as a 'respectful, negotiated way of working that enables choice, participation and equity within an honest trusting relationship based on empathy, support and reciprocity' (p.208).

Working at the intersection 85

In 2014 the HEA produced a set of principles and values for successful partnerships which, whilst including some of the more familiar values such as inclusivity, reciprocity, responsibility, empowerment and trust, also highlighted 'challenge' as a key element that enhances the effectiveness of partnership working: 'Challenge – all parties are encouraged to constructively critique and challenge practices, structures and approaches that undermine partnership, and are enabled to take risks to develop new ways of working and learning' (HEA, 2014, p.4).

What follows in this chapter is the discussion of two challenges for partnerships, firstly the challenge of clarifying the form of partnership working in relation to its purpose and secondly placing the notion of challenge and mutual critique within partnerships as a vital, dynamic element for developing practice.

Uncritical approaches to partnership working: an example

I began my career as a teacher, specifically a teacher of children with special educational needs. During the 1990s, I was head of a Preschool Service (PSS) for children with special educational needs and their families. At the heart of the work of the PSS was a set of 'mix and match' partnerships that intersected at various points. Those who stood on the corners of the crossroads in these partnerships included teachers and nursery nurses in the PSS, parents, educational psychologists, social workers, paediatricians, speech and language therapists, health visitors, physiotherapists, nurses from the community team for learning disability, educational support staff, nursery school staff and local authority officers. I have used the idea of standing on the corners of the crossroads deliberately here, for in hindsight, although the PSS staff would have described the way we worked as being 'in partnership', our predominant way of working was not intersectional. Rather the partners would meet together to share/provide a perspective (state our case), debate our case with the perspective of others currently at various corners, and when one view predominated that way was chosen as the way of travel (perhaps with a few compromises here and there). This was seen particularly in the more formal meetings where all parties, brought together to make key decisions about a child's future, reported their perspective and then made a decision about which perspective to choose to work with. The meetings followed a given formula that allowed people to voice their opinions. Discussion about how the partnership might work to greater effect, what might be achieved from bringing the knowledge of different partners together for shared critique, were not part of the process. Agreement was achieved through a process likely to adopt a 'least worst' approach, choosing a way forward that was most acceptable to most people, rather than considering whether there could new ways of understanding and shaping practice.

Not defining the form of a partnership can result in partnerships that are unlikely to meet their perceived function, especially if that function is also not defined and shared within the partnership. For instance, if the perceived function

86 *Tina Cook*

Table 6.1 Form, function and impact on generative practice

Partnership	Purpose	Impact on practice
Bureaucratic	To demonstrate to others that relevant parties are connecting.	Limited: parties likely to continue on own preferred (or directed) pathway.
Organisational	To ensure that all involved parties know what others are doing.	May affect the framework for practice (timings etc.) but is unlikely to affect the practice itself. In this process 'Worlds and people are what we meet, but the meeting is shaped by our own terms of reference' (Heron, 1996, p.11).
Democratic	To find out what all involved parties are doing and decide a shared way forward: to choose, in a rational way, between a range of options for practice.	Leads to streamlining practice according to an agreed way of working based on a current practice: shared action.
Participatory	To engage with the perspective of involved others with the intention of shared learning for developing practice.	Leads to new, shared understandings not defined by given frameworks for understanding ways of working: innovative.

is shared learning, yet the form of the partnership is 'organisational', then the space for shared learning is compromised and that function is unlikely to be realised. Table 6.1 demonstrates the relationship between form and function in partnership approaches.

In the PSS, this way of working, where the foundations (form and function) of partnership are not actively and collaboratively defined, could be seen in the day-to-day working relationships with parents.

Partnerships with parents: form and function

The Preschool Service included a home visiting service as part of its remit. The principle for developing partnerships with parents was to develop a relationship that was harmonious, trusting and co-operative, the reasoning for this being that if teachers and parents 'got on' together we could work together for the best outcome for the child. Parents and teachers worked together and rubbed along in what was, for the most part, seen as a good relationship. It was a well-respected service. As the 'visiting' teacher, we saw ourselves as forming learning partnerships with parents, working with parents to better understand their child's needs and develop learning opportunities together. The rationale for working together was that everyone would learn, the child who was at the heart of our endeavours,

Working at the intersection 87

the parents from the experience and expertise of the teachers and the teachers from the particular knowledge held by the parents of their child's likes, preferences and behaviours. The partnership could, therefore, have been conceptualised as an intersection, a place where knowledge from different parties could be brought together to build a bigger picture. In hindsight, however, a key issue was that partnerships tended to be formed serendipitously, their form not being shaped by a conscious, shared exploration of purpose. The nature of the engagement was not openly discussed and debated with parents, and so it varied according to pragmatics. Whilst there were many undefined and generally un-negotiated ways of being in that partnership, three of the approaches that could be recognised as being played out in the home visiting partnerships with parents could be termed delivery, instructive/informative and collaborative.

Delivery: for some parents the partnership/relationship was preconceived as a space with clearly defined, but different roles, for themselves and the teachers. Teachers were positioned as deliverers of learning, i.e. the person who came to teach their child whilst they, the parent, provided the space for this. Some might sit in the room, on the settee, and observe the teacher as they played with their child on the floor; others would take the opportunity to get on with other things until the teachers had finished. It was rather like sending your child to school, but having the teacher come to the house provided the added opportunity for the teacher to explain what had been done and why and to give parents ideas for things to carry on with their child until the following visit. The parent was then likely to say to the teacher 'thank you very much' and 'see you next time', but the commitment to continuing the activities with their child was not necessarily enhanced by engagement and thus could be limited.

Instructive/Informative: in this scenario parents welcomed the teachers into their homes, listened to what they had to say about their child's learning and worked with them and their child on tasks suggested by that teacher. Although teachers were seen as deliverers of knowledge about children's learning, and the model of education adopted fell into a more hierarchical approach, parents would be engaged with their child, trying out the ideas, making an assessment of the impact of the suggested approach with the teacher and contributing adaptations to improve the approach to make it better suited their child and their own way of being together with their child and others in the family.

Collaborative: here teachers were the adult who came into the lives of the families with whom parents could discuss their child and talk about what was happening for them and their child. Discussion would start from what the child was achieving, successes would be celebrated and there would be joint discussions about how to build on that success. Teachers and parents would throw their shared knowledge into the pot and decide what to do next. Strategies for developing opportunities for learning were not pre-formed but forged through those discussions. This was the hoped for approach by the PSS staff.

All the above forms of working were not overtly formed through discussion with the parents but rather serendipitously shaped through unspoken expectations with an overlay of habit and custom. The impact of this was that whilst a key

88   *Tina Cook*

rationale for partnership working within the PSS was the opportunity for shared learning, many of the working partnerships were unable to deliver this aspiration. Recognising what a partnership is for should dictate the way in which it is enacted. Different forms of partnership, different levels of engagement, are, however, likely to offer different opportunities for joint working. Partnerships have, as McLaughlin (2004) states, 'no a priori right to being the most effective service delivery method in all situations' (p.112). Neglecting the process of articulating purpose can result in expectations from partnerships that cannot be actualised, resulting in less than optimal outcomes.

> A collaborative educational process needs to open a space in which participants are both invited to engage in work which is important and meaningful for them, and also insist that they reflect on the manner in which they perform that task so that together they learn how to move toward a more genuine collaboration.
>
> (Reason, 1998, p.153)

Challenge within partnerships: the purpose of mutual critique

The approach to developing partnerships in the PSS was pragmatic. Whilst some partnerships might develop in a participatory way that enhanced learning opportunities, many were democratic and others could be described as organisational or even purely bureaucratic. In a partnership that consists of a range of people with multiple viewpoints, if these viewpoints are merely debated and prioritised, if partners merely stand on the corners of the crossroads without entering the intersection, the opportunity to find new ways of seeing and working can be lost. To develop practice rather than choose from a proffered range of current ways of practising, partnerships need to provide the opportunity for disrupting given working practice through a shared critique. Developing a space for mutual reflection and critique of taken-for-granted knowledge, an intersection, provides a springboard for improving practice through the disruption of current norms.

The following example from a research project carried out in a health service setting (Cook, 2011) describes a strong relationship between partners, but where mutual critique is not undertaken, the status quo is left undisturbed. This has a direct impact on the effectiveness of practice.

A man recovering from a stroke attended regular appointments with a physiotherapist at a Neuro-Rehabilitation Centre. The aim of the clinical visit was to assess his needs and provide physiotherapy but also to provide him with exercises he could do at home between visits to the clinic. The man attended with his partner and both really liked the physiotherapist. They described him as 'a hands on man' who spent time explaining things to them, talking with them about the issues and what needed to be done to help improve mobility. Both the man and his partner said they felt included in the discussions and decisions made with the physiotherapist at the clinic. They were happy with the treatment and the way they all 'worked well together'. Although they did not use the term, it could be described as a strong working partnership: a democratic partnership that brought together interested and relevant parties, providing a basis for working together built on mutual trust, respect and conversation. During the process of the research project, however, the man and his partner revealed that although they liked the physiotherapist very much, and engaged with him during the clinic time, the exercises were not continued at home. The reason for this was that by the time they arrived home they could not always remember exactly how to do them. Rather than risk doing the exercises incorrectly, which they believed might 'do more harm than good', they did not do them. Asked why they did not explain this issue to the physiotherapist, they replied that because he had said he was a very 'hands on' practitioner, and they appreciated and respected that, they did not want to ask him to write things down. They interpreted his positioning as a 'hands on' practitioner as meaning it would be against his practice to do so. By asking for written information, they believed they might disrupt his way of working or even offend him by seeming to criticise his practice. They did not want to lose access to him, despite the fact that the effectiveness of the intervention was drastically reduced by not embedding it into daily life at home. A shared discussion of what was really happening, and why, a mutual critique of the impact of the treatment was therefore not instigated.

As demonstrated above, even where partnerships are built on a strong and positive relationship, if the point of the partnership becomes to maintain equilibrium rather than engage in reflexive critique, it is unlikely to provide a generative space for developing effective practice. Whilst critique is not the same as conflict, general use tends to conflate the two and in common parlance in the UK, to be critical is seen as negative and hence to be avoided. As the notion of partnership has the connotation of a non-critical space, as Clarke and Glendinning (2002) suggest, the difficulty in adopting a critical approach is its link to conflict, and: 'Like "community", partnership is a word of obvious virtue (what sensible person would choose conflict over collaboration?)' (p.33).

Developing generative partnerships: the role of challenge, conflict and collaboration

To learn something new about an element of practice in which you already have considerable expertise may mean that you have to let go of some of your own ideas/beliefs about working practices. This is not easy for any party. A conceptualisation of partnership where the very essence of that is not about building on received shared understandings brought to that partnership, but using that partnership to seek out different understandings, involves what Habermas (1998) termed reciprocal perspective taking 'mutual recognition, reciprocal perspective taking, a shared willingness to consider one's own conditions through the eyes of the stranger, and to learn from one another' (Habermas, 1998, p.159)

90   *Tina Cook*

This is at the very heart of a generative, participatory partnership approach. It challenges partners to create a mutually enhancing process for learning together as a catalyst to developing more effective working practices, to develop a co-constructed approach where:

> strands of knowledge and learning are unearthed and critiqued. These strands ultimately act as catalysts for new knowing leading to development and change. It is the space for imaginative freedom and new ideas. It is a place to celebrate 'The importance of not always knowing what you are doing' (Atkinson and Claxton 2000).
>
> (Cook, 2009, p.281)

It is, however, difficult to let go of long-held, cherished certainties and beliefs about 'good' and 'appropriate' services and to unpick taken-for-granted rationales. Hauling apart general awareness to reframe and develop new ways forward is likely to be a variable, unstable and messy process as partners zigzag between intuitive and critical modes of thinking. This necessitates a kind of collaboration that goes beyond the building of a harmonious relationship to reach a common goal. It involves co-labouring, defined by Sumara and Luce-Kapler (1993, p.393) as 'toil, distress, trouble: exertions of the faculties of the body or mind . . . an activity which is at times likely to be uncomfortable'.

This deconstruction of the term 'collaboration' embeds challenge as part of the process. Understanding the term collaboration as co-labouring allows us to reconceptualise partnerships as a place where partners expect to do some hard, reflexive work together to mutually challenge common understandings and expectations. Partnerships thus become places that offer a strong, relationally driven space where 'mutually incompatible alternatives' (Feyerabend, 1975) can be debated and wrestled with; where co-labouring takes place. Here well-rehearsed notions of practice and belief can be deconstructed to allow for the dawning of the new. Through surfacing a range of perspectives not merely to be ranked but to be jostled with, critiqued and subjected to engaged dialectical discussion, co-labouring provides a space for new theories and practices to be developed. It disturbs what the philosopher Roland Barthes (1982) describes as 'studium', the general awareness, recognition and even enthusiastic commitment we have for ways of acting that we recognise, and with which we can affiliate and associate. Co-labouring disturbs the 'studium', the common 'rules' through which we frame our seeing and understanding. The outcome is a co-authored, mutually developed approach to practice. A characteristic of effective partnerships would then be that partners undertake an element of reconceptualisation, not in terms of the principles of respect, trust and strong relationships partnerships might be formed upon, but a reconceptualisation of their form and processes.

> A collaborative educational process needs to open a space in which participants are both invited to engage in work which is important and meaningful for them, and also insist that they reflect on the manner in which

they perform that task so that together they learn how to move toward a more genuine collaboration.

(Reason, 1998, p.153)

Conclusion: partnerships as spaces for critique and communicative action

Whether it is for the development of educational practices, the forging of a new business or the researching of an area of shared interest, a solid relationship needs to underpin partnership working. A strong relationship can provide the space not only to enable the 'work to be done' but to reconceptualise and build understandings of what could be achieved. For this to happen the term 'partnership' needs to be conceptualised beyond taking a shared stance and towards forging shared understandings, with critical challenge being the catalyst for change. The difference between what I have termed democratic and participatory partnerships will determine whether people are standing at the corners of that partnership or engaged at the intersection, choosing from the menu they already have for practice or generating new ways of working. Participatory partnerships are intentionally disruptive to enable the reframing of viewpoints. They necessitate active participation by those involved and an openness to questioning their own perspective and practice in the light of that of others. It requires seeing the positives of critique and challenge, recognising that as difficult but not disrespectful, contesting but not discourteous, a way of learning rather than a way of maintaining status quo. The development of partnerships built on relationships that value critique purposefully opens up the gap between what Reason (1998) described as 'the clarity of the present and the as-yet undefined possibilities of the future, a gap which stimulates the imaginative capacities of the participants' (p.154).

This stimulation of the imaginative capacities is articulated below by a researcher, a man with learning difficulties, who had been engaged in a collaborative research partnership. I would like to suggest that in any taxonomy for effective participatory partnership working that includes challenge, critique and co-labouring, 'enthusiastic engagement' should be an essential element.

> The more things just got blown into the air, the more fun it was . . . When we were discussing and debating stuff, during some of the discussion that we had, your mind slipped a few times before it settled. It's like you started it off and someone would say something and it would be like, 'Erm, I'm not quite sure of . . .' And then it started a bit of a debate up. And then by the time you finished the debate you had most of the answers and then it was like, 'Eh . . . you know, we've just answered it.' . . . I just love information. I just love having information and coming up with new things for it. Just love it. And doing this meant that . . . I've got my little drug going where I've had all the discussion and everything going. And information going and flying all over the place. And it's just like, Yessss! Aye. I just love learning. (David).

(Cook and Inglis, 2008, p.63)

92   Tina Cook

References

Atkinson, T. and Claxton, G. (eds) (2000). *The Intuitive Practitioner: On the Value of Not Always Knowing What One Is Doing.* Bristol: Open University Press.

Ballock, S. and Taylor, M. (eds) (2001). *Partnership Working: Policy and Practice.* Bristol: Policy Press.

Barthes, R. (1982). *Camera Lucida.* London: Jonathan Cape.

Bidmead, C. and Cowley, S. (2005). A concept analysis of partnership with clients. *Community Practitioner*, 78(6), 203–208.

Clarke, J. and Glendinning, C. (2002). Partnership and the remaking of welfare governance. In: C. Glendinning, M. Powell and K. Rummery (eds), *Partnerships, New Labour and the Governance of Welfare*, pp.33–50. Bristol: Policy Press.

Cook, T. (2004). Reflecting and learning together: action research as a vital element of developing understanding and practice. *Educational Action Research*, 12(1), 77–97.

Cook, T. (2009). The purpose of mess in action research: building rigour through a messy turn. *Educational Action Research*, 17(2), 277–291.

Cook, T. (2011). Towards inclusive living: a case study of the impact of inclusive practice in neurorehabilitation/neuro-psychiatry services. *DoH Policy Programme Long Term Neurological Conditions.* Available from: www.ltnc.org.uk/research_files/impact_inclusive.html (accessed 4 August 2015).

Cook, T. and Inglis, P. (2008). *Understanding Research, Consent and Ethics: A Participatory Research Methodology in a Medium Secure Unit for Men with a Learning Disability.* Available from: http://nrl.northumbria.ac.uk/id/eprint/890 (accessed 4 August 2015).

Easen, P. (2000). Education action zones: partnership is no panacea for progress. *Westminster Studies in Education*, 23(1), 55–69.

Edelman, M. (1964). *The Symbolic Use of Politics.* Urbana: University of Illinois Press.

Education Scotland (n.d.). *Transforming Lives through Learning.* Available from: www.educationscotland.gov.uk/learningandteaching/partnerships/about/index. asp (accessed 4 August 2015).

Eisner, E.W. (1988). The primacy of experience and the politics of method. *Educational Researcher*, 17(5), 15–20.

Feyerabend, P. (1975). *Against Method: Outline of an Anarchistic Theory of Knowledge.* London: Verso.

Habermas, J.M. (1998). *The Inclusion of the Other: Studies in Political Theory.* Cambridge: The MIT Press.

Higher Education Authority (2014). *Framework for Partnership in Learning and Teaching in Higher Education.* York: HEA.

Heron, J. (1996). *Co-operative Inquiry: Research into the Human Condition.* London: Sage.

Le Riche, P. and Taylor, I. (2008). *The learning, Teaching and Assessment of Partnership Work in Social Work Education.* Workforce Development: SCIE Guide 23.

Mayo, M. and Taylor, M. (2001). Partnerships and power in community regeneration. In: S Balloch and M. Taylor (eds) *Partnership Working*, pp.29–56. Bristol: The Policy Press.

McLaughlin, H. (2004). Partnerships: panacea or pretense? *Journal of Interprofessional Care*, 18(2), 103–113.

Reason, P. (1998). Political, epistemological, ecological and spiritual dimensions of participation. *Studies in Cultures, Organisations and Societies*, 4, 147–167.

Rummery, K. (2002). Towards a theory of welfare partnerships. In: C. Glendinning, M. Powell and K. Rummery (eds), *Partnerships, New Labour and the Governance of Welfare*, pp.229–247. Bristol: The Policy Press.

Sumara, D.J. and Luce-Kapler, R. (1993). Action research as writerly text: locating co-labouring in collaboration. *Educational Action Research*, 1(3), 387–396.

7   Student partnership and a university legitimation crisis

Morgan White

Introduction

The concept of student partnership has different functions: it is meant to address challenges facing a higher education system under increasing threat from global competition, limit problems associated with asymmetrical power relations between producer and consumer, while also, at the same time, mediating between students as passive consumers of education though retaining the intimacy of pedagogical relationships. In this chapter, I examine problems with the idea that student partnership addresses a passive consumerist approach to education. I have in mind the higher education context in England, where marketisation is particularly advanced. However, the tendencies I try to describe pertain in any overly instrumental education system.

Student partnership takes on various forms intended to encourage students to 'engage' by helping them to determine their own modes of assessment and curriculum content, participate in institutional governance and complete feedback questionnaires. However, in a marketised higher education environment where there is a tendency towards instrumental attitudes to studying, I argue that these practices will tend to undermine the legitimacy of higher education. The argument here is that the concept of student partnership is problematic insofar as it brushes the legitimate authority of academic teachers under the carpet of consumer preference satisfaction. As Russell Keat points out, the difficulty with the neo-classical market model is that consumers' preferences are conceived in value-neutral terms (Keat, 1994, p.29), while educators hold value-laden preferences over what counts as a good education (which, of course, may well vary to some degree between teachers and between different academic disciplines).

Voice and authority

Student partnership gives university students voice within higher education: it shifts the student's role from passive consumer (with freedom of exit from the marketplace) towards active participation with freedom of voice (Anderson, 1995). The student partnership policy is an important acknowledgement that a simple market model of academic producers and student consumers is flawed in

Student partnership and a legitimation crisis   95

relation to education. However, in seeking to give voice to students by bureaucratic imperative, the policy misunderstands the role that authority plays in education, and ignores a fundamental distinction between authoritative teaching and an exploitative relationship between academic educators and their students. In effect, power relations between academic teachers and students are confused with relations of authority. The focus on partnership increases student voice but in so doing disrupts academic authority.

There is a risk that the meaning of academic authority may be misunderstood here. A complex notion of authority lies at the heart of a higher education. Education is a process of recognition that builds authority in students. The concept of students as partners is superficially appealing because it aspires to recognising student authority, but the authority involved is legitimated by policy assertion rather than diligent application to learning and understanding an academic tradition. This chapter traces Hannah Arendt's development of the notion of authority in her essay 'What is authority?' (1993b) and explores how it can be related to higher education. Arendt's conception of authority forms the focal point for two reasons. First, her view of authority connects with action and participation in the world (Jessop, 2011). Indeed, Arendt conceives of education specifically in terms of preparation for action (Arendt, 1993a). Secondly, parallels can be drawn between the 'child-centred', 'progressive' education Arendt attacked in 'The crisis of education' and an instrumental model of higher education encouraged by high tuition fees and a focus on employability. These forms of education provide insufficient insulation for the development of the student and resist the notion of authority in the tutor, and therefore negate the development of authority in students themselves.

What is authority?

Arendt argues that the concept of authority is often misunderstood. It is not about less freedom or more orderliness. Neither, in a higher education context, should it be concerned with less student voice or more university teachers with a teaching qualification. A simplistic view of authority hides important differences between tyranny, democracy, authoritarianism and totalitarianism in politics. Similarly, to confuse authority with mere power in education obscures differences between valuable and trivial forms of education. Arendt points out that the lack of clarity over the concept of authority goes so deep that parents face a crisis of authority in raising children because of an absence of tradition that can be passed on from one generation to the next. In the same way, university teachers face a crisis in authority when they lack an ethical tradition to pass on to their students. A higher education that is oriented towards the future in terms of employability, happiness and income will inevitably confront a crisis of authority. An inability to grasp authority, for Arendt, except in terms of freedom and orderliness, is a result of the dominance of liberal and conservative political thought which conceal meaning in their focus on the purely functional level (Arendt, 1993b, p.103).

96 Morgan White

Authority demands obedience, so it is not surprising that the concept is confused with lack of freedom, or with power or violence. But, in fact, authority is not concerned with external means of coercion; rather it is recognised. As Arendt says, 'where force is used, authority itself has failed' (Arendt, 1993b, p.93). Neither is authority concerned with persuasion because persuasion 'presupposes equality and works through a process of argumentation' (Arendt, 1993b, p.93). It is worth noting that authority explicitly rules out the 'co-constructive', egalitarian relations involved in students as partners. Higher education involves a relation of isonomy, or equality of reason in teacher and student, but this operates against a backdrop of the teacher's authority. In normative terms, education, therefore, occurs in a relation of trust. Authority concerns the recognition (from those under authority) that those with authority hold power legitimately.

Freedom and the passions

The execution of Socrates (for corrupting the youth of Athens) demonstrated that persuasion and reason cannot control the passions of the public sphere (Arendt, 1993b, p.107). A polis regulated only by free speech and reason will not sustain freedom, given the 'crooked timber' of humanity. Free speech alone is insufficient for freedom because we also need a public inclined towards listening to and thinking about this speech. Liberty needs people inclined to hear, and those listening to others should also be free, with open-minded, but critical, attitudes and ready to use their own reason to form judgements. Not everyone, unfortunately, is subject to the force of reason. In part, the problem of authority in contemporary higher education comes from students and academic teachers who struggle to recognise the force of reason because their focal points of interest (love of a subject or future employment, for instance) bypass each other. Recognition of entrenched divergent interests between academics and students demonstrates the difficulty universities face in grounding their legitimacy among those working and studying within them. Authority commands an obedience to listen, but this obedience is uncoerced. This suggests that authority involves trust, as Zdenko Kodelja explains:

> [O]bedience can be the result either of the use of coercive power or of authority. However, in the first case obedience depends on the person who possesses power, but in the second, just the opposite is true: it depends on those who recognize and acknowledge the authority of the person who has the right to command obedience . . . T]he correlative of authority is trust.
>
> (Kodelja, 2013, p.320)

To reconcile freedom with obedience, Plato looked to the household for a model of authority (Arendt, 1993b, p.106). Here, he saw the authority of the despotic father who preserved freedom for his family. Authority can enable freedom. Political freedom for the citizen requires a force external to those in power. In *The Republic*, Plato proposes that law takes on this role of an external force, beyond the powerful. The democratic government, to maintain freedom, must operate within the rule of law, and can only alter law through due process. In order to force those many for whom reason is unpersuasive to follow the law, Plato provides the myth of hell: the idea of an afterlife that punishes the law-breaking bad for eternity. Thus, fear of hell reins in the passions of those unable to control their passions through reason (Arendt, 1993b, p.111). Authoritative education also works as a source of freedom under democratic conditions.

The student as partner, with an overriding fear of indebtedness and future underemployment, might be said to have reined in passion for learning. Those of our students who arrive at university with overwhelmingly instrumental attitudes towards their studies are obedient: present in lectures and tutorials (when not working part-time jobs), and they hand in their essays, but they do so while operating under a misconception of what their higher education is about. The intellectual passion of the academic and student working in partnership under an idea of mastery of a craft is dissolved in the acidity of instrumental higher education. What is required is some external force, beyond fear (of hell, or future unemployment), that will help re-balance attitudes back towards a deepening of intellectual understanding.

Authority of the philosopher king

Plato sees authority in black and white terms; when we are ill, we defer to the doctor; in sailing, to the helmsman. In politics, we should defer to the expert in ideas and laws. The wisest, for Plato, hold the authority to rule because the 'compelling element lies in the relationship itself and is prior to the issuance of commands' (Arendt, 1993b, p.109). However, it is the relationship or shared interest between student and academic teacher which is under threat in market-ised higher education. Shared interests ('inter-est' – a relational ontology, as Arendt puts it in *The Human Condition* (Arendt, 1998, p.182) will not be recaptured by imposing a policy of students as partners from above. It is more likely that partnership (in terms of governance, assessment modes and course content) will throw divergent interests into sharp relief. For Arendt, however, Plato's position is absurd – there is no expert in human affairs. Political matters, relationships between people, in a democracy, can only be considered through free and open discussion where the words of the speaker hold the power to persuade. Whoever best understands the situation is the person we want to listen to. This person, however, is unlikely to have the best grasp of all situations. Therefore, even when we listen to the speaker with the best understanding of the situation we should be inclined towards a sceptical attitude. The 'expert' who supports his authority through threats of violence, or hell in the afterlife, diminishes freedom for the citizen or congregation, just as the threat of grades too low to impress future employers diminishes freedom for the real student or teacher. Teachers and students in higher education ought to incline towards scepticism, yet also tend towards listening to one another in the context of interpreting, understanding and judging the subject matter of their discipline.

98   *Morgan White*

The skills involved here are empathetic and rhetorical: an openness to listen to others, sharing views about the good or justice. The seminar room, then, is a vision of the polis requiring:

> Skill in explaining one's own views, skill in listening to the views of others, skill in bringing the two into relation with one another in a way that highlights their strengths and diminishes their weaknesses, and skill once again in explaining the tentative synthesis that one has arrived at for the benefit of others (who are, of course, engaged in a similar exercise).
>
> (Waldron, 1995, p.575)

The Roman tradition

The political model for Arendt's understanding of authority is Roman. Rome grew and developed; the Empire was built upon a central founding. The development of the Roman Empire meant that life (the private sphere of survival and necessity) and the world (the public realm which we are born into and continues once we are dead and gone) involved constantly keeping Rome in view as the founding idea. Auctoritas, the Latin word for authority, Arendt tells us, derives from augere, to augment, and what those in authority build on is the foundation. Authority, therefore, rested upon the wisdom of the elders who held the foundation in view for all things to come (Arendt, 1993b, pp.121–122). Ultimately, therefore, authority rested on the founders who were no longer alive, with the ancestors rather than those who held actual power. Authority resides in an idea of how the founders would have understood, in a particular attitude.

For Arendt, politics rests on the trinity of religion, tradition and authority (Arendt, 1990, p.117). It is maintained in attitudes, in ethics, rather than in ideas. Religio means to tie back, in the sense that the present is 'tied back' to the past. Those in authority were those who could interpret the meaning of the foundations. Those in authority had to be old and plausibly connected with the foundation itself.

When the Roman Empire collapsed and the church filled its space, it founded itself not as a community of believers, not in obedience to the commandments of God, but upon a foundation of the birth, death and resurrection of Jesus. The church drew its authority from the stories of the Bible and its ability to interpret these. The foundation of Rome was repeated in the Christian church. Upon becoming political, replacing Rome, the church altered its own self-understanding: it gave itself a foundation. And, of course, the church developed institutions, which in time became universities, founded for the education and training of its clergy.

The fathers of Roman thought and culture were not Romans at all, but Plato and Aristotle, so the church adopted a Roman foundational authority and the Platonic problem of how to control the passions. Rather than the law, the church employed the commandments. Without justification, the commandments required the threat of violence, the threat of hell, to ensure obedience. With this came the

Student partnership and a legitimation crisis 99

corruption of the elite as political space was closed down. Where violence is used, authority is already dead. But fear of hell didn't last. Once hell had lost its coercive power, people no longer feared violating the notion of 'good'.

We might ask whether the coercion of debt and redeeming employment is enough for students to fear violating the idea of a good higher education. We might go further still and ask whether the university teacher, stripped of the authority of the foundation, will be able to teach the students what it means to study well, what it means to inquire and study deeply. The absence of this ethical understanding poses a risk to the sustainability of higher education.

Revolution and foundations in the present

By the early modern period, the time of Machiavelli, church and state were already thoroughly corrupt. Machiavelli attempted to re-establish the state. He wanted a new foundation, made in the present, rather than harking back to the past. But creating a foundation in the present, as in a revolution, required a willingness to use violence. As far as Arendt is concerned, to think of 'making' or fabricating a foundation is to invoke a household category and to use it inappropriately in a political situation: a category relevant to the oikos is applied to the polis. Fabricating foundations, in order to build a world, does violence to pre-existing understandings of higher education.

To carry authority, the foundation must carry some respected presence in order to persuade people that it should be built on. The Roman Empire and the church had foundations in the past. This made it easier for it to command respect and to be considered as carrying the wisdom of the ages. For Arendt, the only successful, modern attempt at creating a foundation in the present is the American Revolution. American citizens regard their Declaration of Independence and the Constitution as sacred documents, framed by the 'Founding Fathers'. It succeeded, she thought, because it emerged not out of revolution, but out of a war with England. The Constitution was not a document intended for the victors to rue the defeated. Moreover, it was a based upon a framework (Montesquieu's analysis of the English constitution) which already existed, so it did appeal to the notion of reaching back in time to the elders. A higher education constitutional arrangement founded on student partnership has to acknowledge the foundational idea of the university. This will mean passing authority from one generation to the next, but harking back to what is being passed on, not just forward to student employability or some other weak promise. Higher education, however, also requires political space for those involved. Students and their teachers require room to determine what constitutes higher education for themselves. Regimes without political space are quickly exhausted; they become increasingly irrational. Real life is lived, Arendt maintains, in political space, and when that space is closed off, a person trying to act within it becomes 'embarrassed'. She cannot be herself and the result is a deep sense of alienation.

In relation to our higher education system in the 1960s in Britain, we had our own foundation in the present: the social-democratic expansion of the universities

100 *Morgan White*

after the Robbins Report in 1963. While this system briefly opened up a moment in democratic political space this has since been closed down by a technocratic political class, administering a technocratic higher education. While Arendt hoped to enable the vita activa, direct participation in the political world, we certainly do not have a politics where the wisdom of the ages is passed to us by elders with authority. It should, therefore, come as no surprise that the universities provided by a bureaucratic state lack a strong political aspect and students emerge from their studies without the authority to act and work effectively either in the workplace or in the public sphere.

Education has been undermined by this distance from authority and it can be seen most sharply in higher education. The idea that education develops judgement and practical reason where a 'foundation' of understanding is passed down through the generations is increasingly substituted by an instrumental training. Of course, many academics resist an instrumentalist view of education, but this does not prevent functionalist tendencies in policy change. Knowledge continues to be taught, but its purpose is to provide material to test against. The purpose of this is two-fold: on the one hand to generate certificates and credentials (for future employees to take to higher levels of education and, eventually, to the labour market) and also to monitor the efficiency via 'accountability' of the educational institution itself. This knowledge is not regarded as good in itself. It is not knowledge that is valued but the 'skills' in the trainee or the function of using knowledge to police the educational institution. The more productive these skills are, the more value attached and the higher the wage paid to the owner of 'human capital'. The authority of a knowledge foundation that harks back to the past is displaced by the power of skills that are anticipated as useful in the future. In the case of accountability through performativity, the knowledge involved itself holds no authority, for its purpose is to test and monitor the value of the institution. Authority, or rather, what is taken to be authority, but lacks legitimation through recognition, clearly resides in the monitoring agency rather than the educational institution. Under an Arendtian view of authority, the teacher becomes a servant to the bureaucracy. Rousseau, of course, tells us in Emile that the tutor must never allow himself to be seen as a servant to the student (or anyone else) because this fundamentally undermines the idea that education leads to autonomy. (See, for example, Plamenatz, 1972.)

World turned upside down

Consider a higher education system where education has become completely instrumental. In generating future-oriented credentials and qualifications, the 'purchaser' in the labour market (the future employer) has an interest in pushing down the price of the purchase: pay less for more qualifications. There is also an interest on the part of the educational institution in increasing the qualifications awarded. There is a 'cost-push' and a 'demand-pull' side to this equation. Employers demand more and schools, colleges and universities award more qualifications. The result is qualification or grade inflation.

Student partnership and a legitimation crisis 101

But this is not the only result. For in the process of inflation, the currency is degraded and devalued, like a gold coin that has been snipped away at the edges until it is no longer valued as legal tender. The education involved here rarely carries the wisdom of ages, rarely harks back to the foundation and rarely carries authority. Authority in education, then, is not directly about a hierarchy between teacher and student. Authority is not a curtailment of freedom. Rather, it is concerned with the passing on of culture through knowledge, skills, practices and attitudes and involves the trust of the student. Education is augmenting and building on the foundation of the world. Education, then, makes authority possible, and public education (resourced by revenues collected by the state from citizens) should attempt to open up political space in order to create institutional structures capable of carrying and building upon authority.

Authority demands obedience, yet is not power, violence or persuasion. It harks back to the past, to the foundation of culture. The deepening relationship with ideas in the past is not, however, familiar to the student as partner. For the student as partner does not identify with the notion of scholarship as craft, an apprentice working under a master (Wright Mills, 2000). In stark contrast, the student as partner stands between present and future, without reference to tradition. The student here holds more power but the authority of the academic teacher is weakened. In weakening the teacher's authority, the possibility of the student acquiring authority is lost. The (supposedly) higher education received is one with an eye firmly on an imagined employer rather than 'outmoded' ideas. The authority brought through mastery is lost on students and staff operating in an unsustainable world of high fees, high debt, employability, skills for work and student satisfaction. The system is unsustainable, in part because of practical problems such as unaffordable debt write-downs by the Treasury (the most recent UK government estimate suggests 45 per cent of student debt will not be repaid), but also because of the forces that push higher education away from an ethical attitude to the foundation of intellectual mastery and it consequently loses its legitimate authority. Higher education (in the sense of authoritative, legitimate higher education rather than merely the hollow appearance), in the absence of political space, will be quickly exhausted. The idea of student partnership, where it undermines academic authority, removes the purpose of studying. Teachers and lecturers should not allow the concept of student partnership to be regarded as a panacea for the cleavage in interests between the academic and the student caused by high-level fees and a shift in the cultural understanding of the goals of university study.

Authority in the seminar

Roland Barthes maintained that the seminar was a site where authority was conspicuous in its absence. The seminar was a space for 'changing hands', for passing on and sharing understanding, and not about master and servant relations (Barthes, 1992, p.339). Jürgen Habermas' use of the 'ideal-speech situation' as a regulative ideal led to frequent charges that his theory of communicative

102 *Morgan White*

rationality amounted to little more than an attempt to regard moral, social and political relations as a university seminar writ large. The seminar, however, does involve authority since the to-and-fro of learning and discourse is a back-and-forth movement of (sometimes) small struggles for recognition and trust where we either tacitly or expressly rest on the foundations of tradition, of the understandings that went before.

In the concrete situation of the seminar, attitudes to authority and confusions between authority and power might manifest in a variety of ways. There is the student who persistently confronts the tutor or even insistently quarrels with the 'authority' of the texts or authors under discussion; there is the student who prefers to command the attention of his tutor rather than listening to his peers; there is the student who persistently seeks praise from the tutor or listens intently to everything she says as he writes it down; there are the students who chat amongst themselves instead of joining the discussion; there is the student who tells the tutor what she wants to hear, mindful of the fact that she will be marking his assignment. In the flow of discourse, within the carefully tended ground of the seminar, authority develops in the student, and the sense of embarrassment to speak out diminishes.

The tutor who attempts to give away authority by claiming 'we are all on the same level' in order to create an atmosphere of openness and participation makes it impossible for students to recognise her authority and implies a false equality. By denying the presence of authority, she denies her students the means of recognising and acquiring authority for themselves.

The authoritative tutor

Within the etymology of the words 'seminar', 'student' and' tutor' lies an understanding of the type of authority suggested here. 'Seminar' literally means 'breeding ground or plant nursery'. 'Student' derives from studere meaning to apply diligently, and 'tutor' derives from tueri, meaning watcher, protector, or guardian. The tutor, then, might be conceived to guard or watch over the seminar from which ideas and judgement can develop; he protects the conditions for those who are diligently applying themselves to a matter at hand in order to enable growth. Watching or guarding over conveys a pastoral dimension that extends beyond promoting acquisition of knowledge or skills, although these might also comprise an important element of the seminar. The seminar tutor might give space for the hesitant student to air her views, gently restrain the overbearing or arrogant student, make connections between ideas and suggest new ways of thinking about a topic.

The tutor holds authority over the student through connections to past foundations. He has read the text under discussion, but has also read other works by the same author and that author's contemporaries or predecessors and successors. Perhaps he has written about the text himself or discussed and clarified his own ideas with scholars in the field. He recognises patterns of ideas and can clarify meanings when the seminar begins to flounder.

Student partnership and a legitimation crisis　103

The tutor as protector hopes for students to acquire authority too. The criterion employed to distribute authority is effective reasoning, and this might take different forms from discipline to discipline. The good tutor recognises good arguments, insightful critical comments or exceptional cases and shows students that he recognises them too, in effect bestowing an increasing authority onto them. He might use subtle cues of recognition to indicate when the kind of authority he hopes to nurture is present. The authoritative tutor shows rather than tells the students how to exercise judgement. At the same time, the authoritative tutor guides students towards the idea that no one is expert at everything. Students are encouraged to become sceptical, to listen carefully to others and to discern.

Initially, the sovereignty to distribute authority resides in the tutor, but over time it may be devolved throughout the class. The tutor might use tactics to distribute authority by asking students if they would like the seminar to be organised differently, owning up to a mistake, or exposing himself in some way to destabilise his position as an authority figure. The role of the tutor here might be to watch over or protect authority itself as it grows within the seminar group. In this setting, we see students as more genuine partners in a joint project of study. Good pedagogy is fundamentally about the acquisition of authority in the student. The policy idea behind student partnership asserts the student's authority, but in so doing precludes recognition from the tutor through a pedagogical relationship.

Conclusion

The pedagogic process is a dynamic one whereby students in higher education acquire authority over time, under the guardianship of an educator who accepts and exhibits her own authority within a relationship of trustful obedience. The authoritative educator is concerned with both developing knowledge and cultivating judgement that are rooted in the past but project into the future.

In contrast, the notion of students as partners fetishizes the new and assumes that past foundations are unimportant; it creates a foundation in the present to limit the possibility of a dissatisfied future. Students uncoupled from past foundations and encouraged to take an instrumental approach to their learning are detached from the tutor; they cannot be expected to recognise the authority of the tutor to protect and watch over their progress. This puts tutor and student at cross-purposes rather than in relations of meaningful partnership. The misaligned relations between academic teachers and students rob contemporary, marketised higher education of a sense of legitimate authority in the eyes of both students and teachers, for the university no longer effectively mediates between them but forces them together.

References

Anderson, E. (1995). *Value in Ethics and Economics.* Cambridge, MA: Harvard University Press.
Arendt, H. (1990). *On Revolution.* London: Penguin.

104 *Morgan White*

Arendt, H. (1993a). The crisis in education. In: H. Arendt, *Between Past and Future*, pp.173–196. London: Penguin.

Arendt, H. (1993b). What is authority? In: H. Arendt, *Between Past and Future*, pp.91–141. London: Penguin.

Arendt, H. (1998). *The Human Condition*. Chicago: University of Chicago Press.

Barthes, R. (1992). *The Rustle of Language*. Oakland, CA: University of California Press.

Jessop, S. (2011). Children's participation: an Arendtian criticism. *Educational Philosophy and Theory*, 43(9), 981–996.

Keat, R. (1994). Sceptism, authority, and the market. In: R. Keat, N. Whiteley and N. Abercrombie (eds), *The Authority of the Consumer*, pp.23–42. London: Routledge.

Kodelja, Z. (2013). Authority, the autonomy of the university, and neoliberal politics. *Educational Theory*, 63(3), 317–330.

Plamenatz, J. (1972). Rousseau: the education of Emile. *Journal of Philosophy of Education*, 6(2), 176–192.

Waldron, J. (1995). The wisdom of the multitude: some reflections on Book 3, Chapter 11 of Aristotle's Politics. *Political Theory*, 23(4), 563–584.

Wright Mills, C. (2000). *The Sociological Imagination*, Appendix 'On intellectual craftsmanship'. Oxford: Oxford University Press.

8 Teacher development through professional partnership

Harnessing the power of professional learning communities

Geoff Baker

Introduction

In the last few decades academic studies have highlighted the need to re-evaluate approaches to teacher development. Commentators have called on school leaders to recognise both the power and complexity of teacher development, with the strength of teacher development opportunities provided by a school being seen by many as indicative of the school's overall standing, as well as a vitally important vehicle to improve it (Hargreaves and Fullan, 2012). Traditional, didactic approaches have been the subject of a barrage of criticism, with studies suggesting that sending staff on one-day courses, the content of which often remains the preserve of the member of staff who attended, is 'generally ineffectual' (Opfer et al., 2008; Opfer and Pedder, 2011a). Yet huge components of school budgets continue to be directed at such teacher development courses, and there is now a multi-million pound industry providing day courses for teachers (Desforges, 2014). The title of Opfer and Pedder's 2011 article, 'The lost promise of teacher professional development in England', succinctly summarises an attitude that has arisen in light of the failure of many school leaders to rethink the opportunities for development that they are providing their staff (Opfer and Pedder, 2011a). This chapter explores the view that teacher development that centres on collaboration and partnership can have a transformational impact on staff as individual practitioners and on the school in which they teach, impacting in turn on colleagues and students.

Teacher development and professional networks

A number of broad principles for effective teacher development can be drawn from the literature, notably that teacher development should be:

- interactive;
- located within the professional domain;
- focused on student learning; and
- bespoke to the needs of individual teachers.

106   *Geoff Baker*

A brief discussion of each of these principles is offered here as a context to interpret the direction of this chapter.

In the first place, it is now generally accepted that teacher development should be interactive, giving opportunities for teachers to share and reflect (Kelchtermans, 2004). One of the biggest criticisms levelled at more traditional approaches to teacher development, which often involve an auditorium full of professionals passively listening to a lecture, is that they fail to adhere to the basic tenets of teaching that are widely accepted as good practice when engaging a class of young people (Opfer and Pedder, 2011a, 2011b). It is generally accepted that for meaningful learning to take place in any context simply listening is not enough, and more active approaches are necessary, a view that is transferable to any learning domain, whether the school classroom or a hall full of teachers completing a CPD session (Wright, 2015). Next is the view that teacher development should be located within the communities in which professionals practise. Although in many schools it can feel like an individual endeavour, teaching cannot be isolated from the professional community in which it happens as that is where norms are shaped and shared (Clement and Vandenberghe, 2000). This has led Lieberman and Miller (2008, p.1) to criticise the 'mistaken belief that teachers can increase their effectiveness and deepen their practice outside of the professional communities to which they belong'. Another principle is that teacher development must focus on student learning, the core business of teachers and one that is often lost in more traditional approaches (Hadar and Brody, 2013; Hairon et al., 2015). Finally, the literature clearly suggests that teacher development is most effective when professionals are empowered in the process – it should not be something that happens to them, but happens with them or is led by them (Kelchtermans, 2004; Webb et al., 2009). This in turn highlights the importance of a model of teacher development that gives the individual professional an opportunity to focus on areas of need specific to them. This model is more labour intensive than traditional approaches to teacher development, but by zoning in on areas of need for the individual it can be far more effective (Campbell and Jacques, 2003). The principles for effective teacher development make traditional models of teacher development all but redundant.

The guiding principles that have been identified in the literature on teacher development have a remarkable degree of convergence with work on professional communities. The term 'professional community' is used here to denote when professionals meet together to explore aspects of their practice. The term is used loosely, deliberately so, as a catch-all reference that includes a variety of different models. In the last few decades a significant body of work has emerged that has analysed the role of community in acculturating professional norms (Palincsar, 1999; Stoll and Louis, 2007; Vescio et al., 2008). Increasingly, this work has not only explored professional communities as a sociological phenomenon but has also outlined the different types of professional community that might exist and considered the extent to which they facilitate effective development of the professionals contained within them. Analyses of professional communities have posited the view that empowering professionals in their own development and

Teacher development – professional partnership   107

encouraging them to collaborate is a powerful model (Wenger and Snyder, 2000). This is seen particularly in the literature on teacher development. A myriad of studies have extolled the virtue of professional communities as a vehicle that has the power to 'transform' teaching and raise the profile of the profession (see, for example, Stoll and Louis, 2007; Warren Little, 2002). This is exemplified in the view of Palincsar (1999, p.272) that community is often 'the most important ingredient to change'. While studies have provided a sociological commentary on the impact of professional communities, there are fewer academic works that provide guidance on how to develop a professional community that has a positive impact on the constituent members.

Conceptualising professional communities

Those working on professional communities and teacher development owe a lot to the work of Levine (2010). In an effort to synthesise the material on teacher communities, he provided an analysis of the existing literature, drawing out four broad categories of teacher community that are currently used, often without precision, by commentators in this field. Levine argues that all have a common core in that they are based on a presupposition that collaboration amongst teachers can lead to the development of professional knowledge, yet each of the four conceptions has a different way of interpreting or engaging with these communities.

The first conception of teacher community that Levine (2010) identifies is 'inquiry community', which exists when teachers critique and reflect on their practice together. This form of community might involve peer observations or shared analysis of student work. Lesson study – a model discussed later in this chapter, which involves teachers collectively planning and delivering a lesson – is one example of an inquiry community approach (Lewis and Hurd, 2011; Dudley, 2012; Lieberman, 2009). Levine's (2010) second conception, 'teacher professional community', has a sociological focus and looks at the shared norms that exist when teachers work collaboratively whilst focusing on the student. As various commentators have noted, teacher community can be positive or negative depending on the nature of the norms that are being reinforced (McLaughlin and Talbert, 2001). In recent years this notion has been developed further with the emergence of the conception of 'professional learning communities', which highlights the importance of learning and critical reflection and offers the potential of using sociological insights to inform prescriptive guidelines about how best to harness the capacity of professional communities (Stoll and Louis, 2007). This links to Levine's third conception, 'community of learners', which exists when there is a state within an organisation when all actively seek to develop their professional knowledge led by the principal, who models this through her or his commitment to their own professional development (Levine, 2010; Barth, 1985). The final model Levine identifies is 'communities of practice'. The community of practice model maintains that learning is a social process in which the learner is acculturated into a profession through their participation in it (Lave and Wenger, 1991; Wenger, 1998, 2000). Although the communities

108 *Geoff Baker*

of practice approach has received huge attention from commentators, the bulk of work using this paradigm has had a sociological bent, focusing on interpreting how communities of practice function, particularly in relation to the way in which novices (NQTS) become experts.

There are some limitations to Levine's work. In the first place, the huge attention given to professional communities silences other influences on the development of professional knowledge and identity (Levine, 2010). For this reason, activity theory and the third space have been posited as a fifth paradigm, as they allow for incorporation of a more inclusive view of the range of influences in professional development that include official and unofficial spaces (Levine, 2010; Daniels and Edwards, 2010; Engleström, 1999; Gutiérrez et al., 1999). Also, as Levine recognises, the different conceptions of professional community that he identifies are not completely discrete. It is, for instance, possible that a professional learning community model might be developed that uses inquiry community based approaches with an aim to create a community of learners. The interactions within that community may be interpreted using a community of practice approach. Nonetheless, the distinctions that Levine identifies draw light on both the breadth of literature on professional communities and allow for a framework in approaching and applying them.

The research project

When the project began I was working as Deputy Director of Teaching and Learning across a Multi-Academy Trust. During this period I was contacted by the lead for teaching and learning at one of the secondary schools in the Trust who wanted to move away from a didactic, lecture-based approach to teacher development. We discussed the findings of literature on lesson study and decided on a model that we felt was most 'authentic' and followed the literature most closely. All staff in the school, including members of the senior leadership team, were put into lesson study triads. In every triad each of the three colleagues came from a different subject area, but they chose one particular subject that all three delivered a lesson on. Given the difficulties this posed for some subjects, in terms of colleagues not having any background knowledge, most chose lessons on subjects that were deemed more accessible – history, geography and English being the most popular. The study discussed here involved gathering feedback from all participants, but specific, in-depth work with one triad only, chosen on the advice of the lead for teaching and learning at the school, who believed that they had a 'typical' level of investment in the project.

The research tool

Interviews constituted the core research tool used with the participants. Interviews receive a far better response rate than do questionnaire surveys. Not only that, but in face-to-face interviews the interviewer can also draw on information derived from body language as well as be certain that the answers given are genuinely their answers and they have not received help from others in coming up with the response (Barriball and While, 1994). It has also been noted that face-to-face interviews stimulate interest in a project in a way that few other research tools can, encouraging deeper more meaningful responses (Galletta, 2013). The interviews conducted were semi-structured. Semi-structured interviews by their nature have a degree of structure, usually in a common core of questions, but the interviewer and interviewee have the capacity to probe particular areas more deeply (Carruthers, 1990). Semi-structured interviews also give an opportunity to confirm that the respondent has understood the question as they can check understanding with the interviewer (Barriball and While, 1994). In the same way, the interviewer can push the respondent to deepen answers or clarify responses through the use of probing (Rubin and Rubin, 2012; Coleman, 2012). However, the main reason that semi-structured interviews were chosen as the research tool for this project was that they elicit the kinds of information on which this study will be centred as they can help us to develop an understanding of people's beliefs and attitudes. The participants were asked a series of questions before taking part in the lesson study process and after that considered the practicalities of the lesson study process and deeper questions about the impact that involvement had on their practice and their professional identity.

Discussion

The interviews conducted before the lesson study triads began suggested a level of anxiety amongst colleagues. They had never been involved in this style of continuing professional development before and were concerned about sharing their teaching with colleagues. As one respondent noted, 'I am a little bit worried that they will laugh at me – I have a particular style which they won't see normally' (R2, I1). Another respondent remarked that 'this is different, you put yourself out there . . . not like sitting in a conference where you are safe, as long as you don't ask a question' (R1, I1). This notion finds some wider corroboration in work that has argued that teaching has generally become a closed-door, secretive profession, where colleagues are often hesitant about sharing their practice for fear of criticism (Lieberman and Miller, 2008). However, while they were anxious about sharing their practice in this manner, as we will see, the participants also indicated a real sense of excitement at being involved in what was seen a novel and unusual approach to continuing professional development.

The particular triad that is the focus of this case study spent just over an hour as a group planning the initial focus and getting to know each other a bit better, a time that all three respondents felt was particularly valuable. An English lesson was chosen to be the first of the lesson study subjects as it was felt that this was the most accessible topic of the three taught by the respondents. The English teacher in the triad gave the participants an overview of the topic being taught. To ensure that new approaches were considered, each member of the triad then brought in one piece of research that they had found that discussed ways of engaging students, then all three worked together to devise ways of teaching the

110   *Geoff Baker*

lesson in line with the research they had studied. The participants then took turns teaching the same lesson to different Year 7 groups, with the remaining two participants observing, giving feedback and then developing the lesson accordingly. Students were aware of what the staff members were doing, and all three respondents noted that the students were very 'positive' and 'liked the idea' of knowing that their teachers were doing something different (R1, I2). While the whole process initially sounds labour intensive, the participants noted that they only spent about six hours on the whole cycle, for which staff development time was allocated and cover provided so that they could observe each other teach. At the end of the process the participants got together and reflected on what had been learnt, following which a second interview was conducted that considered what had been learnt in the interim.

The approach to lesson study that was adopted here stuck closely to the method used in Japan where it was first developed, which involved the triad teaching the same, but tweaked, lesson three times to different groups. From the initial interviews it was quite clear that the fact that the participants would all need to teach the same lesson, which meant two members of the triad would be teaching outside their subject area, was a significant area of concern. Even though the group being taught was Year 7 and consequently the background knowledge needed was not substantive, one member of the triad noted fearing being 'exposed' (R2, I1). For ethical reasons, it was felt important to share with the students what was going on, which alleviated these worries somewhat, but there was still a sense that this would somehow be too much to manage. In the triad that was interviewed all three of the participants taught an English lesson, despite the fact that one of the members of the triad was a music teacher and one a science teacher. In the first interview all three respondents noted concern at the notion of teaching a lesson in a subject that was not their own: for example, 'it would be better if we were with teachers from our subject' (R2, I1) and 'I remain to be convinced of the point of me teaching an English lesson' (R3, I1). A stark finding from the feedback was that there was universal praise for this approach from respondents once the programme was complete. Respondent two noted that 'I was really tested, took me right outside of my comfort zone' (R2, I2) and respondent three said that 'it made me think in completely new and unexpected ways. It didn't always feel comfortable to start, but I am a better teacher of my own subject as a result' (R3, I2). Even the English teacher felt that in the act of supporting others, she too developed an increased understanding of her own discipline – 'helping the others with the kinds of things they can do made me think about what was, like, at the core of what I am trying to do, as well as giving me new ideas' (R1, I2). In allowing the teachers to move outside of their comfort zones, but in a manner that was dictated and controlled by the participants, it appears that it facilitated a space in which the participants felt able to be creative and take risks.

All three participants who took part in the lesson study triad that was the focus of this case study noted that the experience had a definite impact on their practice. The overwhelming sense of the feedback from the interviews was that the lesson study approach that was utilised gave teachers a space in which to reflect on their

Teacher development – professional partnership 111

teaching. In the first interview all three respondents noted feelings of positivity, with expressions such as 'optimistic' (R2, I1), 'looking forward to it' (R1, I1) and 'excited to see if it really helps' (R3, I1). Once the lesson research cycle was complete all three noted that they found the experience beneficial and were able to give numerous examples of how their experiences had changed their practice. So, respondent 1 noted that 'it has changed the way I think of learning, I now try to include more kinaesthetic aspects to keep students engaged' (R1, I2). The third respondent included a number of positive examples also, notably 'seeing my colleagues in action made me think about how I could take bits of what they do and put into my own teaching, like their approach to differentiation' (R3, I2). The second respondent who had recently entered the profession stated 'it was like being on the PGCE again, but this time the people watching me and who I watched I really trust. I keep thinking of the different ways you can do something and I am trying new ideas now in lessons to take me outside the comfort zone' (R2, I2). The comments from the participants clearly demonstrated that for this triad the experience of taking part in the lesson study programme had made them rethink areas of their teaching and led to changes in practice.

An unexpected development of the project from the perspective of those facilitating it was that all three noted that participating in the lesson study triad had not only had an impact on their practice, but also on their professional identities. Despite the comparatively small amount of time that had been spent on this activity, participants specifically felt that it had made them rethink how teachers should practise. In the first instance, all three participants said that they would be opening up their practice to far more scrutiny from colleagues. They noted that they would continue to plan lessons together, regardless of whether it was accorded CPD time. Not only this, but one respondent noted that they would be keeping the door to their classroom open in a bid to get more colleagues to come in and offer support/feedback on their teaching. Another stated that since they had qualified as a teacher the only observations they had, had been the performance management observation that occurs three times a year. 'But I am usually so panicked for that, that the observer doesn't see me as I normally am – if feedback is going to help me they need to see how I am every day' (R2, I2). This sentiment was explored on a deeper level by another respondent who stated that 'The fact I have never seen another teacher since qualifying until now is surely the biggest failing of the profession . . . sharing with other teachers should surely be one of our main responsibilities as teachers' (R1, I2). In the same way, it was also remarked that seeing how different the approaches of colleagues were had helped participants reformulate their view of what successful teaching actually was. 'We had a load of lectures on what made questioning good, but to see it in action I now realise how important it is to actually doing any teaching – good teachers really need to be good questioners' (R2, I2). Although unexpected by the facilitators of the project, the literature on professional learning communities alludes to the notion that even a short exposure to this type of activity can lead participants to fundamentally reconsider the profession they are in, reformulating professional norms and leading to the development of new

112 *Geoff Baker*

ways of engaging with the profession that are sustained long after the activity is complete (Wenger, 2000).

Conclusion

The use of a professional community approach to teacher development and the specific approach seen in the case study initially appear labour intensive. While they certainly required the school to be more flexible than giving a day off per year to send someone on a course, ultimately the resources required for completion of an entire lesson study triad was less in terms of time and monetary cost. A wide range of different approaches to professional communities can be utilised. While the lesson study model used in the case study initially promoted a mixture of anxiety and excitement amongst participants, all felt that teaching outside their subject area was an incredibly valuable experience and forced participants to consider approaches they were not familiar with. Both the literature and the experience documented in the case study clearly indicate that when colleagues collaborate and work with each other as part of a professional community, then meaningful developments are possible. This is not to say that community is a panacea to every teaching problem identified in a school, but these kind of approaches empower staff in their own development and when practitioner knowledge and experience are brought together with analysis of research on a particular issue then the conditions are ripe for transformation of practice along with the possibility of reflection on what it means to be a professional.

References

Barriball, K.L. and While, A. (1994). Collecting data using a semi-structured interview: a discussion paper. *Journal of Advanced Nursing*, 19(2), 328–335.

Barth, R.S. (1985). The Principalship. *Educational Leadership*, 42(6), 92–94.

Campbell, A. and Jacques, K. (2003). Best practice researched: teachers' expectations of the impact of doing research in their classrooms and schools. *Teacher Development: An International Journal of Teachers' Professional Development*, 7(1), 75–90.

Carruthers, J. (1990). A rationale for the use of semi-structured interviews. *Journal of Educational Administration*, 28(1), 63–68.

Clement, M. and Vandenberghe, R. (2000). Teachers' professional development: a solitary or collegial (ad)venture?. *Teaching and Teacher Education*, 16(1), 81–101.

Coleman, M. (2012). Interviews. In: A.R.J. Briggs, M. Coleman and M. Morrison (eds), *Research Methods in Educational Leadership and Management*, 3rd edition, pp.250–265. London: Sage.

Daniels, H. and Edwards, A. (2010). Introduction. In: H. Daniels, A. Edwards, Y. Engleström, T. Gallagher and S.R. Ludvigsen (eds), *Activity in Theory and Practice: Promoting Learning Across Boundaries and Agencies*, pp.1–8. Oxon: Routledge.

Desforges, C. (2014). Lesson study as a strategic choice for CPD. In P. Dudley (ed.), *Lesson Study: Professional Learning for Our Time*, pp.xv–xx. Oxon: Routledge.

Dudley, P. (2012). Lesson study development in England: from school networks to national policy. *International Journal for Lesson and Learning Studies*, 1(1), 85–100.

Englestrom, Y. (1999). Activity theory and individual and social transformation. In: Y. Englestrom, R. Miettinen and R. L. Punamäki (eds.), *Perspective on Activity Theory*, pp.19–38. Cambridge: Cambridge University Press.

Galletta, A. (2013). *Mastering the Semi-Structured Interview and Beyond: From Research Design to Analysis and Publication*. New York: New York University Press.

Gutiérrez, K.D., Baquedano-López, P. and Tejeda, C. (1999). Rethinking diversity: hybridity and hybrid language practices in the third space. *Mind, Culture, and Activity*, 6(4), 286–303.

Hadar, L.L. and Brody, D.L. (2013). The interaction between group processes and personal professional trajectories in a professional development community for teacher educators. *Journal of Teacher Education*, 64(2), 145–161.

Hairon, S., Goh, J.W.P. and Chua, C.S.K. (2015). Teacher leadership enactment in professional learning community contexts: towards a better understanding of the phenomenon. *School Leadership and Management*, 35(2), 163–185.

Hargreaves, A. and Fullan, M. (2012). *Professional Capital: Transforming Teaching in Every School*. New York: Teachers College Press.

Kelchtermans, G. (2004). CPD for professional renewal: moving beyond knowledge for practice. In: C. Day and J. Sachs (eds.), *International Handbook on the Continuing Professional Development of Teachers*, pp.217–237. Berkshire: Open University Press.

Lave, J. and Wenger, E. (1991). *Situated Learning: Legitimate Peripheral Participation*. Cambridge: Cambridge University Press.

Levine, T.H. (2010). Tools for the study and design of collaborative teacher learning: the affordances of different conceptions of teacher community and activity theory. *Teacher Education Quarterly*, 109–130.

Lewis, C.C. and Hurd, J. (2011). *Lesson Study Step-by-Step: How Teacher Learning Communities Improve Instruction*. Portsmouth: Heinemann.

Lieberman, A. and Miller, L. (2008). Introduction. In: A. Lieberman and L. Miller (eds), *Teachers in Professional Communities: Improving Teaching and Learning*, pp.1–3. New York: Teachers College Press.

Lieberman, J. (2009). Reinventing teacher professional norms and identities: the role of lesson study and learning communities. *Professional Development in Education*, 35(1), 83–99.

McLaughlin, M.W. and Talbert, J.E. (2001). *Professional Communities and the Work of High School Teaching*. London: University of Chicago Press.

Opfer, V.D. and Pedder, D. (2011a). The lost promise of teacher professional development in England. *European Journal of Teacher Education*, 34(1), 3–24.

Opfer, V.D. and Pedder, D. (2011b). Conceptualising teacher professional learning. *Review of Educational Research*, 81(3), 376–406.

Opfer, V.D., Pedder, D. and Lavicza, Z. (2008). *Survey Report: Schools and Continuing Professional Development (CPD) in England – State of the Nation Research Project (T34718)*. Cambridge: Report for the TDA.

Palincsar, A. (1999). A community of practice. *Teacher Education and Special Education*, 22(4), 272–274.

Rubin, H.J. and Rubin, I.S. (2012). *Qualitative Interviewing: The Art of Hearing Data*, 3rd edition. London: Sage.

114 *Geoff Baker*

Stoll, L. and Louis, K.S. (2007). Professional learning communities: elaborating new approaches. In: L. Stoll and K.S. Louis (eds), *Professional Learning Communities: Divergence, Depth and Dilemmas*, pp.1–13. Berkshire: Open University Press.

Vescio, V., Ross, D. and Adams, A. (2008). A review of research on the impact of professional learning communities on teaching practice and student learning. *Teaching and Teacher Education*, 24(1), 80–91.

Warren Little, J. (2002). Locating learning in teachers' communities of practice: opening up problems of analysis in records of everyday work. *Teaching and Teacher Education*, 18(8), 917–946.

Webb, R., Vulliamy, G., Sarja, A., Hämäläinen, S. and Poikonen, P. (2009). Professional learning communities and teacher well-being? A comparative analysis of primary schools in England and Finland. *Oxford Review of Education*, 35(3), 405–422.

Wenger, E. (1998). *Communities of Practice: Learning, Meaning and Identity*. Cambridge: Cambridge University Press.

Wenger, E. (2000). Communities of practice: the key to knowledge strategy. In: E. Lesser, M.A. Fontaine and J.A. Slusher (eds), *Knowledge and Communities*, pp.3–20. Woburn: Butterworth-Heinemann.

Wenger, E. and Snyder, W.M. (2000). Communities of practice: the organizational frontier. *Harvard Business Review*, 78(1), 139–146.

Wright, D.E. (2015). *Active Learning: Social Justice Education and Participatory Action Research*. London: Routledge.

9 The changing role of the teacher in multi-agency work

Elizabeth Parr

Introduction

The concept of multi-agency working has become embedded in the discourses and recent legislation governing practice as well as policy-making in England. This has culminated in documents such as the *Working Together to Safeguard Children* document, which states, 'Ultimately, effective safeguarding of children can only be achieved by putting children at the centre of the system, and by every individual and agency playing their full part, working together to meet the needs of our most vulnerable children' (DfE, 2013, p.8). However, prior to considering the rationale behind multi-agency work, it is necessary that the definition of this term is established. Lloyd et al. define multi-agency working as 'more than one agency working with a young person, with a family or on a project (but not necessarily jointly). It may be concurrent, sometimes as a result of joint planning or it may be sequential' (2001, p.2). This is opposed to inter-agency working, which is defined as 'when more than one agency work together in a planned and formal way' (2001, p.2). This is an important distinction as schools, for example, are both an agency themselves and a place in which different agencies work. As a result, most agencies work in both ways – multi-agency and inter-agency; however for the purposes of this chapter, predominantly the multi-agency aspect will be considered.

Payne argues that 'the case for treating social problems in a holistic fashion is overwhelming. People know, in a simple everyday fashion, that crime, poverty, low achievement at school, bad housing and so on are connected' (1998, p.12). The DfES built on this in the Green Paper *Every Child Matters* (2003), stating that the government aimed to 'put children at the heart of our policies, and to organise services around their needs. Radical reform is needed to break down organisational boundaries' (DfES, 2003, p.9). This is a significant element of multi-agency working as the boundaries between the agencies are to be crossed and explored to ensure that an effective service is being provided. This is to say that multi-agency working is a holistic method of working with a range of issues rather than agencies dealing with individual issues independently. With this crossing of organisational boundaries and a holistic approach to dealing with problems, multi-agency work also allows for a range of differing professional

116   *Elizabeth Parr*

perspectives to be presented to a situation (Atkinson et al., 2005; Milbourne et al., 2003).

Despite a persuasive and clear rationale, when reading a range of the literature and DfES documents discussing multi-agency working practices, it is notable that a range of terminology continues to be used interchangeably. As Soan highlights, the phrases '"multi-agency" . . . "multi-disciplinary", "integrated services" and "inter-agency"' are all used within three pages of the document (2006, p.212). Soan suggests that despite such a range of terminology, they all point to the same outcome. However, Soan also highlights that there are issues with such a range of language being used. The variety of words may be interpreted by different agencies in different ways, and if the agencies are all aiming to work collaboratively, the language needs to be shared. This highlights a key problem within multi-agency work. If a range of agencies are to be working alongside each other, it is essential that they can communicate clearly with each other.

In a majority of the literature, there is a mixed response to multi-agency working. Most of the research highlights that it has a positive impact on practice; however, challenges concerning tensions between agencies and changing professional roles are ubiquitous. Raffo et al. (2007) clearly present the factors which assist the development of multi-agency working and the challenges to it. The assisting factors include clear management of the programme and non-hierarchical management structures based on mutual respect (p.27). This is supported by Hatcher and Leblond (2001), whose research demonstrates that unequal power relations can undermine multi-agency working. This suggests that when multi-agency working there needs to be equal relations between all agencies working with the family. This is challenging as it brings into question who takes responsibility for implementing an intervention or solving a problem. A further assisting factor which is significant is trust between agencies. Trust is necessary to ensure that agencies have the confidence to communicate; however, trust is also developed through multi-agency working (Atkinson et al., 2002). As a result of this, the multi-agency work builds confidence and trust to discuss tensions between the agencies, therefore furthering practice.

The challenges documented in the research are numerous, from staffing and time commitments to confidentiality issues. However the main challenge is tension between agencies and their approaches to situations (Machell, 1999; Milbourne et al., 2003). Milbourne et al. found that the pressures to perform well under the quantitative measurements imposed on the different agencies limited the multi-agency boundary crossing as agencies continued to be marked against their own individual measures of success (2003, p.28). This is a key factor in multi-agency working as each agency is still bound by restrictions such as targets and league tables. This ensures that although agencies are all working with one family, the agencies' expected outcomes are dependent on how the agency is measured. This may be a source of tension when multi-agency working as there can be a conflict regarding the anticipated outcome. Another significant challenge to multi-agency working is the expectation of professionals to deal with the complex relationships and demands that multi-agency working requires

The changing role of the teacher 117

(Anning, 2005; Engestrom, 2001). This is to say that dealing with such complex relationships when multi-agency working requires the professional to consider their own practices, the demands of their professional values and beliefs and also consider the families they are dealing with. Such questions can lead to a shift in professional identity from their previous identity to their identity within the multi-agency team (Robinson et al., 2005). This can be a positive transformation to acquiring new skills and a development of practice. However, it can also strengthen competitive approaches and entrench professionals further within the boundaries of their own agencies. The literature points to joint training for all multi-agency professionals to overcome these barriers and to support the development of a common language and common outcomes (Hallett and Stevenson, 1980; Bloxham, 1996).

To support the development of such a common language and common outcomes, England's inspectorates reconsidered their 2013 decision not to implement joint inspections. The inspectorates believed they could have a greater impact if they focused their attention into a shorter, sharper joint targeted inspection looking specifically at how well agencies work together to protect children in a locality area and targeted on specific areas of concern. These joint, targeted or 'integrated inspections' aimed to enable inspectorates to explore how partnership working in relation to a particular issue in a particular context improves the experiences and progress of children and young people (Ofsted, 2015). This approach, exploring multi-agency working in one context and in relation to one particular case family, is the approach that was used in the study below to investigate the role of the teacher in such work.

The study

In my professional practice, I have worked as a Key Stage One teacher in a primary school located in an area of significant deprivation. The school was co-located on a site with a Sure Start centre and as a result of this, in my professional practice I worked with Sure Start, families accessing Sure Start and a wide range of agencies on a daily basis. This study aimed to address the research question: how do Sure Start and the school coordinate their practices with other agencies to benefit families? The research took the form of a case study, investigating how a Sure Start centre and school worked with other agencies to achieve positive outcomes for a case family. As part of this research I examined two main areas:

- How is practice influenced by particular forms of coordinated multi-agency working?
- What types of impact does this form of multi-agency working have on disadvantaged families?

In doing this, the working practices of the school and Sure Start professionals were researched and as a result, the local dimensions of practice were analysed in

118   *Elizabeth Parr*

light of these. The impact these services have on the case family was investigated and their experiences analysed. In doing this, multi-agency practices could be analysed and the impact of this on the case study family could be investigated, then used to illuminate existing ideas in this area.

The research questions request information regarding the how and why of Sure Start and the school. It was necessary that the data was from an individual's viewpoint in order to construct a wider picture of what was happening. In this sense, the data collection process informed the direction of analysis, rather than testing a specific hypothesis. Rather than quantifying how many people have attended, or how many times an event has occurred, this research aimed to construct an understanding as to how Sure Start is being used and what impact the service is having on the whole lives of the families. In light of this, qualitative research was chosen as the most appropriate methodology; as Denzin and Lincon (2005) suggest, qualitative research involves an interpretive, naturalistic approach in which the observer is located. They assert that 'qualitative researchers study things in their natural settings, attempting to make sense of, or interpret, phenomena in terms of the meanings people bring to them' (p.3). This is to say that such qualitative data is heavily reliant on the context of the setting and participants' interpretation of events. In this research, this is fundamental as schools and Sure Start centres are managed individually, and therefore each has its own principles, practices and perspectives. From this, however, the existing ideas about multi-agency work can be illuminated in order to resonate with a wider audience. In this, it will be highlighted where the research further corroborates the theories considered below and where there are tensions between theory and practice.

Context

Sure Start was set up as part of the Labour Government's Comprehensive Spending Review 1998 and is based on the Head Start and Early Head Start initiatives, which aimed to improve developmental and educational provision in pre-school children in America (Eisenstadt, 2002). Sure Start's primary aim is to 'enhance the life chances of young children growing up in disadvantaged neighbourhoods' (Melhuish et al., 2008) by providing 'joined-up thinking' in terms of local services to build social capital (Bagley and Ackerley, 2006). This is based on the fundamental belief that pre-school experience and social capital have a direct impact on the achievement and development of children in the future. Sure Start promotes a holistic approach to dealing with families, recognising the relationships between poverty, family circumstance, health, social development and educational achievement (Hannon and Fox, 2005).

Current literature suggests that pre-school experience has benefits to children, compared with none (Sylva et al., 2003), and that the majority of participants benefit in terms of social and academic development (Schneider et al., 2006; Garces et al., 2000; Belsky et al., 2006). Research has also been conducted into the different types of families accessing the service and the impact of Sure Start on different types of users. Belsky et al. (2006) observe disparities between different types of families accessing Sure Start. Although teenage mothers were in the minority of the research sample, they also observe that the most socially deprived groups account for many social problems, and therefore the adverse effects of Sure Start could far outweigh the benefits to society (Belsky et al., 2006, p.4). Another key issue in this area is that Sure Start is dependent on local services and the needs of the local area (Glass, 1999). Therefore, comparing Sure Start and the impact of the services it provides is problematic. As Rutter (2006) argues, the vast variation in programmes and services ensures that definite quantitative answers on effective and ineffective services cannot be sought.

Theories of multi-agency development and learning

The effectiveness of Sure Start, therefore, is dependent on how it and other agencies work together to orchestrate change. This highlights the social and cultural dimension of Sure Start and how it joins with other services to deal with a set of problems and issues. In light of this, the main theories which will be considered are communities of practice and activity theory. The theory of communities of practice is proposed by Wenger (1998) and argues that people are continually learning as part of a community on a daily basis. This theory further suggests that when communities come together, the potential for development and new thinking is strong.

Activity theory, proposed by Engestrom (1987), suggests that an activity system (a group of people, for example an organisation, team or business) involves rules, tools and signs. These activity systems work toward an object which can be interpreted in different ways and, depending on its context, can be transformed. This theory was furthered by Daniels (2002), who considered the potential for new learning and the transformation of current practices.

This model would provide opportunity for tension between the two resulting objects (Object 3). This may be an opportunity for development and to discuss the priorities for each agency. However, if the object is transformed, the impact of this requires consideration as the initial object requires either review in future or justification for its transformation. Ludvigse, Havnes and Lahn (in Tuomi-Grohn and Engestrom, 2003) discuss the relationships between and within activity systems and highlight the significance of the interactions between participants. They suggest that, in reality, individuals move in and between different activity systems, and as a result new practices are formed through the boundary crossings. This could be observed when considering relationships between schools and Sure Start centres, which are continually altering. However, professional identities need to be considered when individuals cross boundaries into different activity systems as their role may become blurred and require renegotiation. These theories can be used as a lens through which the Sure Start activity system can be examined as well as the way it interacts with other activity systems i.e. other agencies. From this, the way in which multi-agency working operates in practice can be analysed.

120 *Elizabeth Parr*

Discussion

As the Sure Start centre is on the same site as a school, much of the discussion surrounding communication focused on the proximity of professionals to each other and the benefits of this: 'because this Sure Start centre is so close, I literally just walk across and give it to her'; 'it's easy for me to, kind of just pop in to say "oh, about this child's such and such"'; and 'sometimes . . . you'll see the person and it's kind of like "oh I had this to tell you"'. Such informal relationships support Wenger's argument (1998) that when frequent, informal discussions occur, knowledge is continually being reflected on and shared, which further develops a community of practice. However, some comments highlight that although such informal communication is useful, there was a feeling that such informality was not always reliable: 'it's not always as quick and efficient as it should be'; 'she's constantly being pulled to and fro, for various roles et cetera, so it is, it can be very difficult to get hold of her'; and 'what she really needs is a debriefing session every day about the children because there are so many issues'. This highlights that although the informal style of communication between the professionals is convenient and supports daily practice, this can be problematic in terms of access and accountability. This is to say that when two communities of practice merge together, a more formal communication system is required as the informal practices within one community of practice may be quite distinct from another. As a result, there is a tension between the systems when they come together. In order to overcome this, one interviewee suggested a more formal debriefing session for the professionals involved 'every day'. This would deal with the issue raised regarding access to communication; however; it is problematic as the accountability of the professionals meeting would be questioned and who is responsible for each element of this.

Another issue that was raised regarding communication between the agencies was language. There was a sense of 'ours' and 'theirs' with regard to the language of a range of agencies such as the school. For example:

> Sure Start Centre Manager: [T]hey have their own languages as well . . . even though, I mean I've never worked so closely with schools before and because we're on a co-located site, I know that's presented challenges, I would never have thought about before and sometimes even though we all speak the same language I didn't know NQTs, I didn't know . . . some things that were being said as very commonplace, your assessments, we had to have them explained to us because we're not teacher trained, but then other things, I can see how our practices particularly our parental involvement has started to rub off with some members of school, some people will now come and say 'will you be able to do that because you're better at that?' or 'will you organise that for the parents?' because you're engaging with them.

This suggests that although the two agencies work together often, they still view themselves as completely separate entities, with their own languages. However,

The changing role of the teacher   121

this also reinforces the 'Object 3' theory in third generation activity theory (Daniels, 2002; Engestrom, 1999, in Leadbetter, 2005). This demonstrates that although there are significant differences in terms of the tools, language and systems each activity system uses, where these systems come together, Object 3 is where development can occur. In this instance, the Sure Start manager states things 'rub off' on each of the activity systems, providing them with a new perspective or way of working. Such collaborative working is evident in the data above with the school asking the Sure Start Centre Manager, 'will you be able to do that because you're better at that?' This signifies that the strengths of each agency are being utilised in order to provide the most effective service.

Communicating different outcomes is also an area of tension between the agencies:

> Teacher: [W]e've also been a little concerned about some of the children who've come straight to Reception: the lack of phonic skills compared to those coming from the school nursery, so I've met with the head of centre, the head of the children's centre and the teachers from the children's centre and erm, we're trying to get staff from the off-site children's centre to come and observe Letters and Sounds because they don't actually do it as formally as we do now but they need to be doing it because [it is] the legal requirement, so it's working that way that, because we know the staff, it's sort of not a threatening type thing, it's working together.

> Teacher: Children who come straight to Reception from the children's centre; they tend to come in at a lower level than those that come from our nursery, but it's a completely different set-up, the care, it's, I would think it's more care at the [Sure Start] children's centre, and it's education in the schools ... the differences are quite noticeable, that the children that are coming in from the children's centre rather than the nursery are at a lower level academically.

This demonstrates that although the agencies are involved in working together and developing their practices together, each of the different agencies has its own agenda and outcome. Clearly here, the teacher's outcomes are academic and children are assessed according to their academic development. However, when she discusses the Sure Start centre, she observes their outcomes to be 'care' focused. This is problematic to activity theory as third generation activity theory depends on the two activity systems having the same outcome. If the systems both have different outcomes, when they work together there will be an issue regarding how the outcome is transformed to incorporate both foci. It is notable that the teacher states that Sure Start 'need to be doing it' and that 'it's a legal requirement', strengthening her argument that her outcomes are the most important. However she does defend her actions, stating that it is 'not a threatening type thing'; however, Sure Start may observe this as a threat to their

122   *Elizabeth Parr*

own outcomes, which they value highly. This is highlighted in the Sure Start manager's response to different working outcomes:

INTERVIEWER: Have you experienced any problems in terms of different working outcomes?

SURE START CENTRE MANAGER: Because the parents are coming in and staying with the children to do our activities we'll get to know the family situation and I think sometimes then when they maybe be questioning a parent for something we will actually know the situation behind it and I think that is quite replicated in other things as well, I know, erm, coming from another background other than schools that sometimes the child is seen in isolation not as part of the family as nature and nurture . . . We don't know what chaotic lifestyles our children, little children, have had before they come to see us, and this is a place of safety, so what you don't want is when they come in feeling judged. But that's because our backgrounds are very different. And equally we still want the same outcomes that the child will achieve higher outcomes, I think when we look at a cold target, really, it's quite difficult, until we all know a little bit more.

The emphasis on 'coming from another background' and 'backgrounds are very different' highlights that the Sure Start manager is aware of the differences between the outcomes valued by the different agencies. It is clear from this that the outcomes for Sure Start are distinctly different from that of the teacher. They are instead focused on 'nature and nurture' and, as fundamental as academic achievement is to the teacher, here she demonstrates that Sure Start's outcomes are as important to her. The emotive use of the words 'cold target' highlights that this is how she may perceive the targets of the school or other agencies and will not compromise the outcomes of Sure Start for those of another agency. From this, although the Sure Start centre is working and communicating effectively with a range of other agencies, different perspectives on appropriate outcomes can be sought, and both the school and Sure Start centre ultimately are accountable to their own outcomes and assessment frameworks.

Conclusion

The results highlight the complexity of multi-agency working within Sure Start and the challenging dilemmas faced by professionals within Sure Start. This research aimed to consider how Sure Start coordinates its practice with other agencies to benefit families. I used a case study to research one Sure Start centre, its practices and its impact on a family. Through this, I investigated the relationships, language and systems operating within the Sure Start centre. The study has found that professionals from the Sure Start centre as well as the school build relationships with a range of agencies and work with these to challenge and develop their practices. This is significant as it illuminates existing theories regarding multi-agency working and learning within them.

The changing role of the teacher 123

This research underlines the challenges of multi-agency working and the complex nature of crossing a range of agency boundaries. For multi-agency work to continue developing, knowledge of other agencies requires constant updating and transformation. To achieve this successfully, further research into joint training and development across agencies may be a starting point. Atkinson et al. (2002; 2005) suggest the role of a 'hybrid' professional who has the knowledge, experience, language and structures of a range of other agencies. This notion of a 'hybrid professional' is not a new one as teachers have long been expected to not only assume the role of a teacher but also work with a range of agencies, provide social support and actively engage with the local community, all outside of the classroom and beyond the limited description as a teacher. Such an amalgam of roles and responsibilities indicate that teachers might be viewed as 'hybrid professionals'. However, this can lead to conflict within educational professionals' identity – as what they desire to do as teachers and what they are expected to do within the wider role of the multi-agency work may not align (Beijaard, Meijer and Verloop, 2004). The challenge for teachers, therefore, is how they navigate their way through the multi-agency landscape while constantly negotiating and renegotiating their role and identity as dependent on the agency, family and context in which they are working.

References

Anning, A. (2005). Investigating the impact of working in multi-agency service delivery settings in the UK on Early Years practitioners' beliefs and practices. *Journal of Early Childhood Research*, 3(1), 19–50.

Atkinson, M., Doherty, P. and Kinder, K. (2005). Multi-agency working; models, challenges and key factors for success. *Journal of Early Childhood Research*, 3(1), 7–17.

Atkinson, M., Wilkin, A., Stott, A., Doherty, P. and Kinder, K. (2002). *Multi-Agency Working: A Detailed Study*. Berkshire: National Foundation for Educational Research.

Bagley, C. and Ackerley, C. (2006). 'I am much more than just a mum'. Social capital, empowerment and Sure Start. *Journal of Education Policy*, 21(6), 717–734.

Belsky, J., Melhuish, E., Barnes, J., Leyland, A., Romaniuk, H. and the National Evaluation of Sure Start Research Team (2006). Effects of Sure Start local programmes on children and families: early findings from a quasi-experimental, cross-sectional study. *British Medical Journal*, dol:10.1136/bmj.38853.451748.2F

Beijaard, D., Meijar, P. and Verloop, N. (2004). Reconsidering research on teachers' professional identity. *Teacher and Teacher Education*, 20(1), 107–112.

Bloxham, S. (1996). A case study of inter-agency collaboration in the education and promotion of young people's sexual health. *Health Education Journal*, 55(4), 389–403.

Daniels, H. (2002). *Vygotsky and Pedagogy*. London: Routledge.

Denzin, N. and Lincon, Y. (eds) (2005). *The Sage Handbook of Qualitative Research*. Third Edition. London: Sage.

DfE (2013). *Working Together to Safeguard Children: A Guide to Inter-Agency Working to Safeguard and Promote the Welfare of Children*. London: Crown.

124 *Elizabeth Parr*

DfES (2003). *Every Child Matters.* Norwich: The Stationery Office.

Eisenstadt, N. (2002). Sure Start: key principles and method. Editorial. *Child: Care, Health and Development,* 28(1), 3–4.

Engestrom, Y. (1987). *Learning by Expanding: An Activity-theoretical Approach to Developmental Research.* Helsinki: Orienta-Konsultit.

Engestrom, Y. (1999). Activity theory and individual and social transformation. In Y. Engestrom, R. Miettinen and R.-L. Punamäki (eds), *Perspectives on Activity Theory.* Cambridge, UK: Cambridge University Press.

Engestrom, Y. (2001). Expansive learning at work: toward an activity theoretical reconceptualization. *Journal of Education and Work,* 14(1), 133–156.

Garces, E., Thomas, D. and Currie, J. (2000). Longer term effects of Head Start. *The Journal of Human Resources,* 35(4), 755–774.

Glass, N. (1999). Sure Start: the development of an early intervention programme for young children in the United Kingdom. *Children and Society,* 13, 257–264.

Hallett, C. and Stevenson, O. (1980). *Child Abuse: Aspects of Interprofessional Cooperation.* London: George Allen and Unwin.

Hannon, P. and Fox, L. (2005). Why we should learn from Sure Start. In: J. Weingberger, C. Pickstone, and P. Hannon (eds), *Learning from Sure Start: Working with Young Children and Their Families,* pp.3–12. Berkshire: Open University Press.

Hatcher, R. and Leblond, D. (2001). Education action zones and zones d'education prioritaires. In: S. Riddell and L. Tett (eds), *Education, Social Justice and Inter-agency Working: Joined up or Fractured Policy?* pp.29–57. London: Routledge.

Leadbetter, J. (2005). Activity theory as a conceptual framework and analytical tool within the practice of educational psychology. *Education and Child Psychology,* 22(1), 18–28.

Lloyd, G., Stead, J. and Kendrick, A. (2001). *'Hanging on in There': A Study of Inter-agency Work to Prevent School Exclusion in Three Local Authorities.* London: National Children's Bureau.

Machell, J. (1999). *The Lost Boys or the Great Unwashed? Collaborative Strategies to Address Disaffection.* Paper presented at the BERA Annual Conference, 2–5 September, University of Sussex at Brighton.

Melhuish, E., Belsky, J. and Leyland, A. (2008). *The Impact of Sure Start Local Programmes on Three Year Olds and Their Families.* Nottingham: DfES.

Milbourne, L., Macrae, S. and Maguire, M. (2003). Collaborative solutions or new policy problems: exploring multi-agency partnerships in education and health work. *Journal of Education Policy,* 18(1), 19–35.

Ofsted (2015). *Integrated Inspections: Consultation Outcomes, Learning from Pilot Inspections and Next Steps.* London: Crown.

Payne, J. (1998). The attractions of joined up thinking. *Adults Learning,* 10(4), 12–14.

Raffo, C., Dyson, A., Gunter, H., Hall, D., Jones, L. and Kalambouka, A. (2007). *Education and Poverty: A Critical Review of Theory, Policy and Practice.* York: Joseph Rowntree Foundation.

Robinson, M., Anning, A. and Frost, N. (2005). 'When is a teacher not a teacher?': knowledge creation and the professional identity of teachers within multi-agency teams. *Studies in Continuing Education,* 27(2), 175–191.

Rutter, M. (2006). Is Sure Start an effective prevention intervention? *Child and Adolescent Mental Health,* 11(3), 135–141.

The changing role of the teacher 125

Schneider, J., Ramsey, A. and Lowerson, A. (2006). Sure Start graduates: predictors of attainment on starting school. *Child: Care, Health and Development*, 32(4), 431–440.

Soan, S. (2006). Multi-agency working: Are the needs of children and young people with social, emotional and behavioural needs being served within a multi-agency framework? *Support for Learning*, 21(4), 210–215.

Sylva, K., Melhuish, E., Sammons, P., Siraj-Blatchford, I., Taggart, B. and Elliot, K. (2003). *The Effective Provision of the Pre-School Education (EPPE). Project: Findings From the Pre-School Period*. Nottingham: DfES.

Tuomi-Grohn, T. and Engestrom, Y. (2003). *Between School and Work: New Perspectives on Transfer and Boundary Crossing*. Oxford: Elsevier Science.

Wenger, E. (1998). *Communities of Practice: Learning, Meaning and Identity*. New York: Cambridge University Press.

10 Partnership and teacher formation for global social justice

Philip M. Bamber and Andrea Bullivant

Introduction

> We are addressing not just the future of humanity in an abstract sense, but the future of our families and our friends. No generation has faced a challenge with the complexity, scale, and urgency of the one that we face.
>
> (Brown 2011, p.xi)

> In an increasingly interconnected and interdependent world, there is a need for transformative pedagogy that enables learners to resolve persistent challenges related to sustainable development and peace that concern all humanity. These include conflict, poverty, climate change, energy security, unequal population distribution, and all forms of inequality and injustice which highlight the need for cooperation and collaboration among countries which goes beyond their land, air, and water boundaries.
>
> (UNESCO, 2014a, p.11)

What is the role of teacher education in responding to the challenges of our time, illustrated by the reflections above? One option is to dismiss the narrative of global crises as alarmist or irrelevant. Those who take this short-term view invoke pressures to increase standards of numeracy and literacy, an already over-crowded curriculum and accountability measures to justify their position. This approach not only fails to provide a solution to the challenges we face but is arguably a fundamental part of the problem. Indeed, 'without significant precautions, education can equip people merely to be more effective vandals of the earth' (Orr, 2004, p.5). Instead, we suggest teacher education must play a pivotal role in alerting 'society to possible changes that lie ahead and to prepare teachers and young people to face those changes with as much confidence as possible' (Hicks, 2010, p.1).

This chapter will demonstrate how exposure to issues of social injustice in a global context, such as child poverty, climate change, Fairtrade and the plight of refugees, alongside a period of community engagement, can impact upon who the future educator is as a person. The findings of a multi-agency research project and case studies, selected to highlight the diversity of community engagement experiences that can lead to these outcomes, will be drawn upon to illustrate the ongoing impact of such intervention upon the professional identity of future educators. It will be argued that a genuine worldwide horizon must be grounded in a concern for the local as much as the global and does not demand international experience. This chapter highlights the importance of collaboration and partnership in achieving these aims whilst reiterating the need to focus upon individual change: the importance of who the educator is becoming as a person, including their values, attitudes and associated dispositions.

Global education for global social justice

Global education is practised and theorised under multiple guises, including Education for Sustainable Development (ESD), Education for Global Citizenship (EGC), Global Learning (GL), Development Education and Peace Education. This activity, when guided by a social justice orientation, puts the inequities of our times under scrutiny and challenges us to be hope-full that a better world is possible. For example, the UK-based non-government organisation Think Global seeks to promote education for a just and sustainable world. It defines Global Learning (GL) as:

education that puts learning in a global context, fostering

- critical and creative thinking;
- self-awareness and open-mindedness towards difference;
- understanding of global issues and power relationships; and
- optimism and action for a better world.

(Think Global, 2015)

Substantial evidence has been collated in the UK to advocate for this form of global education (DEA, 2009). This includes evidence that educators embrace course content that incorporates a global perspective: for instance the vast majority of teachers (94 per cent) agree GL is important and schools should prepare pupils to deal with a fast-changing and globalised world (ibid.). Nevertheless, the same research also found that only 58 per cent of teachers felt that the current school system actually does this. In the same survey, 85 per cent of young, less-established teachers identified 'thinking about the potential contribution of teaching to making the world a better place' as a reason for remaining in teaching. That learning about global issues may be a significant factor in retaining teachers, particularly amongst those recently qualified, provides a compelling incentive to incorporate this perspective, especially when the number of entrants to the profession in the UK is falling and those leaving is at an all-time high (Morrison, 2015).

There is a long history of attempts to include global issues in education in the UK, often initiated and led by non-government organisations. Between 1997 and 2010, legislation and non-statutory recommendations by the Labour government encouraged schools to promote a 'Global Dimension' in education, including through the Sustainable Schools initiative, and placed a duty upon

128   *Philip M. Bamber and Andrea Bullivant*

schools to promote Community Cohesion. Currently, schools are required to promote pupils' spiritual, moral, social and cultural development (SMSC), including development of positive 'attitudes towards different religious, ethnic and socio-economic groups in their local, national and global communities' (OFSTED, 2014, p.35) and at secondary level there remains a statutory requirement to teach citizenship, although this is rarely taught discretely or by experts in this field. The Department for International Development also funds a national Global Learning Programme for schools.

An international survey (Tye, 1999) found that only a small number of teacher education courses in the world promoted global education explicitly. Despite a number of initiatives taking place in the UK since 2000 which sought to 'embed' a global perspective in teacher education (Barr, 2005), the quantity and quality of provision for Education for Sustainable Development (ESD) and Education for Global Citizenship (EGC) in teacher education has been found to be patchy (Hunt at al., 2011). TEESNet, the UK Teacher Education for Equity and Sustainability Network, was established in 2008 to share expertise through supporting a UK-wide community of practice in ESDGC within teacher education and has also found evidence that the quantity and quality of provision for ESDGC in teacher education across the UK remains inconsistent (HEA, 2014). An explicit statutory requirement for inclusion of ESDGC in Wales and Scotland, which demands working in partnership across sectors, has ensured provision is enhanced in these nations. This is demonstrated in the case study following this chapter of 'Working in Partnership for Learning for Sustainability in Scotland'.

Irrespective of these local and regional contexts, international calls for teacher education to promote forms of global education have never been greater. For instance, following the end of the United Nations Decade of ESD in 2014, the UNESCO Roadmap for implementing a Global Action Programme on ESD identifies one of five priority action areas to be 'building capacities of educators and trainers to more effectively deliver ESD' (UNESCO, 2014b, p.15). This includes an expected outcome that ESD becomes integrated into pre-service and in-service teacher education programmes. Recognition of the importance of global education is also evident in that the 2018 Programme for International Student Assessment, run by the Organisation for Economic Co-operation and Development, will include measurement of global competence: assessing 15-year-olds' awareness of the interconnected global world we live and work in and their ability to deal effectively with the resulting demands. Nevertheless, it is not clear how 'global competence' can be meaningfully measured through international testing. There is a danger that such metrics intensify the focus of global education upon short-term observable outcomes rather than longer term changes in behaviour, attitude and practice.

Global education as a process of becoming

The paucity of research and evaluation into the impact of global education has been attributed to the embryonic nature of work in this field (O'Loughlin and

Partnership for global social justice 129

Wegimot, 2008, p.19). Bourn and Hunt (2011, p.7) cite additional factors: its relatively marginal nature in education; short-term funding of projects resulting in a tendency to focus on effectiveness and efficiency rather than impact; and a tendency to pursue practice rather than theory. The latter was also identified by UNESCO in a consultation document exploring Global Citizenship Education as an 'emerging perspective' where 'practice is further ahead than conceptual clarity' (UNESCO, 2014b, p.5).

That researching broader values, beliefs and character associated with global education is only now emerging belies the fact that related curriculum developments over the last half-century, such as the World Studies Project (Richardson, 1976), have been underpinned by 'affective as well as cognitive' dimensions. These pioneering initiatives used active and participatory teaching methods to explore the development of particular values and perspectives towards global issues. Former guidance on integrating a Global Dimension into formal education in the UK (DfES, 2005) built upon these earlier models (Richardson, 1976; Pike and Selby, 1988) with explicit focus on developing skills and attitudes as well as knowledge and understanding (DfES, 2005, p.1). This work is now being consolidated through the work of OXFAM and the Global Learning Programme.

Recent guidance for evaluating global education has subsequently argued that 'changes in knowledge, attitudes and actions are at the heart of GL' (Think Global, 2011, p.12). Moving beyond evaluation of short-term effectiveness, a number of studies have explored the ongoing impact of specific initiatives (Hunt and King, 2015). For example, Lowe (2008) uses audit activities to measure attitudinal change in young people as part of education for global citizenship. As Hunt and King conclude, these studies are limited by a lack of baseline evidence in some cases and reliance on respondents' perceptions to questions, so that analysis for the purpose of identifying impact may 'not capture the nuances of impact across individuals and spaces' (ibid, p.30).

As the 2015 deadline for meeting the Education for All goals approached, UNESCO set out a vision for education for global citizenship that explicated the holistic aspects of this approach. They argued it demands

> a conceptual shift in that it recognizes the relevance of education in understanding and resolving global issues in their social, political, cultural, economic and environmental dimensions. It also acknowledges the role of education in moving beyond the development of knowledge and cognitive skills to build values, soft skills and attitudes among learners that can facilitate international cooperation and promote social transformation.
>
> (UNESCO, 2014b, p.9)

This echoes a framework developed by UNECE (2012) which suggested to successfully implement ESD educators must learn to know (develop understanding), learn to do (develop specific abilities), learn to live together (working together with others) and also learn to be (develop personal attributes). Furthermore, this framework highlights a holistic approach, emphasising the importance of

130 *Philip M. Bamber and Andrea Bullivant*

integrative thinking, inclusivity and dealing with complexities (UNECE, 2012, p.16). Who the teacher is as a person is also a central component of a recent European framework for evaluating education for global citizenship (Fricke and Gathercole, 2015). It details the values (including 'justice, curiosity, diversity, empathy and solidarity') and dispositions (including 'care for and solidarity with people over-coming injustices and inequalities') that must underpin the teaching and learning process. The Wider Perspectives in Education initiative, described in the next section, aims to nurture the becoming of future educators through developing values and dispositions such as these.

Partnership for global social justice in practice: nurturing Wider Perspectives in Education in England

Wider Perspectives in Education (WPE) is a compulsory component of the BA Primary Teaching four year undergraduate degree at Liverpool Hope University. In addition to two extended placements in schools as part of their third year, students complete a community engagement project. The overall aim of WPE is to provide students with a broader experience of education beyond traditional teaching practice, to develop their understanding of and disposition towards GL and promote a sense of themselves as active global citizens. At the same time, WPE supports students as they seek to gain evidence of attaining the professional standards for teaching in England. The course introduces them to global education policy and practice in the UK, and students are encouraged to incorporate related methodologies, such as critical literacy and philosophy for children, within their teaching practice. In doing so, it aims to transform student perspectives on the role of education and their own philosophy of teaching.

Integrating community service with the curriculum, WPE is an illustration of Service-Learning (SL): a pedagogical approach that emphasises learning as opposed to teaching, broadening and deepening the impact of the teacher education course. It draws on theorists that have proposed that we learn through combinations of thought and action, reflection and practice, theory and application (Dewey, Kolb, Schön). Crucially, SL allows students to reflect upon their experiences, knowledge and understanding of community issues within a structured framework of learning. This provides the opportunity for educators to draw on real world contexts and develop analytical and problem-solving skills related to a student's discipline. SL is now gaining recognition as an important pedagogical approach to foster GL in the UK (Peterson and Warwick, 2015).

The community engagement project aims to address an educational issue in a local or international setting. An introductory theoretical component is followed by a project planning phase. At the end of the project, students share their eclectic experiences through presentations at a conference to celebrate their community engagement work. In recognizing and supporting the diversity of learning needs, students are encouraged to organise and lead their project through negotiation with schools and other partners, pursuing issues raised through the course that enables them to address the educational needs of children in the

Partnership for global social justice 131

setting or members of the local community. This enables community engagement to be a critical learning experience as advocated by Rosenberger, who argued students need the opportunity:

- to choose needs or issues in the community that connect to the course content;
- to dialogue with stakeholder in framing and defining the problem and action;
- to engage in problem posing education around the social, political and economic issues that arise in the community experience.

(Rosenberger, 2000, p.40)

Projects in diverse educational settings challenge student assumptions underpinning their own philosophy of education. They also reconsider educational issues beyond the school campus such as child poverty, sustainability, diversity, disability, racism and terrorism. This approach is informed by a belief that participation and self-efficacy play an important role in changing attitudes of teachers towards global issues.

Community engagement such as this affords numerous opportunities for students in teacher education and is more widely practised in the USA. Barr (2005) highlights the power of personal experience to encourage and educate advocates of global education. Engagement with the other arouses curiosity and can stimulate and inspire learning. He suggests that structured opportunities such as international exchanges and linking programmes (Barr 2005, p.12) are particularly successful in changing attitudes amongst teacher educators and their students to global education. The impact of WPE challenges the view that immersion in local settings cannot provoke similar outcomes, as demonstrated by the case study of 'Gemma' below.

In order to better understand this process of teacher formation and evaluate this curriculum innovation, the course team collaborated with a multi-agency group of professionals working in local government, teacher education and non-government organisations that promote global education to develop an inventory to measure attitudes towards GL (Bamber et al., 2013). The process of constructing and reviewing the attitude inventory exemplifies an approach to evaluation that is an 'integrated, ongoing, participatory process of measurement, reflection, adjustment and learning' (Storrs, 2010, p.8) by a committed community of practice. The inventory was used at the beginning, middle and end of the WPE course and completed by a cohort of 154 undergraduate students. The findings show positive changes in attitudes towards GL among females and eradication of the most negative attitudes towards GL during the course of study. Data demonstrates that the community engagement project itself is pivotal in influencing students' positive attitudes towards the course, and global education, more broadly.

The development of a teaching philosophy statement alongside a community engagement project followed by a period of teaching practice, as exemplified in

132 *Philip M. Bamber and Andrea Bullivant*

WPE, provokes deep learning but as a pedagogical approach is not unproblematic. For instance, students do not always make links between their community engagement and their emergent professional identity. As the case study of 'Hannah' indicates, this is a complex process that takes place over a longer period of time. Students need ongoing support to incorporate their learning within their subsequent teaching practice. Teacher educators should also be cognisant that this approach may reinforce rather than overturn incomplete worldviews and existing stereotypes, for example as regards poverty and diversity.

Case study of teacher formation 1: community engagement through church international evenings

Gemma describes below her community engagement experience supporting international evenings at her local church.

> The organiser of the international evenings had previously taught English at the church and has mainly taught wives of men who have brought their family over for a job or have sought asylum in the UK. She now has a network of women and lets them know when the monthly events are on; she also visits the families, and I go along with her sometimes. The attendees' nationalities range from countries in Africa to the Middle East and China. Most of the attendees of the international evenings are women aged 20–40 with their children, with numbers ranging from 40–70 in the church hall.
>
> For the dinners, often women from a certain country will come early and cook their own food (recently all of the women from Yemen cooked food in their local style) then it is served to everyone else who attends, and we provide games and activities for their children. The women mostly chat to each other through the evening though a few church members come also to get to know the women.
>
> The local context is that the women who attend usually struggle to get to know anyone in their community besides people from their own culture who speak their native tongue. Most of the women wear hijabs or burkhas and feel isolated from the Western culture they live in and also often don't wish to integrate through a perceived clash of values. There are few opportunities to meet local people and barriers of language/confidence often prevent this. A lack of understanding of cultures (from both sides, from the local population and also from the families who have emigrated/claimed asylum) leads to more fear or isolation.
>
> I have been informed about how difficult it is to become part of a local community when being from a different culture. I have been able to see living in Liverpool from a completely different perspective, one that I could possibly never experience or know myself but am now

able to understand a bit more. I have fewer prejudices or uninformed judgements regarding people immigrating to the UK with little knowledge of my culture or willingness to adapt to my culture which can be threatening or upsetting to me. I have been able to find a commonality and a way to relate through food, socialising and sharing in community. I now have access to women who, on the surface, seem very different to me. I had found this frustrating in the past because I enjoy learning about other cultures and I dislike seeing people who are isolated or rejected from society. This has given me an opportunity to relate to and spend time with women like this and I have seen a side of the global issue of fundamentalist Islam and the isolation and clash of values which often fuel the issues. I believe that this lack of community integration is one of the factors contributing to the issues seen in the London train and bus bombing and I have been able to see one of the small steps to finding a solution. The experience has helped me to re-evaluate the role that education must play in responding to our diverse and complex world.

Case study of teacher formation 2: the ongoing impact of community engagement

Hannah completed the Wider Perspectives course in 2009–2010. Since qualifying as a teacher in 2011, she has worked as a classroom teacher in a local primary school.

My decision to embark on teacher training was influenced to some extent by my father, who was also a teacher. However, gaining some volunteer experience in a school was also influential. I was bowled over by one teacher, in particular the way she embraced wider initiatives in school. However, I was not aware of concepts such as GL and GCE before starting my undergraduate teacher training. I had a narrower view of education then – in my head teaching was still all about the classroom.

On the WPE course, I enjoyed exploring different perspectives on education, and the course encouraged me to think about the use of discussion in the classroom and the importance of encouraging different viewpoints. I worked as part of a group to deliver activities on Fair Trade in a local partner school. This was a very different experience to my other teaching placements. It allowed me to focus on one specific idea, attempt something 'bigger' and increased my confidence to organise similar projects in future: for example, to use activities such as a bake sale to engage parents – something I now feel more confident to do.

134 *Philip M. Bamber and Andrea Bullivant*

> I came to appreciate the impact of the course even more as time went on. Looking back now, it is something I have used more than I realised. The Wider Perspectives experience helped me in job interviews and it has given me the confidence to take on wider roles in school. For example, in my new school I have already become the lead teacher for enrichment, creativity and outdoor learning. Within the last year, I have also supported a Wider Perspectives project to take place in my school. I worked with a group of ten student teachers to lead a project on creating activities and memorabilia to celebrate a move to a new school building. The students struggled initially to understand the purpose of the project in relation to their course, but through our discussions they began to make connections between commemorating the school's history through a period of transition and wider themes relevant to the school in its community. They subsequently worked with the children to explore what it means to be a global citizen and thought about creative ways to produce things sustainably.

Conclusion

This chapter provides a response to concerns that research and practice in teacher education tend to focus upon short-term observable outcomes rather than longer term changes in behaviour, attitude and practice. The case study of Hannah demonstrates how WPE enhanced her appreciation of the broader purposes of education and the value of partnership, as she became the 'more skilled partner' (Rogoff et al., 1996, p.388) in teacher education responsible for the formation of student teachers. This illustrates the important role of mentoring in developing the moral agency of teachers (Arthur et al., 2015). Her case study also suggests professional resilience is developed and sustained through nurturing a sense of vocation and challenging future teachers to consider the broader purposes of education: an area requiring further research.

The WPE course and the two student case studies illustrate how a process of collaboration between a small group of committed university tutors, students, a local Development Education Centre, schools and community engagement project providers enabled the aim of transforming student perspectives on the role of education to be realised. The complementary expertise of the various partners involved in this work nurtured a shared vision that connected theory and practice and promoted a 'community of learners' where students are 'active learners' encouraged to lead projects and negotiate with teachers and others to contemplate possibilities for action for change. The importance of partnership and collaboration to this work is exemplified on a broader scale in the following case study from Scotland, where Learning for Sustainability is being embedded at different levels of the education system.

References

Arthur, J., Kristjansson, K., Cooke, S., Brown, E. and Carr, D. (2015). *The Good Teacher: Understanding Virtues in Practice Research Report*. Birmingham: The Jubilee Centre for Character & Virtues, University of Birmingham.

Bamber, P., Bullivant, A. and Stead, D (2013). Measuring attitudes towards global learning among future educators in England. *International Journal of Development Education and Global Learning*, 5(3), 5–27.

Barr, I. (2005). *In the Situation of Others. The Final Evaluation Report on the Department for International Development's Initiative on Embedding the Global Dimension in Initial Teacher Education in the UK 2001–2005*. Unpublished report.

Bourn, D. and Hunt, F. (2011). *Global Dimension in Secondary Schools*. DERC Research Paper No. 1. London: IOE.

Brown, L. (2011). *World on the Edge – How to Prevent Environmental and Economic Collapse*. London: Earthscan. Available from: www.earth-policy.org/images/uploads/book_files/wotebook.pdf (accessed 20 October 2015).

Department for Education and Skills (DfES) (2005). *Developing a Global Dimension in the School Curriculum*. London: DfES.

DEA (2009). *Teachers' Attitudes to Global Learning*. London: DEA/Ipsos MORI.

Fricke, H.J. and Gathercole, C. (2015). *Monitoring Education for Global Citizenship*. Brussels: DEEEP.

Higher Education Academy (2014). *Education for Sustainable Development and Global Citizenship: Good Practice Case Studies in Teacher Education*. Available from: www.heacademy.ac.uk/resource/education-sustainable-development-and-global-citizenship-esdgc-good-practice-case-studies (accessed 15 October 2015).

Hicks, D. (2010). *The Long Transition: Educating for Optimism and Hope in Troubled Times*. Third Annual Conference of the UK Teacher Education Network for Education for Sustainable Development and Global Citizenship, London South Bank University, July 2010.

Hunt, F., Chung, L.T., Rogers, M. with Inman, S. (2011). *Taking Stock: A Report from the UK Teacher Education Network for Sustainable Development (ESD)/Global Citizenship (GC) – Survey on Provision for ESD/GC in Initial Teacher Education in the UK*. London: CCCI/LSBU.

Hunt, F. and King, R. (2015). *Supporting Whole School Approaches to Global Learning: Focusing Learning and Mapping Impact*. Research Paper No 13 for the Global Learning Programme. London: DERC/UCL IOE.

Lowe, B. (2008). Embedding global citizenship in primary and secondary schools: developing a methodology for measuring attitudinal change. *International Journal of Development Education and Global Learning*, 1(1), 59–64.

Morrison, N. (2015). Number of teachers quitting the classroom reaches 10 year high. *TES*. Available from: https://news.tes.co.uk/b/news/2015/01/29/number-of-teachers-quitting-the-classroom-reaches-10-year-high.aspx (accessed 15 October 2015).

OFSTED (2014). *School Inspection Handbook. Handbook for Inspecting Schools in England Under Section 5 of the Education Act 2005 (as amended by the Education Act 2011)*. Manchester: OFSTED.

O'Loughlin, E. and Wegimot, L. (eds) (2008). *Quality in Global Education: An Overview of Evaluation of Policy and Practice*. Amsterdam: Global Education Network Europe.

136 *Philip M. Bamber and Andrea Bullivant*

Orr, D. (2004). *Earth in Mind: On Education, Environment, and the Human Prospect.* Tenth anniversary edition. Washington, DC: Island Press.

Peterson, A. and Warwick, P. (2015). *Global Learning and Education: Key Concepts and Effective Practice.* Oxon: Routledge.

Pike, G. and Selby, D. (1988). *Global Teacher, Global Learner.* London: Hodder and Stoughton.

Richardson, R. (1976). *Learning for Change in World Society.* London: World Studies Project.

Rogoff, B., Matusov, E. and White, C. (1996). *Models of Teaching and Learning: Participation in a Community of Learners.* In: D. Olsen and R. Torrance (eds), *The Handbook of Education and Human Development*, pp.388–414. Oxford, UK: Blackwell.

Rosenberger, C. (2000). Beyond empathy: developing critical consciousness through service-learning. In: C. O'Grady, *Integrating Service-Learning and Multicultural Education in Colleges and Universities*, pp.23–44. New Jersey: Lawrence Erlbaum.

Storrs, G. (2010). Evaluation in development education: crossing borders. *Policy & Practice: A Development Education Review*, 11(Autumn), 7–21.

Think Global (2011). *Evaluating Global Learning Outcomes: A Guide to Assessing Progress in Intercultural, Environmental and Development Education Projects.* London: Think Global.

Think Global (2015). *About Global Learning.* Available from: http://think-global.org.uk/global-learning/theory-of-change/ (accessed 15 October 2015).Tye, K. (1999). *Global Education: A Worldwide Movement.* Orange, CA: Independence Press.

UNECE (2012). *Learning for the Future – Competencies in Education for Sustainable Development.* Geneva: UNECE.

UNESCO (2014a). *UNESCO Roadmap for Implementing the Global Action Programme on Education for Sustainable Development.* Paris: UNESCO.

UNESCO (2014b). *Global Citizenship Education: Preparing Learners for the Challenges of the 21st Century.* Paris: UNESCO.

International vignette 2
Working in partnership for Learning for Sustainability in Scotland

Betsy King and Gary Johnstone

At the close of the UN Decade of Education for Sustainable Development (ESD), it is clear Scotland's formal education response has been strengthened by the culture of collaboration between government (including Members of the Scottish Parliament, civil servants and government agencies), academia and civil society. This has been an evolution, not a revolution. It certainly hasn't happened overnight.

Critically, there is a strong cross-party political will to support Learning for Sustainability (LfS) in Scotland. Scotland has a distinguished history of individuals who have recognised the importance of learning for sustainability, from John Muir to Patrick Geddes onwards. Notable among these was Professor John Smyth, who co-wrote Chapter 36 of Agenda 21 in 1992, the non-binding UN action plan regarding sustainable development. However, networks are even more powerful, and this was recognised by Professor Smyth, who through collaboration and partnership inspired a process of engagement in all sectors which culminated in the important publication *Learning for Life* in 1993. The Scottish Environmental Education Council was succeeded by Education 21. The Sustainable Development Education Network joined with other networks such as IDEAS, the International Development Education Association of Scotland, to influence policy and inspire practice towards Learning for Sustainability.

In 2005, following joint working with the third sector, Scotland's Sustainable Development Strategy (Scottish Executive, 2005), set out three key outcomes for education: 'Learning for Sustainable Development is a core function of the formal education system; there are lifelong opportunities to learn; and the Sustainable Development message is clear and easily understood' (p.66). This resulted in two Action Plans for the Decade co-ordinated by government (Scottish Government, 2010), developed collaboratively and setting out ambitions and actions for schools, universities and colleges, and lifelong learning. A Curriculum for Excellence was also introduced that embraces active, relevant learning and aims to foster broad capacities in young people such that they can become successful learners, confident individuals, responsible citizens and effective contributors. The Scottish view is that if LfS is to flourish, and if learners are to receive their entitlement, then LfS needs to be embedded within the curriculum and feature in the day-to-day experience of learners. It is too important to be delivered solely

138   *Betsy King and Gary Johnstone*

through a lunchtime club for a few fortunate learners or in an isolated off-timetable experience. The Experiences and Outcomes within Curriculum for Excellence provide an important and flexible framework to allow schools to embed LfS. Global citizenship and sustainability are important themes across learning, and outdoor learning is seen as a key approach to learning.

The Learning for Sustainability Report (One Planet Schools Group, 2012) advocated that LfS must be an entitlement for all learners. It contained 31 recommendations that were all agreed by the Scottish Government and are now being taken forward by a high-level LfS Implementation Group and associated Working Group. It is recognised that partnerships between teachers, schools and their wider community as well as with the wide range of third sector organisations with expertise and opportunities to offer schools are key.

Critically, in terms of teacher education, LfS is also now an integral part of the General Teaching Council for Scotland's professional standards for registration of teachers, for career-long professional learning and for school leadership and management. The standards are underpinned by three themes: values, sustainability and leadership:

> 'Learning for Sustainability' is a whole-school commitment that helps the school and its wider community develop the knowledge, skills, attitudes, values and practices needed to take decisions which are compatible with a sustainable future in a just and equitable world. Learning for sustainability has been embedded within the Standards for Registration to support teachers in actively embracing and promoting principles and practices of sustainability in all aspects of their work.
>
> (General Teaching Council for Scotland, 2012, p.2)

It is explicitly stated within the professional standards that all teachers include LfS in their practice. It provides an expectation that practitioners model the values, attributes and capabilities we hope to nurture in learners. For example, student teachers are expected to:

- have knowledge of current educational priorities such as learning for sustainability;
- stimulate learner participation in debate and decision-making about issues which are open-ended, complex, controversial or emotional;
- use outdoor learning opportunities, including direct experiences of nature and other learning, within and beyond the school boundary.

Registered teachers must:

- connect learners to their dependence on the natural world and develop their sense of belonging to both the local and global community;
- develop the knowledge, skills and practices needed to take decisions which are compatible with a sustainable future in a just and equitable world.

Middle leaders are expected to:

- draw upon knowledge and expertise from other professional partners to enhance programmes for learners.

Headteachers are expected to:

- set clear standards in relation to enacting the principles of inclusion, sustainability, equality and social justice in the teaching and learning processes.

Education Scotland, the executive agency for improving education in Scotland, is heavily involved in both shaping and supporting the development of LfS. It features strongly in its Corporate Plan and links closely to its mission statement and strategic objectives. A team of Development Officers led by Senior Education Officers regularly update and develop advice and resources to support LfS. During school inspection activity, HM Inspectors record evidence of how LfS is helping to support the achievement of children and young people and also how learners' experiences are enriched through appropriate activities. Moreover, through opportunities in the inspection model to engage in professional dialogue with teachers, HMI are able to identify interesting practice, to share that practice across the system and to build capacity. Education Scotland's suite of 3–18 curriculum impact reports also outline how sustainability is being taken forward by practitioners across different curricular areas. *Conversations about Learning for Sustainability* (Education Scotland, 2014), a report compiled for the end of the UN Decade of ESD, reflects on how the reorientation of education towards sustainable development has made a difference at classroom level and how it has improved outcomes for learners, their families and school communities.

In contrast to England, universities remain the only route to qualification as a teacher in Scotland. *Teaching Scotland's Future*, a recent Scottish Government-commissioned review of teacher education, professional development and school leadership, reinforced a commitment to university-based ITE, noting that:

> The most successful education systems do more than seek to attain particular standards of competence and to achieve change through prescription. They invest in developing their teachers as reflective, accomplished and enquiring professionals who have the capacity to engage fully with the complexities of education and to be key actors in shaping and leading educational change.
>
> (Donaldson 2010, p.4)

A key aspect of the Report's 50 recommendations was the recognition that teacher education is a continuum, including selection, initial and early career education, continuing professional development and leadership. Formal partnerships between local authorities and teacher education institutions have been put in place and there is potential to bring other organisations into these partnerships to fully support learning for sustainability.

140 *Betsy King and Gary Johnstone*

In the spirit of collaboration, Learning for Sustainability Scotland, Scotland's UN-recognised Regional Centre of Expertise (RCE) in ESD, was launched in November 2013 as an open network bringing together academia, government and civil society to advance learning for sustainability practice and policy in Scotland. Now with more than 350 members, and part of the growing global network of RCEs, Learning for Sustainability Scotland is well placed to continue and build on the spirit of collaboration developed during the UN Decade in Scotland.

References

Donaldson, G. (2010). *Teaching Scotland's Future: Report of a Review of Teacher Education in Scotland.* Edinburgh: Scottish Government. Available from: www.gov.scot/resource/doc/337626/0110852.pdf (accessed 20 October 2015).

Education Scotland (2014). *Conversations about Learning for Sustainability.* Available from: www.educationscotland.gov.uk/Images/ConversationsaboutLfS__tcm4-844123.pdf (accessed 20 October 2015).

General Teaching Council for Scotland (2012). *Professional Standards for Educators.* Edinburgh: Scottish Government.

One Planet Schools Working Group (2012). *Learning for Sustainability.* Available from: www.scotland.gov.uk/Topics/Education/Schools/curriculum/ACE/OnePlanetSchools/LearningforSustainabilitreport (accessed 20 October 2015).

Scottish Executive (2005). *Choosing our Future, Scotland's Sustainable Development strategy.* Edinburgh: Scottish Government. Available from: www.scotland.gov.uk/Publications/2005/12/1493902/39032 (accessed 20 October 2015).

Scottish Government (2010). *Learning for Change: Scotland's second Action Plan for the UN Decade of Education for Sustainable Development.* Edinburgh: Scottish Government. Available from: www.scotland.gov.uk/Publications/2010/05/2015 2453/0 (accessed 20 October 2015).

Scottish Office (1993) *Learning for Life. A National Strategy for Environmental Education in Scotland.* Edinburgh: HMSO.

Part III

Practice

11 Subject knowledge enhancement courses a decade on

Redefining professional knowledge in mathematics teacher education

Mary Stevenson

Introduction

> The UK is falling behind global rivals in international tests taken by 15-year-olds, failing to make the top 20 in maths, reading and science.
>
> (BBC, 2013)

There is a sensationalist and potentially dangerous narrative in current British government and media concerning perceived pupil underperformance in mathematics in British schools compared to other countries, as demonstrated by PISA tests (Programme of International Student Assessment). It is apparent that the perceived importance of the PISA testing system is starting to outweigh its validity, meaning and capacity to improve education (*The Guardian*, 2014); however, discussion of the merits and problems inherent in PISA is not the purpose of this chapter. Whether or not British children are actually underachieving is a complex question and open to discussion, but there is evidence to suggest that dissatisfaction with current levels of education, especially in the high-stakes core subjects of mathematics and English, has been a recurrent theme in British government and media (Ernest, 2007; Bell, Costello and Kuchemann, 1983) since Victorian times. If governments view the mathematics curriculum from a technological pragmatist viewpoint (Ernest, 1991) that prioritises servicing business, employment and utilitarian societal needs, then the mathematics curriculum, and indeed the school curriculum in general, is destined to always be one step behind, since it can respond to rapid advances in technologies and the needs of industry but cannot anticipate them.

Perceived underperformance in mathematics in Britain is seen to be linked to a shortage in the supply of appropriately trained mathematics teachers. In the last decade there have been various initiatives in the UK to tackle the shortage of mathematics teachers, including: financial incentives for mathematics trainees linked to their degree classification (Warburton, 2014); government-funded opportunities for students to follow a subject knowledge enhancement course (SKE) prior to embarking on initial teacher education programmes (pre-ITT SKE); funded inservice training programmes aimed at non-specialist teachers of mathematics (post-ITT SKE). In this chapter I examine the impact and legacy of the pre-ITT SKE.

144   *Mary Stevenson*

SKE background and context

The pre-ITT SKE is aimed at graduates who wish to train as secondary mathematics teachers, whose mathematics background is insufficient for direct entry to PGCE or other routes to Qualified Teacher Status, but who otherwise are suitable candidates for ITE programmes. The SKE is primarily focused upon the development of subject knowledge. Providers can offer an ITE place to an applicant which is conditional on him/her completing a SKE. The SKE is fully funded by government, and additionally most participants are eligible for a bursary. Since its inception in 2004, it has grown to become an accepted alternative to a degree (or part of a degree) in mathematics as a route into secondary mathematics ITE. SKE courses are also available for other shortage subjects.

The SKE began life as the Mathematics Enhancement Course (MEC). A detailed specification was developed by academic mathematicians together with mathematics education experts. The first pilots took place in two universities (Chichester and Liverpool Hope) in 2004. The course was then expanded nationally in England to twelve institutions in 2006. The main precursor to the SKE had been the two-year PGCE (offered by only a few universities and not subject to government funding), in which the first year was mainly subject knowledge based, and the second was the professional training year. The SKE, therefore, presented an opportunity to broaden and improve the knowledge base of graduate students as beginning teachers and was doing something which had not been done in this way before. In line with the idea of developing 'profound understanding of fundamental mathematics' (Ma, 1999, cited in Teacher Training Agency, 2003), curricula for the SKE were developed in which various strands were interwoven and which included rigorous undergraduate level mathematics topics as well as an in-depth approach to school curriculum topics. An ethos of questioning, understanding why as well as how – in short an emphasis on deep as opposed to surface learning – was encouraged throughout, consistent with a constructivist philosophy of learning mathematics.

The original specification was for an intensive taught course (550 hours over six months). Over time, this was relaxed, and the format of the SKE became more varied, including short and longer courses, and more institutions were allowed to offer them. Some courses even became largely distance learning delivery. Today, it is possible that almost half of mathematics PGCE and School Direct students enter their ITE programme from a SKE. Therefore, a decade on from its inception – a decade which has seen a worldwide recession, policies of austerity and at national level a major shift in government policy towards school-led ITE – it is timely to examine the impact and position of the SKE.

Discussion of literature and relationship to practice

There is a wide literature interrogating the nature of subject knowledge in and for mathematics teaching. Here I discuss selected contributions particularly relevant to the SKE and its position within the teacher education landscape.

Much research in the field has developed from the work of Shulman (1986) and his conception of three key aspects of knowledge: subject matter knowledge (SMK), pedagogical knowledge (PCK) and curricular knowledge. The existence of PCK implies that there is knowledge that teachers need to have, and ways in which they need to hold that knowledge, which are specific to the requirements of teaching the subject and which other mathematicians do not necessarily have. Ball et al. (2008) refine Shulman's model specifically in the context of knowledge for mathematics teaching, retaining Shulman's distinction between SMK and PCK, and further subdividing these categories. Baumert et al. (2010) have produced studies showing that the elements of SMK and PCK can be distinguished. They argue the vital role of PCK in activating SMK and that SMK 'remains inert in the classroom unless accompanied by a rich repertoire of mathematical knowledge and skill relating directly to the curriculum, instruction and student learning' (p.139). The interrelationship between SMK and PCK highlighted by these studies has clear implications for curriculum design and style of delivery of the SKE course. SMK and PCK growth are intertwined, and SKE courses should provide opportunities for students to develop both at the same time.

Ball et al. (2008) suggest that teachers have to be able to unpack mathematics in order to make it accessible to students. This is in contrast to the conventions of the academic discipline of mathematics, in which compact and 'elegant' solutions are valued highly. Indeed, Hodgen (2011) notes that some aspects of mathematics knowledge for teaching 'run counter to the habits and norms of mathematics as a discipline' (p.35). This has important implications for the design of the SKE. SKE students are all preparing to be teachers. Therefore, SKE teaching should model good practice in decompressing mathematical concepts and also provide opportunities for students to unpack mathematics for themselves. This is in contrast to the formal and didactic style of teaching more commonly seen in traditional mathematics degree programmes.

Mathematics knowledge as an active process

Watson and Barton (2011) assert that models of acquisition of types or categories of content knowledge overlook an important aspect – that 'teachers enact mathematics' (p.67). In other words, it is the process of doing mathematics, using it and exemplifying it that is at the heart of teaching and learning mathematics, and a teacher's knowledge is manifest through engagement in these processes. Watson and Barton refer to the teacher's capacity for 'knowing-to' act in the moment (Mason and Johnston-Wilder, 2004, p.289). Referring to Watson and Barton's work, Ruthven (2011) suggests that their conception is one of 'subject knowledge mathematised' (p.90), wherein a teacher's ongoing personal involvement and experience with mathematics is critical to the teaching and learning process. Citing Bromme (1994), he further suggests that, for experienced teachers, an explicit mathematical narrative provides the blueprint for a tacit pedagogical one. This can be seen, for example, in a teacher's selection and sequencing of mathematical tasks or problems to be considered. Thus, the

146 *Mary Stevenson*

mathematics processes lead the pedagogical processes, and the demands of the mathematics provide the context for the pedagogical approaches taken.

Discussing teacher knowledge from a perspective of complexity science, Davis and Simmt (2006) consider mathematics as a learning system that grows within the individual mind, the collective consciousness (classroom) and wider society. They argue that it is important to consider both teachers' knowledge of mathematics (Ball's SMK) and their knowledge of how that mathematics is established (PCK) as 'inextricably intertwined' (p.300). Davis (2011) suggests that teachers' mathematics could be seen as 'a learnable disposition rather than an explicit body of knowledge' (p1507) to enable them to handle the demands of the curriculum and to embrace change. This emphasis upon developing a positive disposition to learn and use mathematics is critical in teacher education for both secondary and primary teachers.

Understanding mathematics in depth

In her seminal (1999) work, Ma suggests that a 'profound understanding of fundamental mathematics' (PUFM) is essential for effective mathematics teachers. Ma contends that a teacher develops PUFM over time and through the practice of teaching, with regular opportunities for professional discussion and sharing of ideas with colleagues. Profound understanding of fundamental mathematics as expounded by Ma primarily concerns SMK (subject matter knowledge) but is situated in and developed through the practice of teaching and so also spans PCK (pedagogical content knowledge) and Ball's SCK (specialist content knowledge). Ma develops some key theory and offers recommendations for practice. Two important recommendations are:

> Address teacher knowledge and student learning at the same time.
>
> (p.146)

> Enhance the interaction between teachers' study of school mathematics and how to teach it.
>
> (p.147)

These suggestions are based upon a belief that teacher knowledge and student learning are inextricably linked.

Within the specification for SKEs, there was an emphasis on the nature of subject knowledge that should be developed by the courses, and this drew explicitly on the work of Ma (1999), in particular the idea of 'profound understanding of fundamental mathematics, emphasising deep and broad understanding of concepts, as against surface procedural knowledge' (Teacher Training Agency, 2003, p.3). Skemp (1976) discussed two conceptions of understanding of mathematics: instrumental understanding and relational understanding. Instrumental or procedural understanding can be described as knowing how (to perform a mathematical procedure, for example), without understanding why. This approach is associated with a focus upon performance and procedures. In contrast, when someone has relational (or conceptual) understanding, they know the bigger picture, see connections and relations between mathematical concepts, and understand why certain steps are being carried out. The distinction between procedural/instrumental and relational/conceptual understanding may be seen as the difference between surface and deep understanding.

The relationship between the two types of understanding is not simple. Hiebert and Lefevre (1986) argue that learners are not fully competent in mathematics if they are deficient in either conceptual or procedural knowledge or if the two exist as separate entities. This view is supported by Rittle-Johnson and Alibali (1999). They conclude that conceptual and procedural knowledge appear to develop in a continuous cycle, the gains in one supporting the increases in the other, which in turn supports the increases in the first. This interrelationship between ways of understanding is highly relevant to current debates concerning the 'mastery' curriculum being promoted in recent UK government initiatives (National Centre for Excellence in Teaching Mathematics, 2015).

The SKE at Liverpool Hope University

This section discusses the SKE programme at Liverpool Hope and how the course, informed by the literature discussed above, engages students to develop their mathematics knowledge for teaching.

A or AS Level mathematics is an entry requirement for some SKEs (including at Hope); others do not stipulate this, and course content varies accordingly. Institutions offer courses of varying duration. The Hope course is taught over 24 weeks. The course includes a broad range of mathematics units of a level and content broadly commensurate with early first degree mathematics and A Level/ Further Mathematics. Topics include Calculus, Group Theory, Matrix Algebra, Complex Numbers, Coordinate Geometry, Mechanics, Statistics and Discrete Mathematics. Units are shaped into series of usually 5 or 6 half-day taught sessions. In most sessions, an interactive lecture-presentation from the tutor is followed by or interspersed with workshop time, during which students tackle questions with tutor support.

Additionally, students engage in extended open-ended investigations in which mathematical processes and communication feature highly, one of which is an individual enquiry of an area of mathematics of their own interest and choice. The intention is that these course components should be particularly helpful in enhancing students' appreciation of the processes of thinking mathematically and making connections within mathematics, and of collaborative approaches.

An important feature of the course is a unit on 'misconceptions and fundamental mathematics' in which key topics from the school mathematics curriculum are explicitly 'unpacked' (Adler and Davis, 2006; Ball and Bass, 2003). Students learn early in the course that it will not be sufficient for them, as mathematics teachers, to operate at an instrumental level of understanding (Skemp, 1976). They are encouraged to think carefully about concepts and processes located in elementary mathematics, which they may previously have taken for granted. It is therefore intended that these students will avoid developing the 'expert blind spots'

148　*Mary Stevenson*

(Ruthven, 2011, p.88) which can for some teachers obstruct effective mathematics teaching. Teachers need to be able to deconstruct or unpack mathematical ideas and processes for the benefit of their own students; they may not take for granted even simple ideas.

The SKE as a site for the interplay between subject matter knowledge and pedagogical content knowledge

The ideas that discussions about content should be relevant to teaching and that discussions about teaching should be mindful of content (Ball et al., 2008) have resonance with the philosophy of the SKE. I believe that the ideas of Ball and Shulman are highly relevant to the course and are readily seen in the learning and teaching that takes place therein. Decisions made by the tutor team about the types of tasks that students undertake, and about what course content is appropriate for SKE and what properly belongs later within the PGCE remit, are all illuminated by the categorisation models of Ball and Shulman. For example, two short school placements and an intervention project working with children in the university setting both provide opportunities for students on the SKE to start to learn about children's common misconceptions in the learning of algebra. When they move on to the PGCE/SD course later, they will learn explicitly about effective approaches in the teaching of algebra and ways to draw out and overcome children's misconceptions. In this instance, the SKE is offering some of Ball's 'specialised content knowledge' (SCK), and the PGCE is offering pedagogical content knowledge in the form of Ball's 'knowledge of content and teaching' (KCT). So students' learning on the PGCE will be underpinned by earlier experience and understanding gained through the MEC. This is supported by Artzt et al. (2012), who argue that opportunities to study the school mathematics curriculum 'from an advanced perspective' are 'essential for teachers' preparation to teach mathematics meaningfully' (p.261).

Implications for practice: deficits in traditional degree routes to teacher education and the place of the SKE

Gibson et al. (2013), Hossain et al. (2014) and Stevenson (2014) all find that outcomes in teacher training and careers for former SKE students are comparable to those for students from degree routes, therefore showing that the SKE is fit for purpose in providing 'an alternative route into teaching which is on a par with traditional entry teacher training and supporting the quality and supply of teachers into the profession' (Gibson et al., p.16). Further, Gibson et al. (p.14) assert that 'the SKE is considered to be ideal preparation' for initial teacher education. Adler et al. (2013) found students perceive the SKE as an intense mathematical experience and that three themes were prominent in the students' discourse about the course – those of connectedness, reasoning and being mathematical. They also argue that students begin to acquire features of 'understanding mathematics in depth' (UMID) during their course.

Subject knowledge enhancement courses 149

Mathematics ITE tutors recognise the limitations of conceptual knowledge held by some graduates coming to PGCE or School Direct course from traditional mathematics degree courses and the fact that the timescale of the ITE year itself leaves little opportunity to tackle this explicitly. Clearly, mathematics degree courses are designed to suit the needs of a wide variety of people and to prepare graduates to enter a range of professions. Some people might think that university or academic mathematics is the same as school mathematics but harder and more in depth and that, therefore, studying university mathematics prepared one well for teaching school mathematics. However, as Lerman points out, 'school woodwork is not carpentry . . . and school mathematics is not (academic) mathematics' (Lerman, 1998, p.34). Many teachers report that they do not use their knowledge of degree-level mathematics explicitly in their teaching, but perceive its usefulness more in their confidence and in their ability to make connections (Zazkis and Leikin, 2010). To further explore this idea, I would suggest a visualisation of the content of MEC and degree courses using a Venn diagram, as shown in Figure 11.1.

Figure 11.1 shows that there is a clear overlap in the content of the two routes, which contains key areas of fairly high-level and in-depth mathematics concepts, techniques and experiences. I suggest that in the UK most mathematics degree courses and SKE courses contain these areas in common. Examining the regions in the diagram outside the intersection, we firstly see that degree courses develop these concepts to a significantly higher level than SKEs, and thus it is exposure to and engagement with such ideas that makes a degree mathematician's

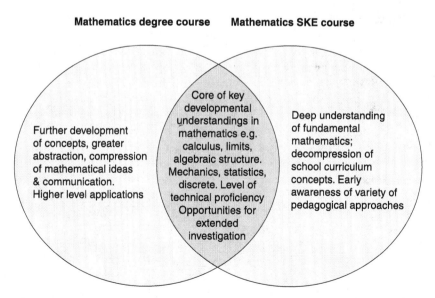

Figure 11.1 Diagram to illustrate typical content areas of mathematics degree and mathematics subject enhancement course

150 *Mary Stevenson*

experience distinctive. There are clearly things that a degree course does which a SKE does not.

Similarly, there are aspects of the SKE which provide a distinctive experience for the student. The SKE region outside the intersection includes in-depth study of aspects of the school curriculum and an implicit focus upon pedagogical approaches – concepts which are not generally found in degree courses. It is also important to note that SKE tutors are often former school teachers and so their teaching approaches may differ from those of other academic mathematicians.

Research suggests that the two routes are preparing students equally well to move into mathematics teaching as a career. Figure 11.1 can help us to understand where the commonality between these two routes lies and also the distinctive 'extra' areas that each route provides. The above analysis of the common and distinct areas of the degree and SKE routes raises questions about mathematics teacher preparation more widely. If it is the case that students on SKEs experience a curriculum that privileges deep understanding of fundamental mathematics and the decompression of mathematics concepts, and degree students do not, then how and where will degree students learn about these things? The simple answer is that they will pick them up (or not) where they have in the past: during school experience in the PGCE year and early years of teaching. However, there are risks inherent in this path. Some novice teachers may spend time handling mathematical concepts in a way which is inappropriately compressed, prior to learning the approach that is needed. During this time, student learning is inevitably compromised. Some novice teachers may take time to attain UMID themselves, having to encounter hurdles in student learning before being able to challenge and reconstruct their own understandings and from that point to adapt their teaching approach. Again, student learning is compromised.

It therefore appears that the knowledge growth within the mathematics education community which has taken place through and in the development of mathematics SKEs now exposes deficits in more traditional mathematics teacher preparation routes. One could argue that all mathematics teachers should have the opportunity to do a SKE. Alternatively, all mathematics degree courses could or should contain units on UMID and decompression of school mathematics. This would provide an intellectually stimulating – and enjoyable – addition to the higher level topics and rigorous approaches taught within other sections of the undergraduate curriculum. Shulman endorsed this idea and argued that university mathematics departments have a responsibility to address this priority:

> Current undergraduate mathematics programs seem to have no place for teaching fundamental mathematics for profound understanding ... such knowledge is misconstrued as remedial instead of recognizing that it is rigorous and deserving of university-level instruction.
>
> (Shulman, in foreword to Ma, 1999, p.xii)

It is now almost two decades since Shulman made these observations. Content of undergraduate mathematics programmes has not changed in the way in which

Subject knowledge enhancement courses   151

he was advocating. Moreover, the rapidly changing landscape in teacher education in England under the Coalition and then the Conservative government has seen funding and allocations for ITE increasingly removed from universities and given to schools, not in a gradual and planned way but in a radical manner which has had the effect of destabilising teacher supply. The government seems unwilling to recognise the place of HEIs in partnership with schools in the preparation of teachers. Teacher education is in a fragile and unstable period. Funding for pre-ITT SKEs continues and now follows the trainee, so that if a trainee is deemed to need a SKE place, funding is provided. In this respect, it does appear that government recognises the value of SKEs in bringing into the teaching profession individuals who otherwise would not gain entry. Thus, the SKE has indeed made its mark in government circles. However, the SKE is currently unregulated. Quality of provision is not monitored by agencies external to providers. There are currently many mathematics SKEs, of varying duration and mode of delivery, across England. Some are run by HEIs, some by school consortia. It is not possible in the public domain to see what SKE courses are available generally (Department for Education, 2015); one has to register and give a home address and subject preference to receive tailored information. There is a diversification of routes and providers. Therefore, it is not clear to what extent the original outcomes of the course, which informed the provision reported on by Gibson et al. (2013) and Hossain et al. (2014), are now generally applicable.

There are pressures on schools to fill their School Direct places on a short-term basis, meaning that currently schools are unlikely to seek a high-quality six-month SKE, for example, as this might mean their trainee starting the School Direct programme a year later than desired. This is not to be interpreted as a criticism of schools but of the larger system that is in play. Over time one would hope that schools will appreciate the importance of workforce planning in the longer term; however the critical shortage of mathematics teachers means that they are constantly dealing with short-term crises in teacher supply.

Conclusion

To conclude, knowledge growth and experience in the mathematics education community over the past decade indicates that SKEs are now an established part of the teacher education landscape and are successful in preparing students for entry to ITE programmes. Diversity and flexibility in SKE provision are to be welcomed insofar as it means that individual needs can be met. However, lack of coherence and accountability is a cause for concern and potentially undermines professionalism. Students applying for SKEs do not really know what they are getting and what their choices are. Unusually within the highly regulated UK education system, SKEs are not monitored; public money is directed into them with little accountability. We therefore need to move towards a situation where providers and policy-makers work together to build upon the progress made so far, and to create a framework for curriculum and monitoring of SKEs which is sufficiently flexible to enable providers to meet the needs of participants but also

152 *Mary Stevenson*

sufficiently rigorous to ensure quality across the piece. SKEs are seen as different from but equivalent to degree mathematics routes, in terms of preparation for entry to ITE. There are important areas of mathematics-for-teaching which are included in SKEs but not in degree routes, and this has exposed a gap in degree provision which needs to be addressed. This would be a fruitful area for further discussion and research involving schools, the academic mathematics community and the mathematics education community.

References

Adler, J. and Davis, Z. (2006). Opening another black box: researching mathematics for teaching in mathematics teacher education. *Journal for Research in Mathematics Education*, 37(4), 270–296.

Adler, J., Hossain, S., Stevenson, M., Clarke, J., Archer, R. and Grantham, B. (2013). Mathematics for teaching and deep subject knowledge: Voices of Mathematics Enhancement Course students in England. *Journal of Mathematics Teacher Education*, 17(2), 129–148. DOI: 10.1007/s10857-013-9259-y

Artzt, A.F., Sutan, A., Curcio, F.R. and Gurl, T. (2012). A capstone course for prospective secondary mathematics teachers. *Journal of Mathematics Teacher Education*, 15(3), 251–262.

Ball, D.L. and Bass, H. (2003). Toward a practice-based theory of mathematical knowledge for teaching. In: E. Simmt and B. Davis (eds), *Proceedings of the 2002 Annual Meeting of the Canadian Mathematics Education Study Group/Groupe Canadien d'Etude en Didactique des Mathématiques*, pp.3–14. Edmonton, AB: CMESG/GCEDM.

Ball, D.L., Thames, M.H. and Phelps, G. (2008). Content knowledge for teaching: what makes it special? *Journal of Teacher Education*, 59(5), 389–407.

Baumert, J., Kunter, M., Blum, W., Brunner, M., Voss, A.J., Klusman, U., Krauss, S., Neubrand, M. and Tsai, Y. (2010). Teachers' mathematical knowledge, cognitive activation in the classroom, and student progress. *American Educational Research Journal*, 47(1), 133–180.

BBC (2013). PISA tests: UK stagnates as Shanghai tops league table. Available from: www.bbc.co.uk/news/education-25187997 (accessed 31 July 2015).

Bell, A.W., Costello, J. and Kuchemann, D. (1983). *A Review of Research of Mathematical Education (Part A)*. Windsor: NFER-Nelson.

Bromme, R. (1994). Beyond subject matter: a psychological topology of teachers' professional knowledge. In: R. Biehler, R. Scholz, R. Strasser and B. Winkelmann (eds), *Didactics of Mathematics as a Scientific Discipline*, pp.73–88. Dordrecht: Kluwer.

Davis, B. (2011). Mathematics teachers' subtle, complex disciplinary knowledge. *Science*, 33, 1506–1507.

Davis, B. and Simmt, E. (2006). Mathematics-for-teaching: an ongoing investigation of the mathematics that teachers (need to) know. *Educational Studies in Mathematics*, 61(3), 293–319.

Department for Education (2015). *Get into Teaching*. Available from: https://getintoteaching.education.gov.uk/subject-knowledge-enhancement-ske-courses (accessed 29 July 2015).

Subject knowledge enhancement courses 153

Ernest, P. (1991). *The Philosophy of Mathematics Education*. Abingdon: Routledge Falmer.

Ernest, P. (2007). *The Mathematics Curriculum* (EdD course handbook). Exeter: University of Exeter School of Education.

Gibson, S., O'Toole, G., Dennison, M. and Oliver, L. (2013). *Evaluation of Subject Knowledge Enhancement Courses Annual Report Year 3 2011–2012*. London: Department for Education.

The Guardian (2014). OECD and PISA tests are damaging education worldwide – academics. Available from: www.theguardian.com/education/2014/may/06/ oecd-pisa-tests-damaging-education-academics (accessed 31 July 2015).

Hiebert, J. and Lefevre, P. (1986). Conceptual and procedural knowledge in mathematics: an introductory analysis. In: J. Hiebert (ed.), *Conceptual and Procedural Knowledge: Case of Mathematics*, pp 1–28. Hillsdale, NJ: Lawrence Erlbaum Associates.

Hodgen, J. (2011). Knowing and identity: a situated theory of mathematics knowledge in teaching. In: T. Rowland and K. Ruthven (eds), *Mathematical Knowledge in Teaching*, pp.27–42. London: Springer.

Hossain, S., Adler, J., Clarke, J., Archer, R. and Stevenson, M. (2014). Trajectory into mathematics teaching via an alternate route: a survey of graduates from Mathematics Enhancement Courses. In S. Pope (ed), *Proceedings of the 8th British Congress of Mathematics Education*. Manchester: British Society for Research into Learning Mathematics.

Lerman, S. (1998). Learning as social practice: an appreciative critique. In A. Watson (ed.), *Situated Cognition and the Learning of Mathematics*, pp.32–44 Oxford: University of Oxford Dept. of Educational Studies.

Ma, L. (1999). *Knowing and Teaching Elementary Mathematics*. Mahwah, NJ: Lawrence Erlbaum.

Mason, J. and Johnson-Wilder, S. (2004). *Fundamental Constructs in Mathematics Education*. Abingdon: Routledge Falmer.

National Centre for Excellence in Teaching Mathematics (2015). *Mastery*. Available from: www.ncetm.org.uk/resources/47230 (accessed 29 July 2015).

Rittle-Johnson, B. and Alibali, M.W. (1999). Conceptual and procedural knowledge of mathematics: does one lead to the other? *Journal of Educational Psychology*, 91(1), 175–189.

Ruthven, K. (2011). Conceptualising mathematical knowledge in teaching. In: T. Rowland and K. Ruthven (eds), *Mathematical Knowledge in Teaching*, pp. 83–96. London: Springer.

Shulman, L. (1986). Those who understand: knowledge growth in teaching. *Educational Researcher*, 15(2), 4–14

Skemp, R. (1976). Relational understanding and instrumental understanding. *Mathematics Teaching*, 77, 20–26.

Stevenson, M. (2014). *Understanding Mathematics in Depth: An Investigation into the Conceptions of Secondary Mathematics Teachers on Two UK Subject Knowledge Enhancement Course*. EdD thesis (unpublished), University of Exeter.

Teacher Training Agency (2003). *Specification for Mathematics Enhancement Course*, unpublished.

Watson, A. and Barton, B. (2011). Teaching mathematics as the contextual application of mathematical modes of enquiry. In T. Rowland and K. Ruthven (eds), *Mathematical Knowledge in Teaching*, pp.65–82. London: Springer.

Warburton, R. (2014). SKE courses and bursaries: examining government strategies to tackle mathematics teacher quantity and quality issues. In S. Pope (ed.), *Proceedings of the 8th British Congress of Mathematics Education*. Manchester: British Society for Research into Learning Mathematics.

Zaskis, R. and Leikin, R. (2010). Advanced mathematical knowledge in teaching practice: perceptions of secondary mathematics teachers. *Mathematical Thinking and Learning*, 12(4), 263–281.

12 Challenging dyslexia

Owen Barden

Introduction

Dyslexia remains a troublesome concept. Despite reportedly affecting around one person in ten, and therefore just about every classroom, it continues to elude satisfactory definition. Neuroscientists, theorists and other researchers working in the dominant psychomedical paradigm continue to search for, and disagree vehemently over, neuroanatomical causes of dyslexia. So there is no consensus within this research community on what dyslexia is, nor how it comes about. And dyslexia advocates are among the first to acknowledge that 'dyslexics' are a diverse population and that every dyslexic person's experience of dyslexia is unique. Yet anyone who publicly doubts the usefulness or validity of the dyslexia concept – the idea of dyslexia as a 'thing' that can be found in some people's brains if only we look hard enough – is on treacherous ground. Consider, for example, the case of Julian Elliott. Elliott is both a professor of education at the University of Durham and a qualified educational psychologist. Educational psychologists are trained to assess for and diagnose dyslexia, and so we would perhaps be wise to listen carefully when one of their number expresses doubt over this process. But when Professor Elliott raised his head above the parapet in 2005 by appearing in the Channel 4 Dispatches documentary 'The Dyslexia Myth', publishing an article in the *Times Educational Supplement* (Elliott, 2005) and later another in the *Journal of Philosophy of Education*, in which he criticised the theoretical basis, empirical validity and educational justification for the dyslexia concept (Elliott and Gibbs, 2008), he was met with scepticism from the mainstream broadsheet press, opposition from high-profile academics and outright hostility from representatives of dyslexia charities.

Dyslexia is evidently a profoundly political and emotive issue; clearly there are vested interests at work in dyslexia research and charities, and the experiences of literacy and learning differences and difficulties for those people labelled with dyslexia cannot and should not be denied. The importance of this second point cannot be overemphasised. However, to suggest that dyslexia is not ultimately a helpful concept to explain such literacy and learning difficulties is not the same as denying the existence of those difficulties. Unfortunately, political and emotional investment in dyslexia, together with media distortion and misrepresentation of

156   *Owen Barden*

the dyslexia-sceptic position, have obscured this crucial aspect of the argument. In this chapter, I will step onto the treacherous ground occupied by dyslexia doubters and explore three ideas which challenge the way we tend to think about dyslexia: firstly, that the way in which we label some children as having dyslexia is problematic because it has negative consequences for them and also for some of their classmates; secondly, that 'biologising' (Lopes, 2012) dyslexia has not yet produced any effective educational interventions, and despite advances in research technology we are still a long way from understanding the mental operations required for literacy. Yet to question the psychomedical paradigm's attempts to explain how dyslexia causes literacy and learning difficulties is dangerous, not only because it challenges received wisdom around literacy, learning and 'dyslexics' but also because it threatens the vested interests of the significant dyslexia industry and the organisation of education provision. The third idea relates to changes in 'what counts' as literacy these days, and as dyslexia is usually defined in terms of perceived underperformance in literacy, these changes imply a challenge to deficit models of dyslexia.

Labelling

The issue of labelling certain people as having Special Educational Needs, including perceived learning difficulties such as dyslexia, presents a serious dilemma. The four main reasons given in favour of such labels can be summarised as:

1   To inform specific, appropriate individualised teaching interventions and adaptations to the learning environment.
2   To establish rights and eligibility for legal protection, including the educational opportunities and access to accommodations such as assistive technologies and alternative assessment arrangements which result from the relevant legislation.
3   To call attention to particular difficulties, informing research and developing and using alternative pedagogies and interventions.
4   To help teachers and parents as well as pupils and students by offering an explanation for the observed difficulties. Labelling a child as 'dyslexic' can offer some comfort because their difficulties can be attributed to a morally neutral neurological condition, rather to them being lazy, which is reprehensible.

(Adapted from Ho, 2004 and Riddick, 2000)

There are significant problems with each of these justifications as they apply to dyslexia. The assumption that the label will provide a passport to appropriate, individualised intervention in order to improve the individual's learning is problematic on at least three fronts. Although many mainstream teachers report feeling that the dyslexia label is helpful in enabling them to understand a child's difficulties, and wanting to act positively towards dyslexic children, they also feel that they do not have the skills, knowledge or training to implement the kind of intervention the label is meant to prompt (Gwernan-Jones and Burden, 2010). There can be only two outcomes from this. The teacher could continue to differentiate the intended learning as best they can in order to take account of their perception of the child's needs – but this is not necessarily the same as providing a specific, appropriate, individualised intervention. The other possible outcome is to transfer responsibility for the intervention to somebody else, quite likely a specialist teacher or TA. This in itself is problematic on two fronts. Firstly, although prompted by an inclusive ethos, such interventions mark students out as inferior or lacking and isolate them from the curriculum and the social environment of the classroom (Hart et al., 2004). Secondly, although these specialist interventions purport to be individualised, experience suggests that they are only superficially so. For three years, I taught an MA in Specific Learning Difficulties at a large university in northwest England. This was a demanding Continuing Professional Development course for qualified teachers wishing to specialise in dyslexia, accredited by the British Dyslexia Association (BDA), who also oversaw the curriculum and assessment of candidates. The guidelines for professional accreditation, and the way the course was presented to participants, placed great emphasis on participants designing 'structured, sequential, multisensory teaching programme to meet specific individual needs' (BDA, 2012). Yet the reality was that in order to gain approval and accreditation from the BDA, specialist teachers were expected to operate within severe constraints to individuality and personalisation. They were strongly encouraged to stick to a rigid, formulaic pattern of teaching and learning activities. They were expected not only to follow a standardised lesson structure and scheme of work but also to use particular approved 'multisensory routines' within that structure, and even to keep to recommended durations for each activity (for examples, see Kelly and Phillips, 2011). Thus, the level of 'individualisation' only really extended to the entry point of an almost 'off the shelf' literacy programme based on a proprietary, highly structured approach to synthetic phonics. This is despite the fact that for a significant proportion of people identified as dyslexic, phonological processing is not the main difficulty and phonics is not an effective approach to literacy learning for them (Cooper, 2012). Moreover, the virtual insistence on a highly structured, synthetic phonics approach even extended to dyslexic students in Further and Higher Education, many of whom have developed their own literacy strategies in order to be able to continue their studies that far, and would see synthetic phonics as irrelevant if not childish and patronising. In sum, the claim to specific, individualised interventions seems, to me at least, somewhat overstated.

The process by which we select some learners (and not others) for dyslexia assessment and subsequent intervention is also highly problematic. It is well known that many parents, unless they can afford an educational psychologist's fees, have to fight, sometimes for years, to have their child assessed for dyslexia. Many schools and local authorities are often reluctant to support this process and even contest the decision to grant protections and accommodations when the assessment confirms that the child is dyslexic. Meanwhile, the child continues to struggle at school. Of course, many children who are assessed will be told they are dyslexic and will receive interventions such as specialist literacy teaching, access to assistive technologies and examination access arrangements. But what of the child who seems to be struggling with literacy or learning but who is deemed not

158   *Owen Barden*

to be dyslexic for one reason or another? The child who, for example, has a 'borderline' or atypical assessment profile that means the assessor cannot conclude that they are dyslexic? (In my former professional capacity as a BDA-qualified assessor and teacher-trainer, I conducted hundreds of dyslexia assessments, and oversaw many more, and such 'problematic profiles' were very common.) Or the child whose literacy difficulties are put down to English being their second language, or to their membership of the traveller community? Or the child whose difficulties are ascribed to them simply not being very intelligent, rather than dyslexic? These students are far less likely to receive any of the accommodations and support granted to students deemed dyslexic, even though their difficulties with literacy and learning may be just as frustrating and limiting. There is a Dyslexia Friendly Schools kitemark – but no Moderate Learning Difficulty Friendly kitemark. For such reasons, it is possible to conceive of 'dyslexics' as, in some ways, a privileged group who have access to teaching, support and resources denied to other students whose needs may be just as great. There are no literacy and learning pedagogies which have been shown to be effective for students identified as dyslexic and yet not to work for other students. Given this, the fact that supposedly individualised interventions are often only superficially so, and that the assessment process itself may obstruct rather than facilitate access to educational opportunities for some pupils, it is perhaps worth considering whether the alternative literacy pedagogies and other interventions do in fact need to be tied to the dyslexia label – or whether more students would learn better if we attended more closely to their individual capabilities and needs, without the dyslexia labelling that empowers some children but stigmatises and denies others.

Biologising dyslexia

So far I have discussed difficulties with two of the justifications given for labelling some children as dyslexic. I will start this section by considering the second two, before moving on to examine the heretical proposition that we should abandon the untenable concept of dyslexia.

Since first identified as 'word blindness' and then 'strephosymbolia' over 115 years ago, the conundrum of apparently inexplicable literacy difficulties in otherwise capable children has motivated a colossal amount of research. The first investigations into what we now call dyslexia were by doctors (Miles, 1996), and the vast majority of research continues to use the psychomedical paradigm. Having a group of people identified as 'dyslexic' is helpful in providing both a justification for research and a population to research. As access to technologies like fMRI scanners becomes more widespread, investigations continue to try and identify a neurobiological cause for dyslexia; *Science*, for example, recently published an advance on the currently favoured phonological deficit hypothesis which claimed that impaired access to mental representations of speech sounds underlies dyslexics' reading and spelling difficulties (Boets et al., 2013). However, in over a century of research, with hundreds of books and thousands of scholarly articles published, we still do not have a satisfactory neurobiological or psychological

Challenging dyslexia 159

explanation of dyslexia. Instead, we have a number of contradictory, competing and inadequate hypotheses: the phonological deficit hypothesis, the working memory hypothesis, magnocellular theory, double-deficit hypothesis and numerous others. None of these alone can explain all the cognitive dispositions and behavioural manifestations currently attributed to dyslexia. For example, the phonological deficit hypothesis, which relates to the processing of speech sounds, cannot explain the visual distortions of printed text experienced and frequent letter reversals made by many dyslexic people – only the magnocellular deficit theory offers a (still hypothetical, and highly contested) explanation for this. And the converse of this is true: magnocellular theory cannot explain variations in people's phonological processing ability. Neither is it clear how a phonological deficit can be related to the clumsiness and untidy handwriting often associated with dyslexia, nor to difficulties with accurately estimating time.

Nevertheless, biological research into the causes of dyslexia is often justified on the grounds that it will enable the development of more effective interventions for literacy difficulties, especially in reading. Certainly such research is exciting and has undoubtedly produced a lot of valuable insights into the process of reading. We now know a lot more about which areas and systems of the brain are recruited for the complex set of subtasks that must be performed in order to read fluently, and this body of knowledge looks set to grow. But current methodologies and evidence from this field must both be viewed with some caution. Many brain imaging studies, for instance, use samples made up partly of diagnosed 'dyslexics', partly of 'poor-readers' who have not been diagnosed as dyslexic and partly of 'normally-achieving' readers. Or sometimes the decision to assign participants to the 'dyslexic' or 'non-dyslexic' group is made according to researcher-defined criteria, rather than full diagnosis. Yet the evidence gained from these studies is often used to draw conclusions about the differences between 'dyslexics' and 'non-dyslexics', rather than between 'relatively poor' and 'relatively good' readers. In the excitement about these new technologies, it is also too easily forgotten that the differences in brain activation the images show only demonstrate correlation, not causality. There is a tendency to conclude that 'dyslexics' are worse at reading than non-dyslexics because they are using less efficient mechanisms in different parts of the brain, and they are using those less efficient parts because of some predetermined disposition, influenced by genetic inheritance. However, as Lopes (2012) points out, the eagerness to biologise this relationship overlooks the fact that the observed differences may be effects rather than causes. That is, more proficient readers are more proficient because they have read more, and that this practice effect has resulted in the reallocation of reading function from the less efficient parts of the brain – used when they learned to read, and still used by the less-practised 'dyslexic' readers – to more efficient parts of the brain. A recent MRI study by Kraftnick et al. (2014) suggested just this. A key implication is that there is, in fact, no underlying congenital difference between supposedly 'dyslexic' and 'non-dyslexic' brains: merely differences in stages of reading development, which could potentially be resolved through appropriate teaching intervention and reading practice.

160   *Owen Barden*

A major irony here is that, as yet, the significant body of neuroanatomical research has yet to produce any effective interventions for dyslexia. Genetic and brain imaging studies may have their uses, but they tell us nothing about how to teach people who have difficulty meeting our cultural expectations of literacy. As noted above, the most commonly advocated approach is a systematic, highly structured programme based on synthetic phonics. Yet there is nothing new in this: structured multisensory literacy programmes have been devised and in constant use since before 1920, well in advance of the biological evidence now used to justify them (Orton, 1928; Fernald, 1943; Gillingham and Stillman, 1960; Hinshelwood, 1917). And even eminent researchers in the field have admitted that the psychomedical evidence does not provide compelling justification for the interventions advocated:

> We have had to come to two uncomfortable conclusions – uncomfortable at any rate, for the authors of a book about phonological awareness and reading. The first is that there is very little direct evidence that children who are learning to read do rely on letter-sound relationships to help them read words. The second is that there is a great deal of evidence that these young children take easily and naturally to reading words in other ways.
>
> (Goswami and Bryant, 1990, cited in Thomas and Loxley, 2007, p.73)

From this, it would seem that the idea that the 'dyslexia' label is some sort of passport to scientifically proven, specialised teaching interventions is flawed. To be sure, it may well trigger some sort of teaching intervention, but it is spurious to believe that such an intervention has a robust empirical basis. While it cannot be denied that many people labelled as dyslexic find these approaches helpful, many others don't, and we must bear in mind the fact that there is no teaching approach which appears to be effective for 'dyslexics' which is not effective for other groups of learners experiencing literacy difficulties. Indeed, the opposite seems to be true: the approaches which are advocated initially for 'dyslexics' often end up being implemented with others who are perceived to be underachieving. In addition, there do not seem to be significant differences in levels of improvement in the targeted skill domain between 'dyslexic' and other subgroups of students.

Ideology of literacy

Given the complexity of the sensory and cognitive processes required to be proficient in the invention we call literacy, we should perhaps be more surprised that so many people learn to read and write with relative ease, than that some people experience significant difficulties using these tools. However, the fact that we unquestioningly assume a literate norm means that in the minds of most teachers, students and parents, the concept of dyslexia is inextricably linked to perceived literacy deficits. This is not surprising. It reflects official definitions, teacher-training, research and policy discourse, and media and commercial influence. Yet the deficit view of dyslexia depends on a particular conception of literacy and learning which is itself currently subject to challenge. Historically, teachers and schools have tended to promote a form of 'alphabetic' or 'typographic' literacy in which the essay, or essay-type texts, have been taken as the ideal and which pupils should seek to emulate as closely as possible. Essays and essay-type texts have been widely considered the best way to enable students to evidence not only the most appropriate literacy skills for education and employment but also intellectual abilities like rational thought (Street, 1984). But pedagogy is changing, texts are changing and ideas about 'what counts' as literacy are changing, partly motivated by newly emerging literacy practices, many of which are mediated by digital technologies. As such, there is a significant challenge to the essay-text as an ideal. This is evident in classrooms in the ubiquitous use of PowerPoint and YouTube as well as in digital texts and on social media. Social media provide a wealth of potential authentic literacy and learning experiences and do demand literacy, but many of us would accept that composing a text message or reading a tweet demands a slightly different set of competencies than those required for composing or reading an essay. A common educationalist's response is to decry the 'decline' in literacy standards such technologies are supposedly responsible for. This response ignores evidence which suggests that such informal literacy practices can be used to motivate and scaffold literacies which are more acceptable in schools. For example, studies have shown that the motivated wordplay and increased exposure to language concomitant with high levels of SMS 'texting' may actually enhance traditional literacy skills (Plester and Wood, 2009; Veater, Plester and Wood, 2011). So another way to respond is to realise that rather than there being a single, ideal form of literacy which all pupils should strive towards, there are different kinds of literacies which are more or less appropriate for different contexts, and to promote opportunities for pupils to develop and exploit contemporary literacies.

Texting provides only one example of the way texts, and so reading and writing, are changing. A key idea when thinking about the way texts, reading and writing are changing is multimodality (Kress, 2003). Whereas the essay-text has only one semiotic mode, one way of communicating meaning – the printed word – digital texts are often multimodal. A multimodal text consists of several semiotic modes: it combines text with other modes such as sound, video or graphics, gesture, animation. In contrast to an essay, a school textbook might well contain some images and diagrams and therefore be considered multimodal, though it would most probably still tend to privilege the written word, with the pictures being supplementary. Whilst it cannot be disputed that the Web has made a superabundance of text available to us, and that in some cases people's difficulties with reading and writing have simply been transposed online, the nature of many texts is changing, and multimodality is becoming more commonplace. Consider BBC Online, one of the hundred most-visited websites in the world. Until fairly recently, the main news was presented as text, with supplementary pictures and audio. Now, the main stories are presented through video, with text subservient to images and audio. Moreover, technological innovations such as 3D printing, haptics, holograms, virtual and augmented reality suggest a strengthening

162 *Owen Barden*

challenge to the dominance of the written word as the privileged mode for learning in formal education. Such developments prompt reconsideration not only of what counts as literacy but also how we conceptualise dyslexia and how we organise educational opportunities. For example, dyslexia is often associated with strengths in creative, visual and non-linear thought (West, 2009) such as mechanical construction, 3D mental-mapping or imaging, 'seeing the big picture' and 'making connections between different facets of life' (Ehardt, 2009 p.3), and this propensity invoked to help explain difficulties with producing and interpreting linear essay-type texts. West (1997 and 2009) argues that a societal shift away from privileging textual representations of concepts and processes, towards a much more visual approach, could lend itself to the more visual thinking processes instinctively adopted by many people labelled with dyslexia. If he is right, then because of the perceived power of this mode of thought, some dyslexic people could find themselves at the forefront of academic thinking and research because of their 'different' (or 'abnormal') brain organisation rather than in spite of it. This has the potential to be a seismic shift in power and agency for people labelled with dyslexia as well as others who struggle with traditional reading and writing, who have been seriously disadvantaged and marginalised by both educational and wider cultures which privilege reading and writing over other forms of communication and learning.

Conclusion

We have seen that there is no consensus on what dyslexia is, and therefore who is or is not dyslexic, nor on what causes dyslexia. This is not a controversial assertion. We have also seen that although psychomedical and biological research has given us some useful insights into both cognitive aspects of literacy and the way people's brains can vary in engaging in executing literacy-related tasks, it cannot yet give a full account of these processes, cannot reliably distinguish between 'dyslexic' and 'non-dyslexic' subgroups (Elliott and Grigorenko, 2014), and has not yet produced any teaching intervention which works for 'dyslexics' but not for others. We also know that dyslexia is associated with a very diverse range of characteristics, and that partly because of this every 'dyslexic' person's experience of dyslexia is unique. From this, it would seem that the claim that 'dyslexia' offers a helpful explanation for someone's learning and literacy difficulties might be an illusory one: it appears to offer an explanation because it allows people to give a socially acceptable name to the problem, but provides little of substance beyond that. Here we are about to move onto controversial ground. If nobody can agree on what dyslexia is, or how it is caused; if the assessment and label tell us little about the person or their learning; if even advocates of labelling children 'dyslexic' admit that half find the label stigmatising (Riddick, 2000); if being labelled as dyslexic grants access to resources denied to others who may be experiencing similar difficulties; if psychomedical research is useless for producing teaching interventions and inhibits the allocation of resources for research into teaching – should we continue to label some children as dyslexic and others as not? To suggest we

Challenging dyslexia 163

abandon the dominant psychomedical conception of dyslexia is heretical and dangerous because it provokes and threatens not only our received wisdom about dyslexia but also an influential research community, the vested interests of powerful charities, the dyslexia and broader SEN industries, and the structure of educational provision. We must also acknowledge that, for some, 'dyslexic' can be an affirmative identity (Macdonald, 2009). But given that the approaches which work well with 'dyslexic' learners are also effective with others, that psychological assessments ultimately do little to inform teaching practice, and that individualised interventions are divisive and segregationist, perhaps it would be fairer and more inclusive to offer differentiated and personalised teaching and learning without tying it to the diagnostic label, whilst striving towards a less judgemental society which would not look so harshly upon naturally occurring variations in reading and writing proficiency.

Such differentiated and personalised teaching might take account of contemporary notions of critical literacy, which shift the emphasis away from the essay-text and its derivatives and towards appreciation and production of a range of texts and recognise that (a) 'what counts' as literacy depends on audience, genre, medium and the affordances of mode (Cope and Kalantzis, 2000; Gee, 1996 and 2007), and (b) students with labelled with dyslexia, and others who struggle to master conventional reading and writing, are likely to have talents in some modes to complement talents of non-dyslexics in alphabetic literacy. That is, opportunities to work collaboratively with multimodal texts and digital media can help 'level the playing field' in the classroom for learners who are disadvantaged by traditional literacy expectations and practices (Barden, 2014). There are numerous definitions and interpretations of critical literacy, but they converge around building on students' existing practices and knowledge, whether obtained through formal or informal education, and identifying 'barriers and enablers' to participation in textual practices and cultures (Willett, 2009 p.21; also Davies, 2009). In an important book on the future of education and schools, Facer (2011 p.69) suggests that the critical literacy students will need in the text-saturated near-future for social and academic success has three elements:

1   Discernment: The ability to judge the quality of information, its relationship to other information, and to personal goals and interest. This will include appreciating the power relations embedded in texts (Dowdall, 2009).
2   Multiliteracy: To appreciate the affordances and limitations of different technologies, materials and modes of communication for representation and comprehension, and to be able to work fluently across these.
3   Responsibility: In a world where information is ubiquitous, students must learn to consider the consequences of the ways in which they manage, circulate and control the information flows in their networks.

To adopt a critical literacies perspective is thus not to simply say 'anything goes' – rather, it is to recognise that literacy is not merely an end in itself but a means to learn about and express other things, and that different literate forms

164 *Owen Barden*

are more or less appropriate or effective in different circumstances and for different learners. It is not about saying we should totally abandon the formal structure, grammar and spelling of the traditional essay – with which so many, dyslexic and not, struggle – but about accepting that such an essay is only one literate way of showing what one knows, that it is not inherently superior to other literate forms, and about working inclusively to enable learners to exploit the wealth of expertise they bring, and technologies available, in being and becoming literate 21st century citizens.

References

Barden, O. (2014). Facebook levels the playing field: dyslexic students learning through digital literacies. *Research in Learning Technology*, 22 (February) [online]. Available from: http://dx.doi.org/10.3402/rlt.v22.18535

Boets, B., Op de Beeck, H.P., Vandermosten, M., Scott, S.K., Gillebert, C.R., Mantini, D. and Ghesquiere, P. (2013). Intact but less accessible phonetic representations in adults with dyslexia. *Science*, 342(6163), 1251–1254. DOI: 10.1126/science.1244333

British Dyslexia Association (2012). *Criteria for Recognition of Teachers and other Professionals with Specialist Training.* Available from: www.bdadyslexia.org.uk/files/AMBDA-ATS-Criteria-July-2012.pdf (accessed 19 December 2013).

Cooper, R. (2012). *Neurodiversity and Dyslexia; Challenging the Social Construction of Specific Learning Difficulties.* Available from: http://outsidersoftware.co.uk/wp-content/uploads/2012/11/Neurodiversity-and-Dyslexia-Challenging-the-social-construction-of-specific-learning-differences.doc (accessed 19 December 2013).

Cope, B. and Kalantzis, M. (2000). Introduction: multiliteracies: the beginnings of an idea. In: B. Cope and M. Kalantzis (eds), *Multiliteracies. Literacy Learning and the Design of Social Futures*, pp.3–8. Abingdon and New York: Routledge.

Davies, J. (2009). A space for play: crossing boundaries and learning online. In: V. Carrington and M. Robinson (eds), *Digital Literacies. Social Learning and Classroom Practices*, pp.27–42. London: SAGE/UKLA.

Dowdall, C. (2009). Masters and critics: children as producers of online digital texts. In: V. Carrington and M. Robinson (eds), *Digital Literacies. Social Learning and Classroom Practices*, pp.43–62. London: SAGE/UKLA.

Ehardt, K. (2009). Dyslexia, not disorder. *Dyslexia*, 15(4), 363–366. DOI: 10.1002/dys.379

Elliott, J. (2005). The dyslexia myth and the feelbad factor. *Times Educational Supplement*, 2 September. Available from: www.tes.co.uk/search/story/?story_id=2128733 (accessed 3 June 2008).

Elliott, J.G. and Gibbs, S. (2008). Does dyslexia exist? *Journal of Philosophy of Education*, 42(3–4), 475–491. doi:10.1111/j.1467-9752.2008.00653.x

Elliott, J. and Grigorenko, E. (2014). *The Dyslexia Debate*. Cambridge: Cambridge University Press.

Facer, K. (2011). *Learning Futures. Education, Technology and Social Change.* Abingdon, Oxon: Routledge.

Fernald, G.M. (1943). *Remedial Techniques in Basic School Subjects*. New York: McGraw-Hill.

Challenging dyslexia 165

Gee, J.P. (1996). *Social Linguistics and Literacies. Ideology in Discourse.* Second edition. London: RoutledgeFalmer.

Gee, J.P. (2007). *What Video Games have to Teach us about Learning and Literacy.* Revised edition. New York: Palgrave Macmillan.

Gillingham, A. and Stillman, B. (1960). *Remedial Training for Children with Specific Disability in Reading, Spelling and Penmanship.* Cambridge, MA: Educators Publishing Service.

Goswami, U. and Bryant, P. (1990). *Phonological Skills and Learning To Read.* London: Lawrence Erlbaum.

Gwernan-Jones, R. and Burden, R. (2010). Are they just lazy? Student teachers' attitudes about dyslexia. *Dyslexia*, 16(1), 66–86. doi:10.1002/dys

Hart, S., Dixon, A., Drummond, M.J. and McIntyre, D. (2004). *Learning Without Limits.* Maidenhead: OU Press.

Hinshelwood, J. (1917). *Congenital Word Blindness.* London: HK Lewis.

Ho, A. (2004). To be labelled, or not to be labelled: that is the question. *British Journal of Learning Disabilities*, 32(2), 86–92. DOI: 10.1111/j.1468-3156. 2004.00284.x

Kelly, K. and Phillips, S. (2011). *Teaching Literacy to Learners with Dyslexia: A Multisensory Approach.* London: SAGE.

Kraftnick, A.J., Lynn Flowers, D., Luetje, M.M., Napoliello., E.M. and Eden, G.F. (2014). An investigation into the origin of anatomical differences in dyslexia. *The Journal of Neuroscience*, 34(3), 901–908. doi: 10.1523/JNEUROSCI.2092-13.2013

Kress, G. (2003). *Literacy in the New Media Age.* London and New York: Routledge.

Lopes, J. (2012). Biologising reading problems: the specific case of dyslexia. *Contemporary Social Science*, (7) 2, 215–229.

MacDonald, S. (2009). *Towards a Sociology of Dyslexia: Exploring Links Between Dyslexia, Disability and Social Class.* Saarbrücken: VDM Publishing House Ltd.

Miles, T. (1996). A hundred years of dyslexia. *Dyslexia*, 2 (3), 145–152.

Orton, S.T. (1928). Specific reading disability – strephosymbolia. *JAMA*, 90, 1095–1099.

Plester, B. and Wood, C. (2009). Exploring relationships between traditional and new media literacies: British preteen texters at school. *Journal of Computer-Mediated Communication*, 14(4), 1108–1129.

Riddick, B. (2000). An examination of the relationship between labelling and stigmatisation with special reference to dyslexia. *Disability & Society*, 15(4), 653–667.

Street, B. (1984). *Literacy in Theory and Practice.* Cambridge: Cambridge University Press.

Thomas, G. and Loxley, A. (2007). Thinking about learning failure, especially in reading. In: G. Thomas and A. Loxley, *Deconstructing Special Education and Constructing Inclusion*, pp.66–76. Maidenhead, Berks: Open University Press.

Veater, H., Plester, B. and Wood. C. (2011). Use of text message abbreviations and literacy skills in children with dyslexia. *Dyslexia*, 17(1), 65–71.

West, T.G. (1997). *The Mind's Eye.* New York. Prometheus.

West, T.G. (2009). *The Mind's Eye. Creative Visual Thinkers, Gifted Dyslexics and the Rise of Visual Technologies.* New York. Prometheus.

Willett, R. (2009). Young people's video production as new sites of learning. In: V. Carrington and M. Robinson (eds), *Digital Literacies. Social Learning and Classroom* Practices, pp.13–26. London. SAGE/UKLA.

13 An issue of social justice
Bullying in schools

Babs Anderson

This chapter is dedicated to the School Council for 2014/2015, who articulated their vision for education for a just society.

Introduction

In her work, philosopher Hannah Arendt (1977, p.185) suggests that school is 'the institution that we interpose between the private domain of the home and the world in order to make the transition from the family to the world possible at all'. Thus, schooling largely assumes the function of education in the child's development instead of the family, in order to guide the child to learn the requirements of the world in which they belong. This includes support for individual children to recognise the diverse nature of family, community and culture for other children. The school may therefore be seen as second only to the family and significant others in the socialisation of children from the age of five years in the UK, providing an interactive social space for children to form non-familial relationships with children and adults. The understanding that this space may sometimes present as an unwelcoming and challenging arena is well documented (Layard and Dunn, 2009; Bradshaw, 2011).

The *Good Childhood Report 2015* (Pople et al., 2015) continues the analysis of earlier surveys into the subjective well-being of children in the UK. This identifies key topics and themes from consultation with children aged 14 and 15 years of age. Together with the key topics are six cross-cutting themes of love; support; safety, security and protection; fairness; respect and freedom/ autonomy. One specific key topic is friends, where the issues are friends as a source of support, bullying and peer pressure. The researchers found that the 'most common response to our question about what prevents a good life is bullying' (ibid, p.14). Bullying is one of the key negative experiences that can influence an individual's well-being. Instances of this are present in pre-school, primary and secondary schools, as in other institutions, such as workplaces, prisons and in army settings (Salmivalli, 2010).

An overview of bullying research

In the original view of bullying as a group activity, 'mobbning' (Heinemann, 1972, cited in Salmivalli, 2010) was seen as directed towards an individual or individuals, who had attracted a group's collective aggression. The influential work of Olweus (1978), however, moved this focus to individual actions and relationships away from the collective actions of a group. This led to the categorisation of individual children as bullies, victims, bully-victims and bystanders. The intention underpinning this change of focus was to highlight those individuals who are responsible for initiating bullying situations. In doing so, the aim is to prevent bullying occurring or to offer a means of dealing with this negative behaviour. Further research has led to a consensus that power relations are integral to understanding how school bullying works (Horton, 2011). James (2010) writes in an influential study commissioned by the National Society for the Prevention of Cruelty to Children (NSPCC) that the defining features of bullying set it apart from other aggressive behaviours. One such definition (Olweus, 1993) states that bullying is defined by an explicitly aggressive intention to cause harm on the part of the bully, that there is repetition of this behaviour and that an inequality of power or status exists between the individuals within the interaction. This leads on to the supposition that bullying is proactive aggression on the part of the bully and invited by the victim, either passively or provocatively. However, this does not take account of the social order within the school culture or indeed of the socio-cultural influences within which the school is located. Nor does it take account of peer involvement in bullying episodes, where often peer witnesses are known to be present.

Salmivalli et al. (1996) identify four participant roles in bullying episodes in addition to the bully and the victim. These were termed assistants of bullies, reinforcers of bullies, outsiders and defenders of the victim. Assistants aid the bully, reinforcers give positive feedback, outsiders remove themselves from the bullying situation and defenders take sides with the victim, offering support and comforting them. A key factor in the extent of bullying is the amount of negative and positive feedback given to the bully by their classmates. Where positive feedback supports the bully's behaviour, the likelihood of anxious or rejected children being victimised is greater. Where negative bystander feedback by defenders is more prevalent, the less likely it is that bullying will occur. However, the classroom context influences the extent to which defenders will counteract the bully. Dijkstra, Lindenberg and Veenstra (2008) indicate that bullying is socially acceptable in classrooms where high status (popular) pupils carry out these types of behaviour, rather than all pupils.

Corsaro (2015) takes a socio-cultural view in considering bullying in the United States of America, recognising that societies have cultural norms, which influence the behaviours of those people living within them. In this case, in the US 20–25 per cent of the school population aged between 6 years of age and 18 are regarded as having experienced bullying, compared with 15 per cent in Europe. A potential reason for this differential may be the higher prevalence of status groups and heightened concerns with status in the US.

168   *Babs Anderson*

In the UK context, the Office of Standards for Education (OfSTED) produced a report in 2012, entitled *No Place for Bullying*, indicating that schools have a major role in dealing with bullying incidents. However, the report states that there is a lack of awareness in school staff of different forms of bullying, such as homophobic bullying. This lack of awareness results in reduced recognition of the true nature of bullying situations, with the concomitant failure to take active steps to prevent bullying from occurring. Thompson and Smith (2011) found that the effectiveness of anti-bullying strategies used by schools was variable, so while certain schools were able to succeed in their anti-bullying, others were less successful.

The research project

A single primary school with pupils aged from 3 years to 11 was identified as the research site and acted as a case study to examine the phenomenological experiences of bullying in school. Phenomenology has the advantage of utilising subjective consciousness as bestowing meaning for the participants (Cohen, Manion and Morrison, 2011). This enabled the exploration of the topic of bullying in the form of subjective interpretations of this social phenomenon by teachers and pupils.

Purposive sampling was chosen in order to derive a particular focus on a partner school, active in addressing the issue of bullying. Partnership with schools is increasingly important for Higher Education Institutes' provision of Initial Teacher Education Programmes. When HEIs and schools work together effectively, this enhances programme planning and delivery by mapping ITE provision to the needs of schools. The participating school was identified, namely a large primary school in the northwest of England with a significant diversity of ethnicity and family background within the school population. A series of interviews were carried out on a sequential chronological basis. The first participant held the position of SENCO/safeguarding officer, the second participant was an established classroom teacher and the third group of participants formed the school council with representatives from Year 1 to Year 6. A form of 'iterative reframing' was used to structure the research process; the participant responses from the first interview were analysed, used to formulate the subsequent second interview focus and questions, and a similar process used with the responses in the second interview to inform the third group interview. As in grounded theory (Charmaz, 2014), the analysis of the data from each participant was essential in shaping the following sections of data collection.

The role of the researcher was made clear as part of the research process, so as an ex-practitioner with many years of experience within a primary school setting, some elements of fluidity of insider/outsider perspectives were present. As an outsider, not employed by the school with no responsibility for responding to behavioural issues within the specific pupil population in particular, it was easier to take an objective view of the school and their policy and procedures. As an insider within the broader educational world, having had direct experience and responsibility for anti-bullying work in a similar primary school, it was important to have a shared understanding of the accountability and challenges presented by such a role with the staff participants.

The findings

The SENCO/safeguarding officer had a detailed understanding of individual and group-level strategies, which can be categorised into two major aims. The first aim is reactive in that such bullying incidents that do occur are managed effectively, whereas the second aim is proactive in order to reduce the potential for bullying incidents to occur.

Reactive strategies

Recognition and identification of bullying incidents is essential for all staff, including those support staff with responsibility for children in more unstructured times during the school day, such as playtime, lunchtimes and the end of the school day. During these times, the level of supervision of children on the school site is reduced, with the children afforded more choice as to their movements than commonly offered within classrooms. However, these are also more vulnerable times for children, who may experience peer victimisation and bullying due to lower levels of adult surveillance. Clear lines of support are essential, both for the staff members to be able to discuss their concerns with a more senior member of staff and also for the children involved in bullying incidents, including bystanders.

It is necessary to take the situation seriously. Children may be faced with a situation where adults think they are exaggerating or unable to see someone else's point of view. The value placed by adults on children's well-being needs to be explicitly communicated to the children by the actions taken by the adults. It is insufficient to have a policy which states that all children are valued as individuals if the normative sociological processes within the school culture belie this.

An honest assessment of the situation is called for by all parties, including children, parents and staff. Parents, in particular, may feel very uneasy when their child has been involved in a bullying episode and be unable to apportion responsibility to their own child for these negative actions. They may invoke a potential provocation aspect of the victim's behaviour in order to justify and account for these actions. Likewise, children, particularly young children, may be unable to recognise the effects of their behaviours on others, particularly where Theory of Mind or empathy is underdeveloped. Certain children may be able to manipulate other children to agree with their perspective, due to being perceived as having a high status or prestige within the class so that bullying behaviour is denied.

A more subtle analysis of bullying situations requires the recognition by school staff of the impact of their preconceptions of the children involved. School staff may have internalised beliefs about certain children and their behaviour, so that these beliefs are imposed on the adults' interpretations of any future interactions between the child and other children.

170 *Babs Anderson*

Recording any potential bullying incidents is essential, so that effective monitoring can be carried out. One designated member of staff has the responsibility for managing this log, named here as the safeguarding officer. Thus, the safeguarding officer has a remit beyond that of child protection, with its emphasis on family care and background. In safeguarding, there is the explicit understanding that children's relationships with their peers contribute to the holistic well-being of the child both in and out of the school environment as well as their experience of familial care. A common behaviour management tool used in recording and monitoring episodes of bullying is the ABC system. In this, A stands for the antecedents of the behaviour, B is the identification of the behaviour itself and C is the consequences for the child of the identified behaviour. While this is perfectly adequate, a more sophisticated extension requires personal reflection on their behaviour on the part of the child. In this extension, D and E are included where D is the decision made and E requires an evaluation of how successful this decision has been in its implementation and any alteration that may be necessary. This may be seen as a form of restorative justice (RJ), where an intermediary facilitates a process whereby the child who has bullied is made accountable for their actions. The victim is given the opportunity to express how these actions have affected them and to ask questions. Cremin, Sellman and McCluskey (2012) relate how these types of interventions have been shown to have a potential for a positive impact on school pupils, when challenged as to the consequences of their behaviour for others. They can also support teacher and support staff understanding of the complex, faceted nature of bullying and conflict between peers.

Proactive strategies

Bullying is clearly located within a coherent behaviour policy. It is viewed as being on a continuum of behaviours, and this view is communicated explicitly with children and their parents. The behaviour policy lays down the requirements for prosocial behaviours in peer interactions throughout the school environment as well as general expectations of behaviour in the classroom. While it is made clear that the responsibility for the individual's actions lies with the individual as a matter of conscious choice, nevertheless the possibility of social influence affecting behaviour is discussed, with support strategies provided.

Safeguarding is prioritised within the school system, with effective briefing systems to alert staff once a potential issue has been identified. This may involve extra support for vulnerable children, for example where the family make-up is changing through divorce or bereavement. Inclusion also is seen as a positive value, where diversity is understood as fundamental to human society. Even though cultures, societies, communities and their school curricula are exclusive by their very nature, inclusion is operational and consists of how people treat each other and the respect given to others and their ways of leading their lives (Nutbrown, Clough and Atherton, 2013).

Friendship groups are recognised, valued and promoted as examples of prosocial behaviours, so that the support offered to the individuals within such groups is highlighted as it occurs. Specific examples of a deliberate use of this include 'circle of friends', whereby socially adept children befriend a vulnerable child in a therapeutic use of circle time.

The school is actively working towards the Rights Respecting Schools Award, which is coordinated by UNICEF in the UK. This programme aims to underpin school ethos and culture with the United Nations Convention on the Rights of the Child (UNCRC) (UNICEF, 2015). This includes informing the children of their rights, so that they are able to fully appreciate their entitlements and obligations to others.

Proactive strategies are employed on a number of levels. On an individual level, the children are supported in self-awareness and self-efficacy, so they are aware of their strengths and their challenges, including how others see them. Their intra-personal skills are enhanced through their Personal, Social and Health Education curriculum, with a focus on understanding PSHE education to be more than a limited repertoire of sex and relationships education, drug education and personal finance education. Conflict resolution skills are also taught, so children learn how to negotiate with others and achieve an acceptable solution to both parties. This element also includes recognising the differences between assertiveness, aggression and compliance and the advantages and consequences for each type of behaviour.

On a group level, children are supported in their inter-personal skills, developing their Theory of Mind and their skills of sympathy and empathy. They are able to appreciate the motivations and intentions of others, even where they disagree with their own. Citizenship education comes into play here with its emphasis on democracy, political and social issues, and the requirement for school children to be able to take their place in society as responsible citizens. It must be stated here that, at the time of writing (2015), Citizenship is only statutory on the national curriculum for Key Stages 3 and 4. PSHE and Citizenship do not yet hold the status of statutory subjects in the national curriculum.

On a societal level, the Every Child Matters outcomes, as outlined in the Children Act 2004 (DfES, 2004), state explicitly the responsibilities of parents, carers and families and the children's workforce in enabling children both to stay safe from bullying and discrimination and to make a positive contribution by choosing not to bully or discriminate. The UK as a signatory of the UNCRC (UN, 1989) must adhere to Article 2, whereby no child should be treated unfairly on any basis. Another related aspect is spiritual, moral, social and cultural development and values education, educating children as to specific values, such as respect, love, peace and co-operation in order to promote a more just society.

Issues for practice

The above detail successful strategies put in place within the school environment. The second participant voiced a number of issues about the wider social environment and how this may impact on the children within the school, leaving them vulnerable either to becoming a bully, victim or bystander.

172 *Babs Anderson*

Parents are regarded as the child's first educators, so by the age of five years, they act as the primary agent of socialisation for their child. However, the school ethos may be different from the home ethos, so that conflict arises. This may be true where the family hold a prejudice, so the child is exposed to this and believes it to be true and 'normal'. They may actively discriminate against certain groups of people through this prejudice and the child may then feel threatened and conflicted when the school teaching counteracts these beliefs. Buttelmann et al. (2013, p.428) indicate that in their study of 14-month-old infants, these children are already 'starting to selectively acquire the characteristics and specifics of their own cultural group via social learning from very early in ontogeny'. By the time children start compulsory schooling in the UK at the age of five years, they will have had a wide range of experiences, actively processed to enable them to identify their own social grouping in preference to others.

Another type of situation may arise through the lack of staff awareness of wider societal issues, such as gay and lesbian households. One such example was a child from a lesbian family grouping as part of a class of children, making a mother's day card and feeling unsure as to whether she was expected to make one or two cards. Assumptions with regard to family make-up are common and these can cause a child to feel uncomfortable in their difference. This may also be the result of school staff feeling uncertain as how to respond in an appropriate manner, with a professional fear of 'getting it wrong'. The teacher or teaching assistant may ignore issues, so as to reduce the possibility of creating a more difficult situation to manage.

The media can also promote and perpetuate stereotypical views, whereby a desire for conformity can lead to a rejection of diverse groups. Pratt-Adams, Maguire and Burn talk of the 'lexicon of exclusion' (2010, p.154) as this can be influential in families but also within the professional realm. Teachers have prejudices also, and may believe that certain groups of children in coming from deprived backgrounds may not possess the same potential as others. Their relationships with these children may unwittingly convey an inferior value to other children, which undermines the child's status with their peers.

The school council's views on bullying show an interesting slant on this. They focused strongly on the affective side for the individual, both the child who had bullied and the child who was the victim. They believed strongly that it was the school's duty to teach the children how to behave well. Therefore, in order to reduce bullying, the key condition is social influence within the classroom, whereby any reward or motivation for bullying is reduced as it is for other forms of unacceptable behaviour. The norms of the classroom require that victims are listened to and bullies confronted for their unacceptable behaviour by bystanders as well as school staff.

Conclusion: an alternative view

Horton (2014) suggests that school acts as a microcosm of society, so change is a trigger for social unease, involving moral panics and political battles. One such example is gay marriage in the UK and the response to this from certain sectors of society. School functions as an institution, where relationships are structured by dominance, competition and conformity, thus weakening each individual school's opportunity to promote a more just society, where all individuals are valued equally. Within each school, there exists a range of power relations over which the children have little control. They do not choose which class they are in, nor do they have a choice as to their classmates or their teacher, with whom they spend a large proportion of their waking day.

Teacher education concentrates on the primary function of school as being one of educating the cognitive aspects of the child rather than the promotion of social understanding. It is difficult to enhance student teachers' understanding of the holistic well-being of the child, both cognitive and affective, when their performance is measured against the teaching standards (DfE, 2011). These standards are regarded as the benchmark for effective teaching, yet here the 'lexicon of exclusion' (Pratt-Adams, Maguire and Burn, 2010, p.154) is present with the notion that teachers must only show 'tolerance' and respect to the rights of others. The lack of an appreciation of diversity within the teacher's professional standards is also apparent, seeming to promote conformity to agreed standards, a one-size-fits-all approach. Ball (2008) considers the performativity culture for teachers as promoting a form of accountability, which may only be measured by cognitive gains. This does not lend itself well to the aim of promoting social justice in the school population, either in the short term for the individual as they progress in their school career or in the long term and the impact on social understanding of diversity and democracy. Schools can do so, as is evidenced by the school within the case study research, but this takes diligence, resolution and care.

References

Arendt, H. (1977). *Between Past and Future*. New York: Penguin Books

Ball, S. (2008). *The Education Debate*. Bristol: Policy Press.

Bradshaw, J. (ed.) (2011). *The Well-being of Children in the UK*, 3rd edn. Bristol: Policy Press.

Buttelmann, D., Daum, M., Zmyj, N. and Carpenter, M. (2013). Selective imitation of In-Group over Out-Group members in 14-month-infants. *Child Development*, 84(2), 422–428.

Charmaz, K. (2014). *Constructing Grounded Theory*, 2nd edn. London: Sage.

Cohen, L., Manion, L. and Morrison, K. (2011). *Research Methods in Education*, 7th edn. Abingdon: Routledge.

Corsaro, W.A. (2015). *The Sociology of Childhood*. Thousand Oaks, CA: Sage.

Cremin, H., Sellman, E. and McCluskey, G. (2012). Interdisciplinary perspectives on restorative justice: developing insights for education. *British Journal of Educational Studies*, 60(4), 421–437.

DfE (2011). *Teachers' Standards*. Available from: www.gov.uk/government/uploads/system/uploads/attachment_data/file/283566/Teachers_standard_information.pdf (accessed 26 August 2015).

174 *Babs Anderson*

Dijkstra, J. Lindenberg, S. and Veenstra, R. (2008). Beyond the class norm: bullying behaviour of popular adolescents and its relation to peer acceptance and rejection. *Journal of Abnormal Child Psychology*, 36, 1289–1299.

Horton, P. (2011). School bullying and social and moral orders. *Children and Society*, 25, 268–277.

Horton, P. (2014). Portraying monsters: framing school bullying through a macro lens. *Discourse: Studies in the Cultural Politics of Education*, 1–11.

James, A. (2010). *School Bullying*. Research report. London: NSPCC.

Layard, R. and Dunn, J. (2009). *The Good Childhood Enquiry: Searching for Values in a Competitive Age*. London: Penguin Books.

Nutbrown, C., Clough, P. and Atherton, F. (2013). *Inclusion in the Early Years*, 2nd edn. London: Sage.

Office for Standards in Education (OfSTED) (2012). *School Strategies for Preventing and Tackling Bullying. No Place for Bullying*. London: HMSO. Available from: www.ofsted.gov.uk/resources/110179 (accessed 26 August 2015).

Olweus, D. (1978). *Aggression in Schools – Bullies and the Whipping Boys*. New York, NY: Wiley.

Olweus, D. (1993). *Bullying in School: What We Know and What We Can Do*. Malden, MA: Blackwell.

Pople, L., Rees, J., Main, G. and Bradshaw, J. (2015). *The Good Childhood Report 2015*. London: The Children's Society.

Pratt-Adams, S., Maguire, M. and Burn, E. (2010). *Changing Urban Education*. London: Continuum.

Salmivalli, C. (2010). Bullying and the peer group: a review. *Aggression and Violent Behaviour*, 15, 112–120.

Salmivalli, C., Lagerspetz, K., Björkqvist, K., Österman, K. and Kaukiainen, A. (1996). Bullying as a group process: participant roles and their relations to social status within the group. *Aggressive Behavior*, 22, 1–15.

Thompson, F. and Smith, P. (2011). *The Use and Effectiveness of anti-Bullying Strategies in Schools*. DfE Research Brief DFE-RB 098. London: DfE.

UNICEF (2015). *The Rights Respecting School Award*. Available from: www.unicef.org.uk/rights-respecting-schools/about-the-award/what-is-rrsa/ (accessed 27 August 2015).

United Nations (1989). *Convention on the Rights of the Child*. New York: UNHCHR.

14 Contemporary learners need enlightened environments

Technology, student agency and emergent learning

Susan Rodrigues

Introduction

> Every time I go to school I have to power down, said a high school student.
> (Prensky, 2001, p.3)

In this chapter I provide snapshots of the relationship between ideas and developments in education, digital technology and science classroom practice. I describe how the relationships have influenced how students learn inside and outside formal learning environments. I describe how a formal learning environment that takes on board the potential of digital developments and builds on student agency as evidenced outside the classroom environment has scope to be revolutionary within a classroom environment. The chapter also briefly presents illustrations of more progressive classroom practice. Contemporary learners have an entitlement to enlightened learning environments with more informed access to technology, scope for learner agency and the use of more emergent learning situations.

Rom Harré's work mentions 'oughtness' (Harré, 1993; Harré and van Langenhove, 1999). Many teachers feel that they ought to be using technology in their classrooms with their students. Their sense of 'oughtness' is probably based on an awareness of their situation as educators repositioning learners to develop informed knowledge and based on an assumption that in the current climate teachers are expected to use digital technology when teaching. Consequently some teachers incorporate technology but continue to use methods they have always favoured. This is probably because in many cases teachers assume the methods that worked when the teachers were students still work with students in this day. But as Prensky (2001, p.3) reported over a decade ago, 'The assumption is no longer valid. Today's learners are different.' Kennedy and Levy (2008, pp.328–329) posited that instead of 'taking advantage of a technology that the students already consider an essential part of their daily lives', students are often 'exhorted to 'switch off' their phones when 'engaged in learning activities'. As Harré (1993) observed, people do what they believe their societal duties dictate. What Harré calls rights and duties, in terms of possibilities of action and actual action, are governed by beliefs. In some cases teachers' sense of 'oughtness' is influenced by security concerns and beliefs.

176   *Susan Rodrigues*

Approximately 4 per cent of smartphones/tablets in 2010 had some form of mobile security installed (MobiThinking, 2014). So teacher cautiousness when considering the use of mobile technology in classrooms is understandable. Cautiousness, however should not be used as a justification to exclude innovation.

Moreover, in the world beyond the classroom, digital technological developments have brought about, and continue to bring about, a shift in how students see themselves, see their position in their community and see their communication strategies. Digital technological developments have triggered significant shifts in the structure and function of students' ontology and epistemology. Students' ways of being and their ways of knowing have changed. As a consequence, and despite the teacher sense of 'oughtness', to a certain extent classroom practice (be it primary, secondary or tertiary based) has not kept pace with digital advancement, let alone the changes in students' ways of knowing and being brought about through their informal engagement with technology.

Changes in education policy, classroom practice and digital development

The 1990s

In the 1990s information technology, or IT as it was known then, was advocated in various government documents. The 1997 DfEE White Paper *Excellence in Schools* mentioned better training for teachers, focusing on literacy, numeracy and IT. In England, from 1997–2001, English, maths, science, IT and swimming were to be statutory requirements for primary schools and intended to provide a 'broad curriculum'. In the US, science teachers were encouraged to integrate technology in science inquiry (American Association for the Advancement of Science, 1993).

In tandem with these calls for IT use in schools, in the 1990s several countries were also in the process of reviewing their national curricula. For example, in 1993 the National Curriculum in England underwent its first review (House of Commons, 2009). In 1995 in Victoria, Australia, The Curriculum and Standards Framework (CSF) was introduced. In science education these reviews and the research in science education identified IT benefits in terms of cost, time and the potential of IT to make the microscopic element of science more accessible (see Rodrigues, 1997). Over this decade, an argument that gained prominence with regard to IT use focused on its scope to support context-dependent and content-dependent collaborative knowledge construction rather than simple reproduction (Jonassen, 1994). As such, at the time, it was thought that IT could encourage the development of authentic tasks in classrooms (Jonassen, 1994). This era saw the authentic task research contend that IT could enable formal learning to work with multiple representations of a complicated world. However, in general, in formal science learning environments, IT was deployed to do what was customary in classrooms but with resources with a higher technical specification.

Technology, student agency and emergent learning

Unfortunately, for the most part and despite the hype and rallying calls, in science education IT still appeared to support what was customary practice. It was just done with access to more current technology. This was clearly evident when integrated learning systems were introduced. Integrated learning systems are computerised drill and practice tasks. Integrated learning systems in the 1990s provided students with repetitive tasks, and the computer programme assessed their answers. Interestingly, in this decade, where science (and maths) formal learning environments concentrated on data collection, generation and assessment (or what could be seen as the information and technology aspect), those working in digital environments were increasingly focusing on communication.

Indeed, the digital environment in the 1990s decade saw rapid developments in IT, especially with regard to communication via the worldwide web (www). This was probably as a consequence of Tim Berners-Lee developing HyperText Markup Language in 1989, which resulted in the birth of the worldwide web. In 1993 Mosaic web browser released the first commercial software allowing graphical access to content on the internet. A year later Yahoo was founded and blogging emerged. In 1996, Bhatia and Smith founded Hotmail. A year later Barger coined the term 'weblog' and Merholz shortened this to blog. That same year SixDegrees.com allowed the creation of a social networking site. Google, a product of a 1996 research project (for two Stanford University PhD students) made its debut in 1998.

The new century

The new century saw education policy and practice recognise and report on the important place and tangible potential of technology. Tomlinson's 2004 working group advocated a 'core' of 'functional' subjects (including ICT and communication skills). The Culture, Media and Sport and Business, Innovation and Skill Departments (2009) produced a document entitled *Digital Britain* in which they posited that the digital skills, motivation and confidence of all citizens needed to be developed to enhance participation in the digital world.

In formal learning environments 'communication' joined the term information technology (IT), and information communication technology (ICT) arrived. However the change in nomenclature did not bring about tangible change in the nature of technology use in formal science education settings. The ICT rhetoric and rationale has grown. Now ICT is thought to:

- provide the right information at the right time (Kester, Kirschner and van Merriënboer, 2004);
- be safer and not incur significant material costs (Lagowski, 2005);
- allow for submicroscopic mechanisms to be illustrated in a more dynamic way (Eilks, Witteck and Pietzner 2010);
- represent information in a variety of forms (Rodrigues, 2010);
- support collaborative work and help develop negotiating skills (Mackenzie, 2010).

178 *Susan Rodrigues*

Ten years ago, conference publications (Bradley, Haynes and Boyle, 2005; Naismith and Corlett, 2006) argued that mobile learning was motivating and engaging. More recently, some have suggested that mobile learning encourages: collaboration (van't Hooft, 2013); communication (Shuler, Winters and West, 2013); greater autonomy (van't Hooft, 2013); and anytime-anywhere use (Dhir, Gahwaji and Nyman, 2013). Last year, Reidel (2014) looked at findings from the 2013 Speak Up survey (involving hundreds of thousands of users including teachers, parents, students) and reported that students were using mobile devices to transform their own learning processes.

Given these strong arguments for the use of ICT, one could be forgiven for assuming classrooms saw increasing use of technology for teaching and learning. But studies reporting on ICT indicate that, on average, teachers used computers several times a week for preparation but only once or twice a year for teaching purposes (Russell et al., 2003). Ten years on, and Price (2013) reports that research still suggests that less than 50 per cent of teachers use technology for online lesson plans (49 per cent) or give students access to web-based activity (45 per cent) or access to resources on line (43 per ceny). This may be because teachers have yet to be supplied with evidence for the beneficial impact of technology on teaching and learning and as such are less inclined to buy into the rhetoric.

Teachers should not assume confidence in the students' abilities, for student self-declared competencies may not match reality, and the students might not have the ability to deal with new applications (Burke et al., 2005). Furthermore, teachers also face their own challenge: a gap between 'can do' and 'actually do'. Getting from 'can' to 'actual' is often challenging (Harré, 1993; Harré and Van Langenhove, 1999). Thus far in the new century, change in actual classroom practice is barely noticeable, let alone significant, despite the fact that access to a range of technology has grown and despite the fact that outside the classroom students have engaged with technology to such an extent that they themselves recognise, as stated by Prensky (2001), that they have to 'power down'.

Vignette one shows access to technology has improved in formal learning environments, but in general the nature of use in these environments has seen little change from normal practice.

Vignette 1: access to technology

The issue of access to technology is important if formal learning environments are to become enlightened. Reports from the Department of Education and Childhood Development in Australia show an increase in the number of computers used in schools by students. For example, in 2002 there were 136,559 computers used which rose to 201,861 by 2010. In 2009, across primary and secondary sectors there were 3.93 students per computer, by 2010 that ratio was 2.68 students per computer and by 2013 that was 1.39 students per computer (DEECD, 2009, 2010, 2013). The DEECD reports (2009, 2010, 2013) also showed differences in the nature of the digital hardware over that period of time. There were 140,125 desktop computers and 27,693 laptops in 2009. Four years later there were 31,556 tablets used, the number of laptops increased (256,281), and desktop computer use decreased (104,720). Hardware changes were accompanied by other technology support modifications. In 2006 the Victorian State Government in Australia promoted a $90 million project to provide high-speed fibre optic broadband to all Victorian government schools. By the middle of 2009, a majority of schools had a better-than-forecast connection. Thus the technology hardware/speed access issues that are often used to justify why 'can' does not translate into 'actual' may no longer apply.

Despite the reported increases in access to hardware and despite the possibility of faster access, unfortunately research continues to report that technology in formal learning environments is used predominantly to support existing practice. For example, experiments are the same, but instead of using a thermometer the students will use a data logger. There are publications in the literature reporting on some changes in practice. For instance some have pursued a flipped classroom approach (see for example, Mumper, 2014): learners review material online, and face-to-face time is used for more active learning in the form of tutorials. This is still just replicating tasks. The sequence/delivery in which the tasks occur may be different (for example, a face-to-face lecture is replaced by an online lecture that is viewed prior to a face-to-face meeting). But the nature of the tasks, and one could argue the process within each element, is in essence the same.

Prensky (2005) pointed out that students have short attention spans in classrooms but these same students can play computer games endlessly. Computer games are 'hard fun', and Papert (1998) stated that children disliked school not because the work was too hard but because it was boring. Despite Papert's and Prenksy's statements, Ofsted (2012) reported that digital technologies in school remain underdeveloped.

ICT has continued to move briskly. In a newspaper article, Garreau (2008) suggested that the iPhone in 2008 had more processing power than the sum of the North American Air Defense Command in 1965. MobiThinking (2014) reported there to be nearly 7 billion global mobile-broadband subscriptions (roughly equivalent to 95.5 percent of the world population) and mobile phone subscriptions outnumber fixed lines 7:1. Possibly as a result of this mobile access, student cultural capital now includes websites, virtual gaming environments and social media. Jukes and Dosaj (2006) posited that students under 14 years old have always known about or had computers, the internet, mobile phones and digital games. Extrapolating that 2006 statement means that in 2016 students under 24 will have always known computers, the internet, mobile phones and digital games. Consequently student life experiences have changed significantly. Their ways of 'knowing and being' outside of school have changed.

Allowing students to access technology that is very much part of the fabric of their everyday lives might help captivate them in a formal learning environment. But it also has scope to undermine the current state of moral authority. Some in authority may be circumventing the issue and ignoring the affordances of

180   *Susan Rodrigues*

technology. Interestingly the developing nations or those at a disadvantage may take the lead with regard to closing the gap between formal and informal ways of knowing and being. For as Dr Álvaro Sobrinho wrote online (2014),

> Rigid educational settings, including classrooms, don't offer the flexibility that many on the continent need . . . There is no doubt about it, mobile has the potential to revolutionize Africa's educational development, reaching more people and making learning more personal, relevant and intuitive.

Likewise, Barden (2014, p.101) suggested that, 'digitally-mediated social networks . . . can motivate learning through literacies amongst students traditionally marginalised by school literacy . . .'. In medical education, Alamro and Schofield (2012) found that shy students were more likely to participate online. It is possible that the learning milieu for those often marginalised may match the potential found in the informal learning milieu sooner than the milieu that currently serves the majority in formal environments because it acknowledges student agency.

The role of student agency in formal learning milieus

Learning has been defined, broadly, as acquiring 'knowledge' or the 'capacity for effective action' (St Onge and Armstrong, 2004). As previously indicated, technology and digital literacy have transformed students' ways of knowing, and this has had an impact on their capacity for effective action outside the classroom. Therefore it might be in the teachers' interests to review the role and place of student agency if they want to tap into that capacity for effective action inside the classroom.

Most would accept that there are three key facets responsible for determining a learning environment. These are location, repertoire and agency. In a formal education milieu:

1   Location can be thought of in terms of a digital and physical time and space. As such, locations have different affordances and constraints. For instance, a primary school has a remit with regard to the accepted code of student behaviour.
2   Student repertoire consists of what a student brings to a location with respect to social, physical, and digital skills as well as previous experiences and tools and resources.
3   Agency occurs when a student has control and autonomy.

Location, repertoire and agency help define a student's learning situation. Thus, simply enhancing access to technology hardware or modifying content delivery is not enough to enable a formal learning environment to address changes in student agency. In fact, agency poses a bit of a conundrum. For example, many assume that simulations found in science lessons should pose no difficulty for those students who are familiar with computer games. Yet investigations into the use of fairly typical and common simulations (Rodrigues, 2011, 2012) suggest the transition of skills is not automatic and may be determined by the differences in pre-conceived values and practices found in the formal and informal learning environments.

Vignette 2: transfer between formal and informal learning environments

Students (mid secondary school to first year university) were tracked when they engaged with a chemistry simulation to see if there were differences in engagement patterns as a consequence of user age, prior experience or gender. The researchers reformatted the screen: keeping the information and task the same but changing the screen appearance and presentation style. The researchers found 'selective amnesia', 'inattentional blindness' and 'conditioned behaviour' influenced student progress through the simulation.

For example, one simulation illustrated a microscopic level view of atoms, molecules and ions. Initially the spheres representing these atomic particles were labelled but as the reaction progressed the labels disappeared. Student interviews revealed that they forgot what the spheres represented and assigned them different interpretations that suited the diagram but which rendered the simulation scientifically incorrect. This finding was labelled selective amnesia. Students did not see (inattentional blindness) the obvious. For example, the majority of students using a titration experiment simulation did not see the instruction numbers beside each on-screen sequenced statement. The missed tab (instruction number 3), which supplied a list of chemicals to choose from, was likely due to students' wet lab 'conditioned behaviour'. In a wet lab students are given the chemicals they need to use. In contrast the titration simulation required students to select chemicals. We need to ensure that conditioned behaviour does not undermine student agency. For formal learning environments to be enlightened, we need to address issues pertaining to student agency.

A place for emergent learning

Emergent and prescriptive learning have always co-existed. Prescriptive learning hinges on knowledge that is pre-determined. It tends to be duplicated and delivered via a customary approach. In complex-adaptive zones, learning is self-organised and formed and distributed largely by the learners (Williams, Karousou and Mackness, 2011). Emergent learning arises from interaction between a number of people and resources. Emergent learning is therefore unpredictable; however, retrospectively it is coherent (Williams, Karousou and Mackness, 2011). In many classrooms technology use is shaped by a prescriptive approach. It relies on prescriptive learning outcomes and normative expectations and includes conventional institutional driven hierarchies (Williams, Karousou and Mackness, 2011).

182 *Susan Rodrigues*

With the developments in technology, we now have scope for a radical transformation in terms of how learner agency governs interaction, communication and dissemination in formal learning situations. Collins and Halverson talk of 'the affordances of digital media' as opposed to 'traditional modes of learning,' (2010, p.18). As the vignette below shows there is scope for a transformation in the nature of knowing and the place of student agency in formal settings.

Vignette 3: student agency in formal learning environments

Forensic science is a common theme in school science. Six schools used a forensic science topic and an emergent approach. In terms of location, repertoire and agency the project required teachers and students in school pairings (one secondary and one primary) to solve a fictional crime. Clues to the crime were unequally assigned to school pairs. The community of primary and secondary school students and teachers and scientist communicated face-to-face, or via a real time online face-to-face process or through an online forum. For the students involved, there was a sense of purpose and accountability with respect to who benefitted from their work (other students, teachers, scientist). Having an audience and shared purpose gave their science learning authenticity. The students shared information and guided others (regardless of age). There was evidence of increasing independence and growing agency. For example, young students challenged older students by politely asking for information to be re-analysed, and they also questioned the scientist about the reliability of information she supplied.

Networks are about experiences. In the forensics project, data analysis showed that authenticity, purpose and transferability were important factors in drawing on the affordances of social digital media while combining the wisdom, support and advice found within the online environment. This project mimicked students' informal ways of knowing and being. Access to others enabled them to construct and develop their own understanding of the science involved. In the forensics project, students saw the impact of their contribution on the online community and they drew on social networking in a formal learning environment to help them develop and enhance their knowledge base. Emergent learning needs to find a place in formal learning settings for the settings to become enlightened.

Conclusion

Digital technology is part of a student's everyday existence. Ignoring student familiar contexts and tools signals a lack of empathy for what students value. While formal learning situations have acknowledged the potential of technology to enhance the learning milieu we continue to ignore student agency.

We have better access to hardware and software in formal education environments. We have better connectivity to support access to information outside these environments. Teachers are more confident in digital environments.

Technology, student agency and emergent learning 183

But we ignore the fact that student ontology and epistemology have changed. In formal educational settings, how students come to know and how they come to be is stagnating. In contrast, outside the formal educational setting student ontology and epistemology have experienced a significant transformation and in essence a silent revolution. As a result, a blinkered older generation continues to tout customary practice while the adaptable younger generation have found new ways to add to their epistemology and ontology. In this communication era, balancing teacher oughtness and duty of care while accepting and fostering student agency poses a challenge. But as Sutch (2010, p.6) in the Futurelab report stated,

> Becoming conscious of the range of possibilities covered by the professional demands of the overall role of 'teacher' will be a first step to weighing up priorities, defining one's own practice, and improving how some of the roles are performed.

Emergent learning does not imply teacher absence. Emergent learning requires openness, a different form of interaction and an awareness of student agency.

Science education is about helping students to understand complex ideas while developing their skills and ability to investigate, model, experiment, gather data and problem solve. Why should this be restricted to occurring within a box that we call a primary/secondary/tertiary classroom?

Currently we are doing our students a disservice. For knowledge acquisition and regurgitation per se is of limited use to them in their future. Using technology to simply reinforce a model of learning that does no more than support knowledge accumulation will not help to meet the needs of our future society. That argument is not new. If we want to make the most of our students' cultural capital and ensure they have relevant, authentic and purposeful experiences, then we have to make better use of the technology and support learner agency, rather than settle for demonstrating institutionalised adeptness. An environment that takes into account student agency and access to technology while embracing emergent forms of learning is more likely to support students on their journey to becoming informed citizens in an international society.

References

Alamro, A. and Schofield, S. (2012). Blended problem based learning in the Qatar medical programme. *Medical Teacher*, 34, S20–S24.

American Association for the Advancement of Science (1993). *Benchmarks for Scientific Literacy.* New York: Oxford University Press.

Barden, O. (2014). Exploring dyslexia, literacies and identities on Facebook. *Digital Culture & Education*, 6(2), 98–119.

Bradley, C., Haynes, R. and Boyle, T. (2005). Adult multimedia learning with PDAs – the user experience. *Mobile Technology: The Future of Learning in Your Hands.* Fourth World Conference on Mobile Learning, mLearn 2005, 25–28 October, Cape Town, South Africa, pp.23–27. Available from: www.mlearn.org/mlearn 2005/papers-full.html (accessed 1 June 2015).

184   *Susan Rodrigues*

Burke, M., Colter, S., Little, J. and Riehl, J. (2005). Utilizing wireless pocket-PCs to promote collaboration in field-based courses. *Mobile Technology: The Future of Learning in Your Hands*. Fourth World Conference on Mobile Learning, mLearn 2005, 25–28 October, Cape Town, South Africa, pp.28–31. Available from: www.mlearn.org/mlearn2005/papers-full.html (accessed 1 June 2015).

Collins, A. and Halverson, R. (2010). The second educational revolution: rethinking education in the age of technology. *Journal of Computer Assisted Learning*, 26, 18–27.

Culture, Media and Sport and Business, Innovation and Skill Departments (2009). *Digital Britain: Final Report, June 2009*. Available from: http://webarchive.nationalarchives.gov.uk/+/http:/www.culture.gov.uk/images/publications/digitalbritain-finalreport-jun09.pdf (accessed 5 August 2015).

DEECD (2009). *Computers in Victorian Government Schools*. Available from: www.eduweb.vic.gov.au/edulibrary/public/account/datacoll/census/2009_census_statistics-rpt-v1.00-20090809.pdf (accessed 5 August 2015).

DEECD (2010). *Computers in Victorian Government Schools*. Available from: www.eduweb.vic.gov.au/edulibrary/public/account/datacoll/census/2010 censusstatistics-rpt-v1.00-20100819.pdf (accessed 5 August 2015).

DEECD (2013). *Computers in Victorian Government Schools*. Available from: www.education.vic.gov.au/Documents/school/principals/infrastructure/2013 compcensusstats.pdf (accessed 5 August 2015).

DfEE (1997). *White Paper: Excellence in Schools*. Presented to Parliament by the Secretary of State for Education and Employment by Command of Her Majesty. London: Her Majesty's Stationery Office. ('Excellence in Schools' was prepared for the web by Derek Gillard and uploaded on 4 February 2013.) Available from: www.educationengland.org.uk/documents/wp1997/excellence-in-schools.html (accessed 5 August 2015).

Dhir, A., Gahwaji, N.M. and Nyman, G. (2013). The role of the iPad in the hands of the learner. *Journal of Universal Computer Science*, 19(5), 706–727.

Eilks, I., Witteck, T. and Pietzner, V. (2010). Using multimedia learning aids from the internet for teaching chemistry. In: S. Rodrigues (ed.), *Multiple Literacy and Science Education: ICTS in Formal and Informal Learning Environments*, pp.46–69. Hershey: IGI Global.

Garreau, J. (2008). More mobile but less free. *The Age*, 29 March, p.7.

Harré, R. (ed.) (1993*). Reason and Rhetoric: Anglo-Ukrainian Studies in the Rationality of Scientific Discourse*. Lewiston: the Edwin Mellen Press.

Harré, R. and van Langenhove, L. (eds) (1999). *Positioning Theory: Moral Contexts of Intentional Action*. Malden: Blackwell.

House of Commons. (2009). *The Evolution of the National Curriculum: from Butler to Balls*. Available from: www.publications.parliament.uk/pa/cm200809/cmselect/cmchilsch/344/34405.htm (accessed 5 August 2015).

Jonassen, D.H. (1994). Technology as cognitive tools: learners as designers. *ITForum*. Available from: http://itech1.coe.uga.edu/itforum/paper1/paper1.html (accessed 14 August 2015).

Jukes, I. and Dosaj, A. (2006). *Understanding Digital Children: Teaching and Learning in the New Digital Landscape*. (Prepared for the Singapore MOE Mass Lecture 2006.) Available from: http://edorigami.wikispaces.com/file/view/Jukes+-+Understanding+Digital+Kids.pdf (accessed 18 May 2015).

Kennedy, C. and Levy, M. (2008). Using SMS to support beginners' language learning. *ReCall*, 20(3), 315–330.

Kester, L., Kirschner, P.A. and van Merriënboer, J.J.G. (2004). Information presentation and trouble shooting in electrical circuits. *International Journal of Science Education*, 26(2), 239–256.

Lagowski J.J. (2005). A chemical laboratory in a digital world. *Proceedings of the 18th International Conference on Chemical Education Chemical Education International*, 6(1), 1–7. Available from: www.iupac.org/publications/cei/vol6/02_Lagowski.pdf (accessed on 26 March 2006).

Mackenzie, S (2010). Achieving multiple literacy in science education: a classroom teacher's perspective. In: S. Rodrigues (ed.), *Multiple Literacy and Science Education: ICTS in Formal and Informal Learning Environments*, pp.32–48. Hershey: IGI Global.

Mobithinking (2014). *Global Mobile Statistics 2014 Part A: Mobile Subscribers; Handset Market Share; Mobile Operator*. Available from: http://mobiforge.com/research-analysis/global-mobile-statistics-2014-part-a-mobile-subscribers-handset-market-share-mobile-operators#uniquesubscribers (accessed 11 May 2015).

Mumper, R.J. (2014). The flipped classroom: a course redesign to foster learning and engagement in a health professions school. *Academic Medicine*, 89(2), 236–243.

Naismith, L. and Corlett, D. (2006). Reflections on success: a retrospective of the mLearn conference series 2002–2005. *mLearn 2006 – Across generations and cultures*, Banff, Canada.

Ofsted (2012). *Mathematics Made to Measure*. London: Ofsted. Available from: www.gov.uk/government/uploads/system/uploads/attachment_data/file/417446/Mathematics_made_to_measure.pdf (accessed 5 August 2015).

Papert, S. (1998). Does easy do it? Children games and learning. *Game Developer*, June, 'Soapbox' section, 88. Available from: www.papert.org/articles/Doeseasydoit.html (accessed 12 August 2015).

Prensky, M. (2001). Digital natives, digital migrants, part 1. *On the Horizon*, 9(5), 1–6. Available from: www.marcprensky.com/writing/Prensky%20-%20Digital%20Natives,%20Digital%20Immigrants%20-%20Part1.pdf (accessed 12 August 2015).

Prensky, M. (2005). *Engage Me or Enrage Me: What Today's Learners Demand*. Available from: www.educause.edu/ir/library/pdf/erm0553.pdf (accessed 8 February 2006).

Price, G. (2013). *New Survey Findings Report on How Educational Technology is Being Used in Classroom*. Available from: www.infodocket.com/2013/02/04/survey-looks-at-technology-usage-by-teachers-in-the-classroom/ (accessed 13 August 2015).

Reidel, C. (2014). *10 Major Technology Trends in Education*. Available from http://thejournal.com/articles/2014/02/03/10-major-technology-trends-in-education.aspx (accessed 12 August 2015).

Rodrigues, S. (1997). The role of information technology in secondary school science: an illustrative review. *School Science Review*, 79(287), 35–40.

Rodrigues, S. (ed.) (2010). *Multiple Literacy and Science Education: ICTs in Formal and Informal Learning Environments*. New York: IGI Global.

Rodrigues, S. (2011). Using chemistry simulations: attention capture, selective amnesia and inattentional blindness. *Chemistry Education Research and Practice*, 12, 40–46.

186 *Susan Rodrigues*

Rodrigues, S. (2012). Chemistry simulations. In: K.C.D. Tan and M. Kim (eds), *Issues and Challenges in Science Education Research: Moving Forward*, pp.209–224. Dordrecht, Heidelberg, New York and London: Springer.

Russell, M., Bebell, D., O'Dwyer, L. and O'Connor, K. (2003). Examining teacher technology use: implications for pre-service and in-service teacher preparation. *Journal of Teacher Education*, 54(4), 297–310.

Shuler, C., Winters, N. and West, M. (2013). *The Future of Mobile Learning: Implications for Policy Makers and Planners*. Paris, France: UNESCO. Available from http://unesdoc.unesco.org/images/0021/002196/219637E.pdf (accessed 12 August 2013).

Sobrinho, Á. (2014). *The Insiders' Guide to Mobile Learning (m-learning) in Africa: Dr Álvaro Sobrinho, Chairman, Planet Earth Institute*. Available from: http://mobiforge.com/news-comment/the-insiders-guide-to-mobile-learning-m-learning-africa-dr-álvaro-sobrinho-chairman-planet-earth-ins (accessed 5 August 2015).

St Onge, H. and Armstrong, C. (2004). *The Conductive Organisation*. Oxford: Elsevier.

Sutch, D. (2010). *Education Futures, Teachers and Technology*. A discussion document generated from an expert seminar, led by Futurelab and supported by the Training and Development Agency, investigating the challenges and changes to the role of teachers within educational futures. Available from: www2.futurelab.org.uk/resources/documents/other_research_reports/Education_futures.pdf (accessed 5 August 2015).

Tomlinson, M. (2004). *14–19 Curriculum and Qualifications Reform*. Available from: www.educationengland.org.uk/documents/pdfs/2004-tomlinson-report.pdf (accessed 18 May 2015).

Van't Hooft, M. (2013). The potential of mobile technologies to connect teaching and learning inside and outside of the classroom. In: C. Mouza and N. Lavigne (eds), *Emerging Technologies for the Classroom: Exploration in the Learning Sciences, Instructional Systems and Performance Technologies*, pp.175–186. New York: Springer.

Victoria Board of Studies (1995). *Curriculum and Standards Framework (CSF)*. Melbourne: Board of Studies.

Williams, R., Karousou, R. and Mackness, J. (2011). Emergent learning and learning ecologies in Web 2.0. *International Review of Research in Open and Distance Learning*, 12(3), 39–60.

15 The Hope Challenge

A new model of partnership for school improvement

Jane C. Moore, Michelle Pearson and Sue Cronin

Introduction

The drive to a self-improving school system places the onus on schoolteachers and leaders to find their own solutions to school improvement priorities (Tseng, 2014). Schools draw on a range of external sources of support such as other schools and 'traditional' agencies like local authorities; whilst these measures may become part of a successful strategy, it is nevertheless the case that school improvement is a complex and context-specific issue, with schools managing a range of challenges both within and beyond their walls and control. 'School effectiveness and student success, it is now well established, is explained more by what happens outside schools than within them' (McBeath, 2005); political attention given to the aim of 'narrowing the gap' in achievement and opportunity between the most disadvantaged and others has been demonstrated in a raft of initiatives over some time (Kendall et al., 2008). The impact of teachers and their practice is just one part of this complex picture; however, it is the case that teacher quality is consistently seen as being the most significant element influencing the quality of education. This view attracts popular anecdotal consensus, but is also, as noted in the House of Commons Education Committee's report of 2012, borne out by diverse research findings, which show that 'the impact of a good or outstanding teacher, compared with a mediocre or poor one, is both tangible and dramatic' (2012, p.14).

In England in recent years, and spanning the term of the Coalition government of 2010–2015 and the Labour government before, the quality of teachers has been judged by the quality of educational outcomes, broadly measured in pupil assessment data, relative school performance and ultimately in international league tables. This last, for example, was highlighted in the Schools White Paper (Department for Education, 2010), in which it was stated that 'The first, and most important, lesson is that no education system can be better than the quality of its teachers', putting this firmly in the context of England's performance relative to other countries (Foreword, p.3). The relationship between teacher quality and school improvement as an element of the education system overall is emphasised here, with the White Paper making it explicit that school improvement is the responsibility of schools themselves within a 'self-improving' system

188 Jane C. Moore, Michelle Pearson and Sue Cronin

(Department for Education, 2010, p.73). In reality, there is a great deal of complexity underlying the seeming simplicity of local, self-directed, peer-supported solutions to school improvement priorities.

The Hope Challenge, developed by teacher educators at Liverpool Hope University, addresses some of these long-standing issues from a new angle. This is the name given to a new model of collaborative working with HMI inspectors, local authority officers and colleagues in schools, in which schools in challenging circumstances are mutually identified, and interventions are designed and implemented to target specific areas of concern. The projects demonstrate the capacity for university teacher education providers to engage directly and proactively in school improvement agendas and to work in partnership with a range of organisations, beyond the core function of providing initial teacher training to meet workforce needs. This allows them to engage in a wide range of professional activity that spans both career paths from application to leadership and also reaches across different parts of the wider educational community.

Whilst the quality of teachers is self-evidently significant in the context of pupil achievement and school improvement more widely, the question of what underpins and sustains teacher quality is less clear; the writers of this chapter view this as stemming from a blend of professional attributes and dispositions, including moral commitment and the sense of being a 'change agent' (Day, 1999). It is proposed that teacher educators have a bigger role to play in the formation of new teachers who are fully and explicitly prepared for work in a whole range of schools, including the most challenging – however that is defined. Secondly, whilst school leaders may draw upon a range of external support providers, these may be working independently from another. The Hope Challenge involves collaboration between a range of stakeholders from the outset, so offering an unprecedented level of mutual engagement in pursuing common aims.

It is relevant that this work is also undertaken at a time of acute political challenge for teacher educators as the current Conservative government continues a determined drive to school-led teacher training (Ellis and McNicholl, 2015; Furlong, 2013, p.11). The Hope Challenge offers a retort to the marginalisation of university teacher educators but more widely still, it constitutes a response to the question of what 'good' teaching and 'good' teacher education *are*, when that answer arises from directly addressing some of the most pressing challenges being faced in the country's schools. We hope to show that finding new ways to work in partnership is critical here, echoing Ellis and McNicholl's view that the future of teacher education lies in dealing creatively with the 'ruptures and resistances that complicate educational reforms' (2015, p.152) rather than defending 'territory', vested interests or the status quo.

This chapter will consider the broader context of school improvement over recent years, as the backdrop to the Hope Challenge initiative and within which it operates. The writers will also present some of the guiding principles which shape their approach to teacher education, of which the Hope Challenge forms a small but representative part. Whilst the Hope Challenge has, by its nature, only involved a relatively small number of schools (though also a sizable and growing number of trainee and practising teachers), it is underpinned by a philosophy of teacher education that combines specific pedagogical strategies with attention to the moral dimensions of practice in its widest sense.

We will first of all focus on changes to school improvement services over recent years, which have disrupted established support and accountability structures. It is in the context of this altered sector landscape that we propose there is space for new modes of working, and we explore the contribution university teacher educators can now bring to this area, focusing on one particular innovation.

The existing school improvement landscape

The English education system is one of the most closely regulated in the world. The government's inspectorate, Ofsted, is responsible for compliance, regulation and standards across a range of services for children and young people, including maintained schools and nurseries and providers of initial teacher training. Ofsted inspections are also claimed to have a direct impact on school improvement, by virtue of a range of mechanisms such as setting standards, ensuring that these are being achieved, making recommendations and promoting self-evaluation (Jones and Tymms, 2014). The means by which inspection systems can act as vehicles for system-wide improvement are complex and have changed over time with reforms to the framework and Ofsted itself; for example, in 2006, the main functions of Ofsted were rewritten as part of the Education Act, with a new emphasis on 'promoting' improvement in schools rather than primarily 'informing' the Secretary of State about quality (ibid., p.320). Certainly, the dominance of the role of Ofsted in the school landscape is evidenced by the physical display of (positive) inspection outcomes on banners on school buildings, as well as across websites and recruitment advertisements; conversely, the ultimate consequence of repeated poor gradings may be removal of both governing body and senior leaders. The potential severity of the sanctions have magnified concerns about consistency and transparency, resulting in an increasing emphasis on data and evidence, with tightly formulated criteria for judgements; criticisms that the process thereby becomes a 'tick-box' exercise, removed from professional judgement and jurisdiction, are also common (Baxter and Clarke, 2013).

Alongside this inspection system, school improvement in England has historically been the remit of local education authorities, as part of a raft of services provided to schools and other organisations working with children and young people. This role has changed radically in the wake of both policy agendas and a changing economic landscape, influenced by the global downturn and national austerity measures (HM Treasury, 2013). Nationally, the policy of academisation – begun under the New Labour government in 2000 as the Academies Programme and accelerated by successive administrations – has contributed to the further dismantling of a unified education system, which also now includes Free Schools (Gunter and McGinity, 2014; Ellis and McNicholl, 2015). Much of the political rationale for this process, from the outset, has focused on the imperative to improve the quality of education in England's schools, with a strong rhetorical emphasis on opportunities for 'freedom' and 'innovation' once school leaders and teachers are freed from the 'bureaucracy' of local authority and other centralised control (Gunter and McGinity, 2014, p.301). Notably, whilst advocates and key agents from across the political spectrum have drawn in similar ways on ideas of 'freedom' equating to quality through innovation, these have largely aligned with the language of marketisation (parental choice, for example) rather than educational research and expertise.

As noted earlier, there has been a growing emphasis on the concept of a 'school-led school improvement' system, in which the onus is on school leaders and teachers to identify and manage their own performance targets and trends through robust planning, evaluation and auditing systems and to share their expertise across networks of schools. The academic literature has focused on the impact of various models of leadership on school improvement measures; whilst it is generally accepted that leadership undoubtedly plays one of the most significant parts in how schools improve their performance, there is no consensus as to how exactly this is enacted. Traditional 'heroic' leadership models still have currency, especially in terms of identifying and establishing a 'vision' or 'ethos' with which the whole school community can identify; however, Harris (2004) and others (e.g. Hopkins and Jackson, 2002) note that distributed forms of leadership emerge as most likely to result in 'capacity-building', given their role in releasing potential across school staffing teams, building morale and creating a shared vision across the wider school community. This is also true for schools in challenging circumstances; whilst the nature of certain issues and the urgency to demonstrate progress might necessitate taking an authoritative approach at times, it is generally agreed that sustainable school improvement will only arise from distributed models that enable genuinely collaborative and empowering activity across whole staff teams (Harris, 2004, p.19; Robinson et al., 2009).

This poses challenges for those designing and delivering initial training programmes for teachers, especially considering the extent to which these prepare individual teachers to work with professional autonomy. The constraints imposed by data-driven performance targets, especially in schools in challenging circumstances, can impede innovation and risk-taking where closer managerial control of practice is a mechanism for ensuring and demonstrating consistency and compliance. More widely, it can be argued that the 'technician' conceptualisation of the teacher (as promoted, for example, by Gove, the former Secretary of State for Education) prioritises a narrower range of activities and responsibilities than those associated with full 'professional' status – which might include having the scope to enhance one's practice in various ways and in response to multiple drivers, including current research. Emerging from this, there are clear implications for teacher training programmes, which are themselves closely regulated, and which exist to prepare trainees for the teaching posts they will enter, subject to the performance indicators typical in most schools. For the writers of this chapter, there has been a lengthy engagement with the task of reconciling these potentially conflicting objectives – producing teachers who can work pragmatically and effectively within defined parameters, whilst maintaining a focus on, and commitment to, much broader professional concerns and commitments.

The Hope Challenge – principles and projects

The Hope Challenge arose from concerns in the inspectorate as to how teacher training providers were supporting schools in challenging circumstances, chiefly regarding how trainee teachers should be best prepared to face the rigours of teaching in such schools. The demands of school teaching as a job are widely acknowledged and have been reflected in high attrition rates for a number of years (whilst there is some disagreement as to whether the drop-out rates are as dramatic as reported in the media, there is still legitimate concern regarding the retention of the most able teachers – see, for example, House of Commons, 2012). A significant aspect of this relates to professional resilience, identified as being a key personal characteristic for teachers, though this too is far from straightforward; the factors that can affect personal and professional resilience are many. We would suggest that superficially linking socio-demographic profiles of schools with teacher retention is unhelpfully crude and misses a number of the motivating factors that attract teachers to the profession in the first place (Roness, 2011), as well as neglecting the specificity of school contexts in terms of ethos and values, for example. This knowledge of context is, in fact, a very significant element of a more refined approach to teacher education and will be revisited later in the chapter.

In response to this new and explicit focus on preparing trainee teachers for working in challenging contexts, Liverpool Hope University convened a series of meetings in the summer of 2014, bringing HMI inspectors, local authority officers and school headteachers together with Hope colleagues to establish protocols for the identification of projects in the pilot phase and clarifying aspects such as ethical clearance, data sharing and quality assurance. All those involved in this planning stage were in agreement that issues of both dissemination and sustainability were key. In terms of dissemination, there was a shared commitment to making the knowledge and learning generated by the projects available to the wider educational community; this might be on a variety of levels, from direct school-to-school contact to presentations at academic and professional conferences, all demonstrating a commitment to knowledge mobilisation. The question of sustainability was equally important to all stakeholders; it was of particular concern that interventions should take place in schools with established capacity to improve, that they should be sensitive to school priorities and communities, embedded rather than superficial, and that they should have defined plans for consolidation and continuation beyond the end of the projects.

Underpinned by these principles of collaborative and ethical working, the Hope Challenge projects are based on a philosophy of teaching and teacher education that Hope colleagues had been developing for some time. At national level, the policy direction for teacher education has dictated an increasingly school-led, 'technician' approach, with the emphasis on the development of classroom skills gained principally through observation and practice. Whilst these are also vital components of university-based teacher provision, in university courses they are contextualised, supplemented and enhanced by work undertaken both in the university and in schools under joint university and school guidance. Such work operates at a number of levels, relating both to the practice-specific and also more widely to the values and philosophical positioning that sustain and give meaning to practice. For the Hope Challenge projects, these elements are especially complex and intertwined. The issue of what it is, or might be like, to work in a school in challenging circumstances was one to which we gave a lot of attention; we were aware that trainee teachers have their own educational 'histories' and preconceptions and that these perceptions can only be addressed and refined through direct experience of a range of school contexts (Britzman, 2006). At a 'practice' level, we view the development of pedagogical skills as part of a wider conceptualisation of professional disposition, within which the underlying purposes and overarching aims of any aspect of practice are embedded. This is the 'why', as much as the 'what', of teaching.

The individual projects were each therefore designed according to a common framework, termed the 'Hope Challenge Cycle for Ambitious Teaching' (see Figure 15.1). This model is based on a series of stages, from initial collaborative planning to evaluation of each project against its own specific success criteria. At each stage, explicit and discrete time is made for collective reflection, both anticipatory and critical, creating a space that is vital for both trainee and practising teachers. This has much in common with well-established models for professional

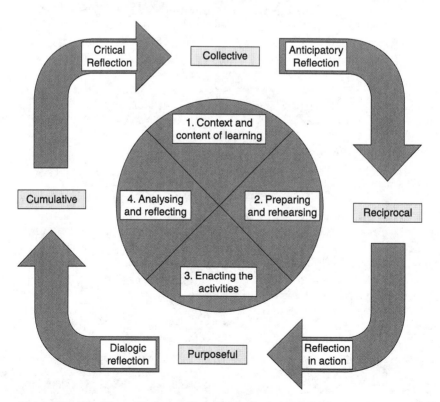

Figure 15.1 The Hope Challenge Cycle for Ambitious Teaching

reflection, from Schön (1991) onwards; overlaid on this cycle, however, is a model for the development of 'ambitious teaching', which draws on the work of Grossman et al. (2009) and Lampert et al. (2013). The concept of 'ambitious teaching' references the theory of 'pedagogies of enactment' (Grossman et al., 2009), which makes explicit the discrete parts of teaching practice so that they can be modelled, learned, rehearsed and refined. The seeming simplicity of teaching is herein problematised; what appears to be effortless and obvious in the work of a skilled and experienced teacher is, in fact, a complex and subtle synthesis of theoretical insight, accumulated practical expertise and real-time adaptation of practice to unpredictable and unfolding events. There are a number of implications arising from this, pertinent to both beginner teachers and teacher educators. One is that, whilst knowledge of context is key for understanding and adapting practice to suit the needs of specific learners in a specific time and place, the actual building blocks of professional knowledge are not context-bound; they can be learned and rehearsed in isolation and in a 'neutral' place, ready to be 'enacted' in the classroom with a greater degree of confidence. As mastery of these pedagogical practices grows, the teacher is increasingly able to give attention to the real-time events of the classroom, developing a level of fluency with regard to routine knowledge (Huberman, 1983), which then requires less conscious thought.

Over the period of the 2014–2015 academic year, a series of nine projects in primary and two projects in secondary schools were completed. In each case, the identified school met the agreed criterion of being in 'challenging circumstances', defined as having at least 25 per cent of pupils attracting pupil premium funding. For some schools, the focus was on a particular aspect of the curriculum (such as science or phonics) or other priority, with a specific cohort or sub-group of pupils, and with the aim of raising attainment in that area. At this level, each project achieved its defined aims and success criteria; it was acknowledged, however, that at small-scale and with a number of variable factors, any claims to impact should be cautious. However, there have been highly encouraging indications of longer-term effects that suggest real strengths in this new model of working. In one participating school, for example, approaches to teaching have been changed as a result of working with Hope trainees on the project; in another, pupil improvement has been sustained well beyond the end of the project, suggesting embedded rather than short-term gain. In each case, further visits to the schools are scheduled to assess sustainability and ongoing impact. In the current academic year, there is a further series of projects with nine primary schools and one secondary school, involving over 150 trainee teachers.

Whilst the successes of the projects represent tangible improvements by sector-defined criteria, we are most interested in structural and cultural changes to ways of working, both in partnership and as teacher educators at a time of profession-wide uncertainty and risk. The Hope Challenge began as a response to concerns about teacher attrition, specifically in schools seen as presenting especially challenging working environments. One part of our response would be to reiterate that university training models, in partnership with schools, allow for professional preparation both within and outside the classroom/school setting, with space for learning, reflection and refinement that is a precursor for resilience. Where training is too context-specific and dependent, it is limited by and to the parameters within which it takes place; we would argue that this compromises transferability and development over time. University programmes facilitate learning in a range of placements, allowing for early experience of, and adaptation to, contrasting school environments. However, the Hope Challenge represents a significant step beyond these models of 'good practice', which are established in providers across the country and have been for some time. On one level, this is through collaboration with other organisations explicitly addressing the school improvement agenda; on another, that trainee teachers gain huge benefits from seeing the development of their practice from a broader perspective, but within a highly supportive framework that ameliorates the fear of risk.

It is in the area of perceptions of challenging schools that we think the Hope Challenge model is especially strong. Trainees were interviewed on their views of what schools in challenging circumstances were like, and their responses revealed a range of preconceptions about deprivation, poor resourcing and social disadvantage; 'children who come from a very negatively influenced home life may have little self-confidence. May need to be made to feel important and special' (trainee). Some may have had their own experience of a challenging school career, and others may be drawn to the profession through a missionary zeal to 'make a difference'; these are not uncommon occurrences. In each case, however, the individual's personal educational experience can be both a burden and a motivation; professional preparation is about challenging preconception, not reinforcing it. We found that trainees reported very different views of what it is like to work in a challenging school after taking part in projects and that some were then determined to look for posts in similar schools after graduating.

This richer, more nuanced and mature perception of what it means to be a teacher is distinctive of what we think of as 'vocation'. 'Vocation' of course has its religious connotations, and, especially in an institution with a unique ecumenical foundation, this aspect may be personally relevant for a number of our trainee teachers and school partners. We also take the concept more broadly, though, in line with the view that 'vocation [is] the moral voice in the teacher's identity' (Estola et al., 2003) and echoing Green's defence of the word – 'I use the term quite deliberately, in the sense of a calling, though thoroughly worldly' (2009, p.2). In both cases, it is taken as given that the formation of teachers involves the acquisition and refinement of a complex blend of skills and knowledge, of practical and technical elements alongside the theoretical and abstract; but underpinning all is a deep sense of care and commitment to those in our charge, of improving life chances and being open to and respectful of the lives of others. So, whilst the Hope Challenge projects are on one level framed and evaluated within the educational structures and criteria defining progress and achievement, they operate more profoundly on the level of opening up new ways of working with and viewing others, of seeing possibility and potential in the place of challenges and barriers. This is true at all levels, from university colleagues working in new ways with those from other organisations, to beginner teachers working with experienced school practitioners outside of the customary 'mentee/mentor' relationship. The Hope Challenge projects emphasise the common purpose that should unite the educational community, at a time when fragmentation and competition are more characteristic.

Conclusion

This discussion has highlighted a number of connected strands. Changes to the ways in which school improvement support services are delivered have resulted in a more fragmented education system. Schools achieving a disappointing Ofsted report will still be monitored and supported by a designated HMI, but there is less capacity for sustained involvement; schools in challenging circumstances generally may be able to access some LA support, but the extent of this will be very variable across regions (including how it is funded). Similarly, there may be support available from schools such as Teaching Schools, which status requires them to share their expertise, but again, the extent and nature of this will be dependent on a number of local factors. And finally, there is the question of how effectively schools themselves can drive their own improvement agendas where capacity might be compromised and in which settings individual teachers are constrained in their freedom to make professional judgements.

Against this sector backdrop, university teacher education departments represent a resource that is increasingly marginalised and under threat. However, engaged in research, working with large and diverse partnerships of schools and centrally involved in the development of new and experienced teachers, teacher educators work at a dynamic nexus of professional interaction, with huge opportunities for both knowledge and relationship brokering. We at Hope have worked hard to re-imagine the role of the teacher educator, acknowledging that the scale and scope of change in the sector is creating at best an uncertain and challenging future. That uncertainty suggests it is wise to revisit first principles and to stay true to our best understanding of what and *who* the 'good teacher' – and specifically, the 'Hope Teacher' – should be. The Hope Challenge demonstrates that others across the sector share these values too, in the emergence of an authentic and dynamic professional community.

References

Baxter, J. and Clarke, J. (2013). Farewell to the tick box inspector? Ofsted and the changing regime of school inspection in England. *Oxford Review of Education*, 39(5), 702–718.

Britzman, D. (2006). Teacher education as uneven development: toward a psychology of uncertainty. *International Journal of Leadership in Education: Theory and Practice*, 10(1), 1–12.

Day, C. (1999). *Developing Teachers: The Challenges of Lifelong Learning*. London: Falmer.

Department for Education (2010). *The Importance of Teaching: The Schools' White Paper*. London: DfE.

196 *Jane C. Moore, Michelle Pearson and Sue Cronin*

House of Commons (2012). *Great Teachers: Attracting, Training and Retaining the Best*. London: Education Committee.

Ellis, V. and McNicholl, J. (2015). *Transforming Teacher Education: Reconfiguring the Academic Work*. London: Bloomsbury.

Estola, E, Erkkila, R. and Syrjala, L. (2003). A moral voice of vocation in teachers' narratives. *Teachers and Teaching: Theory and Practice*, 19(3), 239–256.

Furlong, J. (2013). *Education – The Anatomy of the Discipline: Rescuing the University Project?* London: Routledge.

Green, B. (2009). The (im)possibility of the project. *The Australian Educational Researcher*, 37(3), 1–17.

Grossman, P., Hammerness, K. and McDonald, M. (2009). Redefining teaching, re-imagining teacher education. *Teachers and Teaching, Theory and Practice*, 15(2), 273–289.

Gunter, H. and McGinity, R. (2014). The politics of the Academies Programme: natality and pluralism in education policy-making. *Research Papers in Education*, 29(3), 300–314.

Harris, A. (2004). Distributed leadership and school improvement. *Educational Management, Administration and Leadership*, 32(1), 112–4.

HM Treasury (2013). *Spending Round 2013, CM 8639*. London: The Stationery Office.

Hopkins, D. and Jackson, D. (2002). Building the capacity for Leading and Learning. In: A. Harris, C. Day, M. Hadfield, D. Hopkins, A. Hargreaves and C. Chapman (eds), *Effective Leadership for School Improvement*, pp.84–105. London: Routledge.

Huberman, M. (1983). Recipes for busy kitchens: a situational analysis of routine knowledge use in schools. *Knowledge: Creation, Diffusion, Utilization*, 4(4), 478–510.

Jones, K. and Tymms, P. (2014). Ofsted's role in promoting school improvement: the mechanisms of the school improvement system in England. *Oxford Review of Education*, 40(3), 315–330.

Kendall, S., Straw, S., Jones, M., Springate, I. and Grayson, H. (2008). *Narrowing the Gap in Outcomes for Vulnerable Groups: A Review of the Research Evidence*. Slough: NFER.

Lampert, M., Franke, M., Kazemi, E., Ghousseini, H., Turrou, A., Beasley, H., Cunard, A. and Crowe, K. (2013). Keeping it complex: using rehearsals to support novice teacher learning of ambitious teaching. *Journal of Teacher Education*, 64(3), 226–243.

McBeath, J. (2005). Leadership as distributed: a matter of practice. *School Leadership and Management*, 25(4), 349–366.

Robinson, V., Hohepa, M. and Lloyd, C. (2009). *School Leadership and Student Outcomes: Identifying What Works and Why (Best Evidence Synthesis Iteration)*. Wellington: Ministry of Education.

Roness, D. (2011). Still motivated? The motivation for teaching during the second year in the profession. *Teaching and Teacher Education*, 27(3), 628–638.

Schön, D. (1991). *The Reflective Turn: Case Studies In and On Educational Practice*. New York and London: Teachers College Press.

Tseng, C-Y. (2014). Changing headship, changing schools: how management discourse gives rise to the performative professionalism in England (1980s–2010s). *Journal of Education Policy*, 30(4), 483–499.

Conclusion

Keith Crawford

Teacher educators live in a world where it seems that the only thing that is certain is that nothing is certain. The unrelenting pace and reach of change has produced what Fullan once called 'brute sanity'; characterised by

> the tendency to overlook the complexity and detailed processes and proce-dures required, in favour of more obvious matters of stressing goals, the importance of the problem and the grand plan. Brute sanity overpromises, over-rationalises and consequently results in unfulfilled dreams and frustra-tions which discourage people from sustaining their efforts and from taking on future change projects.
>
> (Fullan, 1990, p.174)

Of course criticisms of teacher education are not new; it has all been seen before. If we were to believe the populist rhetoric we would conclude that those who educate student teachers are left-wing revolutionaries who deliberately embrace mediocrity and teach morally suspect content to unsuspecting genera-tions of students. Aimed at a quite specific audience, this is a tired, cliché-ridden and fatuous perception that ought to have run its course. Nevertheless, teacher educators do face the challenges of a reform agenda that needs to be taken seriously.

We cannot, nor should we, avoid adjustments to the professional nature of our work as teachers. But neither should we react uncritically or passively to proposals that threaten to undermine a 21st century teacher professionalism. Teacher educators have always recognised and responded to calls for change, and what is currently required is a proactive and critically open response to change that challenges the spectre of de-professionalisation with re-professionalisation.

Clearly the social consensus model of educational discourse based upon profes-sional trust and partnership between different agencies has been replaced by one that emphasises a new set of cultural, ideological and political priorities. What is now sought are schools and teachers who 'perform' within constraints and controls shaped by agencies and groups outside what was perceived historically as the secretive and uncommunicative world of the educational professional. The outcome is that, for some, teaching is no longer a profession in the way in

198   Keith Crawford

which it was once defined. That may well be true, but it is also unsurprising; teacher professionalism has never been a static entity – it has always been culturally, ideologically and politically modified to reflect changing circumstances.

So, key questions are: has teacher professional status and identity been mutilated to such an extent that teachers now carry out a role that denies them the standing of 'professional'?; have teachers moved from being the authors of recipes to the followers of recipes, and if so, how might they respond? Many of the chapters in this book have suggested fruitful avenues of progress, but here I want to briefly focus upon aspects of professionalism, professional partnership and the practice of teaching. Some of what I offer suggests reclaiming principles and values that have underpinned teacher education for a generation and making then relevant to the 21st century while also exploring how teacher educators might exploit changing times.

*

If there is a single lesson to be drawn from the papers in this collection, it is that responding imaginatively and resourcefully to the contexts within which they work is the mark of a professionally and ethically knowledgeable, skilled and astute teacher. As ethical professionals, teachers cannot respond submissively to agendas set elsewhere, no matter the extent or status of their legitimacy; to take that road denies their professionalism. A professionally reflective teacher engages in debate, critique and analyses about what it means to be a teacher. Only in that way can they occupy a secure professional space that enables them to retain a re-configurated expertise, autonomy and responsibility. That means reclaiming and colonising broad notions of professionalism – instead of responding to an agenda, teacher educators should be setting one.

Resistance and non-compliance is not an option; it is exhausting and, while it is something teachers discuss and wish for, it is often futile, serving only to increase a sense of disempowerment and frustration. The alternative is to work professionally to re-model reforms by critically evaluating them and blending them with elements of existing practice and values to create a new synthesis. In short, teachers educators ought to engage in what Wallace has called a 'principled infidelity' (Wallace, 2005, p.12). This creates what Sachs has called an 'activist professionalism' that builds new knowledge, creates new communities of practice, is progressively responsive to social change and contributes to it and is future-orientated (Sachs, 2003).

It would be a professional failure if teacher educators accepted a technicist and managerial approach to being a teacher without question; the outcome would be a teaching profession that is docile and compliant. It need not be so. As Bill Ayers has claimed, 'Teachers choose – they choose how to see the world, what to embrace and what to reject, whether to support or resist this or that directive. As teachers choose, the ethical emerges' (Ayers, 2004, p.4). Twenty-five years ago, Stephen Ball and his colleagues observed that given the 'context of text production' and the 'context of practice' policies are open to various interpretations within school and classroom. While policy makers attempt to exercise control over how

Conclusion 199

policies are read, they cannot control the plurality of meanings that emerge, meanings that are contextualised and local (Ball, 1990, 1993, 1995). Thus, there is a strong element of agency within the process of interpreting policy agendas that offers the potential for a new professionalism to emerge. I have never been comfortable with the view that government-sponsored reform agendas are incapable of being interpreted in pursuit of a progressive professionalism that critically responds to the demands of social justice, citizenship and democracy.

Perhaps teacher educators need to remind themselves that they should exercise the right to pursue values and beliefs, moral and ethical concerns, and that they have a professional obligation to contribute to the formation of policy by speaking out if they consider policy parameters to be educationally questionable. Simply put, while policy makers and powerful interest groups seek to re-define what it means to be a teacher, teachers do not have to buy into their agendas in an uncritical and unreflective way.

It is important to acknowledge that a policy document does not teach a student how to be an ethical professional; it does not teach a student how to develop an ethical approach to professionalism or an innovative approach to creating a high-quality learning environment, and nor does it teach them a philosophically grounded view of teaching and learning – that remains the interpretative task of teacher educators and colleagues in schools. Policy documents talk in the language of outcomes, but they should not dictate the route towards meeting those outcomes.

There are some clear statements of principle from which teacher educators might re-colonise their professionalism as a response to technicist bureaucratic managerialism:

- education and schooling is not a commodity; it is a public service committed to providing learners with a high-quality teaching and learning experience;
- teachers ought not to be bureaucratic apparatchiks uncritically implementing decisions made elsewhere; in pursuit of quality teaching and learning, their professionalism requires them to employ ingenuity and insight through critical self-reflection and the analysis of research-based evidence;
- teacher professionalism cannot be reduced to management, supervision and delivery of a product; it must embrace a commitment to positioning itself at the centre of debates about education and schooling;
- instrumentalism denies professionalism, and teacher professionalism must encompass rich and multi-faceted ideas on the nature of education and schooling;
- student teachers need to develop a critical understanding of the structures of education and schooling and the impact they have upon the political, ideological and ethical contexts of their work and student learning;
- student teachers need to pursue reflective educational practices based upon pedagogical and organisational models of schooling that emphasise the critical importance of equity, democracy and social justice in the development of healthy and democratic communities.

200   *Keith Crawford*

A critical part of teacher professionalism must be to recognise that social justice and equity are central in any society that seeks to call itself educated and democratic; one of the most important tasks a teacher can undertake is the quest for social good. Without a professional emphasis upon social justice, we lose much that lies at the heart of what it means to be a teacher. Teaching for social justice

> involves coming to understand oneself in relation to others; examining how society constructs privilege and inequality and how this affects one's opportunities as well as those of different people; exploring the experiences of others and appreciating how those inform their worldviews, perspectives and opportunities; and evaluating how schools and classrooms operate and can be structured to value diverse human experiences and enable learning for all students.
>
> (Darling-Hammond, French and Garcia-Lopez, 2002, p.201)

Herein lays a problem because as teacher education programmes face the challenges of instrumentalism, teaching and learning for social justice runs the risk of being diverted into some obscure cul-de-sac abandoned to a checklist of competencies. Such a position threatens to deny the wider cultural and social demands that a holistic conception of teacher professionalism requires. Even within a climate of bureaucratically managed performativity, it remains the ethical and moral responsibility of teacher educators to see education and schooling as transformative and to ensure that student teachers see themselves as agents of social change. Students must be provided with opportunities to explore the moral and social purposes and values of what teachers teach and why they teach it.

We need teachers who are knowledgeable about the fundamental goals and purposes of education, and we need teachers who have participated in critical discussions about what constitutes effective teaching and learning. Part of this process involves remembering that education is the 'practice of freedom' (hooks, 1994, p.207). This involves celebrating a passion for ideas inside the classroom, encouraging critical thinking through the questioning of competing discourses, being committed to improving the science and art of teaching and offering students the opportunity to join in responsibility for their learning.

*

It is now trite to claim that partnerships between university-based teacher educators and schools are an indispensable aspect of teacher education programmes; of course they are – neither can go it alone in the professional education of teachers. Indeed, I can think of no occasion when anybody who wishes to be taken seriously has said anything different. High-quality and well-mentored practical experience must be embedded into every teacher education course. The real questions focus upon how much practice, within what contexts, in support of what aims and with what measure of negotiation, compromise and control. We need more partnership not less; we also need more creative and innovative partnerships – teacher educators and schools have nothing to fear from the more equal division of responsibility in this sphere. But this does require transforming the structure, function and relationships that exist between universities and schools and, critically, within universities and schools. It cannot just be universities that respond to this climate of change; schools will need to fulfil their transformatory role in teaching and learning lest inertia creates confusion, disappointment and frustration.

A 'self-improving school-led system' requires an enormous amount of carefully considered and strategic planning if it is to have real traction. It needs to respond to society's wider cultural, social and economic needs and the impact these have upon education and schooling. If we acknowledge that being a teacher must move beyond technical competence to understanding the values that underpin what it means to be educated and the role of schooling in society, we must ask whether the majority of schools have the time, inclination, resources or expertise to assume the role of developing broader conceptions of professionalism.

There exists a perfectly understandable immediacy about school-led teacher education that requires schools, or clusters of schools engaged in partnerships, to think of the present rather than to invest in the broad educational, cultural, social and economic needs of society. The danger is that we might see teachers as a professional body of practitioners whose function is simply to deliver specific outcomes locked into specific contexts rather than being furnished with the knowledge and understanding to enable them to respond imaginatively and critically to the wider demands of society, education and learning.

Questions of instability, unrest and worries about the destabilization of university-based teacher education, about funding and recruitment are real enough. But universities will continue to play an important role in the professional development of new teachers and in the continuing professional development of practising teachers. While school-led teacher education programmes offer challenges, the majority of student teachers continue to be based within university teacher education programmes, and many universities already have well-developed partnership programmes. There is also evidence that schools have no wish to abandon links with universities or to expand their role in teacher education beyond what they consider to be their core aims and capabilities (Menter et al., 2010).

As government policy frameworks pursue the concept of school-based teacher education through programmes such as *School Direct*, universities need to carve out a new space in the landscape. At the heart of a genuine partnership must be a common sense of purpose and direction that combines professional expertise; it must be questioning, critical and proactive. The key is to ensure that schools are encouraged to explore the potential of closer partnerships with universities based upon building teaching and learning alliances supporting innovative school development and teaching quality. Here, as intellectual communities, universities have a role to play in re-asserting the claims that:

- teaching is an evidence-based profession, and schools can benefit from the expertise of teacher educators in helping to collaboratively drive local and regional school improvement programmes;

202 *Keith Crawford*

- in enabling students and qualified teachers to become critically reflective practitioners, teacher educators provide them with knowledge, skills and understanding of key foundational aspects of education and schooling, teaching and learning that exploit relationships between theory, research and classroom practice;
- teacher educators can create secure and seamless links between initial teacher education and the further professional development of teachers.

Teacher educators must continue to develop a lead role in the education of school-based mentors (Hobson and Malderez, 2013). This must involve schools having teachers who see themselves as teacher educators as well as classroom practitioners involved in an equal partnership with colleagues in universities. Genuine partnerships might see the creation of 'democratic learning communities' (Alexander, 2001), where teachers, pupils, parents and the wider community are jointly involved in the creation of an active community of learners who collectively act out the processes of education for citizenship and social justice in authentic and meaningful contexts. If we agree that education and schooling are transformative experiences, then partnerships must be transformative in pursuit of socially just change that makes real differences to lives. This then returns us to a broadly-framed model of collaborative partnership that sees teacher educators working with others committed to teaching for a just society. It also reinforces the important claim that teachers have responsibilities that move beyond school and classroom to encompass wider social agendas around critical forms of active citizenship.

*

Teaching is an intellectually challenging profession and we need teachers who, as part of that professionalism, demonstrate idealism, creativity, resourcefulness and ingenuity. But recent years have seen a drift towards a 'training' model of professional education based upon instrumentalism and a technicist vocabulary of competency-base assumptions. The training route is very seductive; it offers a common-sense argument that points to what populist rhetoric assumes are the skills that teachers need. But common-sense arguments are invariably anti-intellectual and anti-expert. Common-sense notions rely upon the belief that when it comes to deciding about education and schooling, good sense does not rest with academics and teachers but within the accumulated experience and knowledge of the community. Common-sense explanations produce shallow and superficial justifications and little in the way of explanation, insight or illumination.

Student teachers must be educated not simply trained. This is not a case of semantics. You can train an individual to follow a prescribed list of procedures and demonstrate competence, but if we seriously think that all we do is train teachers, then we are in trouble. The training argument narrows the conceptualisation of what teaching and learning are and what education and schooling is for and,

Conclusion 203

critically, what it means to be a teacher. It can assume that by the simple act of engaging in a task that you will eventually learn to do it, avoid mistakes and hopefully be 'competent' (such an unambitious and unimpressive word). That might work if you are painting a wall, assembling your flat-pack furniture or following a cooking recipe, but it does not work with teaching and learning where the stakes are far higher than a burnt omelette.

John Dewey once argued that 'nothing has brought pedagogical theory into greater disrepute than the belief that it is identified with handing out to teachers recipes and models to be followed in teaching', claiming that what this did was to 'dispense with [the] exercise of his own judgment' (Dewey, 1916, pp.176–177, 179). A century later we cannot escape the conclusion that for teachers, a critical understanding of education and schooling that moves far beyond the common-sense and taken-for-granted, and that establishes tangible and working relationships between theory and classroom practice, is a very serious and significant goal for teacher education. Teacher educators have a professional obligation to explain, develop and justify that position if students are not to be lost in a quagmire of bureaucratic speak and a deterministic repertoire of cliché-ridden slogans that hide the essential fundamentals of what it means to be a teacher.

Engagement with evidence-based research and theoretical approaches to teaching and learning in pursuit of an intellectually-grounded knowledge base are a fundamental aspect of teaching as a profession. We cannot marginalise theoretical understandings of teaching and learning to an instrumental and technicist discourse – skills are important, but ideas, initiative and inspiration are just as important. The American critical educator Henry Giroux has written of a time when, at the beginning of his teaching career, how he taught and organised his classroom was questioned by the vice-principal of the school in which he worked. When asked to explain what he was doing, he could not because he lacked the knowledge to defend his classroom practice and justify what he was trying to achieve. It was this experience that set Giroux on the road towards ensuring that he was able to defend his educational values and practices by reference to theoretical principles and ideas. Giroux's story illustrates how vitally important it is that in pursuit of professional excellence and progress, teachers are able to explain and justify what it is they do inside schools and classrooms with reference to a body of knowledge and theoretical perspectives. While educational theory is criticised as lacking in practical application, practical application minus a theoretical grounding is just as sterile and unproductive.

Reflections on practice ought to focus more upon what we mean by pedagogy. This too is a significant aspect of what it means to be a professional teacher because debates about pedagogies are always debates about alternative views of education, schooling, society and its future. In recent years, government agencies and their allies, some of whom are in university departments of education, have reduced what we mean by pedagogy to little more than the technical process

204   *Keith Crawford*

of teaching. What happens is that teaching becomes more about planning, management and assessment and less about children, child development and learning. What does it mean to be judged 'competent' as far as children's learning is concerned? There is merit in Shor's claim that:

> Education is not reducible to a mechanical method of instruction. Learning is not a quantity of information to be memorized or a package of skills to be transferred to students. Classrooms die as intellectual centers when they become delivery systems for lifeless bodies of knowledge.
>
> (Shor, 1993, p.25)

On this point, Scott Webster writes: 'Pedagogy has become so highly technicist and limited in its scope that it is causing teaching to be reduced to the compliant application of best principles as if these were universally the "best" for all contexts' (Scott Webster, 2009, p.45). He is right; such a view of pedagogy threatens to reduce it to little more than a technical skill, and we need to reverse that trend. Alexander is also right in suggesting that 'Pedagogy is . . . a purposive cultural intervention in individual human development which is deeply saturated with the values and history of the society and community in which it is located' (Alexander, 2004, p.3).

Pedagogy is inextricably wound up with broader cultural, social and political questions about teaching, learning, the purposes of education and schooling and, fundamentally, the future of democratic societies. Pedagogy is about the practice and theory of education and teaching; it is not just about the teacher as technician, the teacher as programmer, the teacher as manager or the teacher as assessor. Pedagogy must be transformatory and it must embrace the critical analysis of the varied contexts (cultural, social, economic and political) and opportunities and constraints within which teaching and learning takes place. In addition, any meaningful understanding of pedagogic practice must begin with the understanding that teachers teach children first and subjects second. Pedagogical studies must focus upon children, child development and how children learn; without such knowledge and understanding, learning becomes de-contextualised, programmatic and sterile.

*

Teacher educators are living through a time when everything seems exposed to the prospect of change; that is a mark of the 21st century world within which we live. Change is always threatening, and its scope and pace can produce enthusiasm and anticipation or disquiet and anxiety. Change can be an exciting and unsettling experience, with responses lying somewhere between pessimism and doubt, hope and excitement. But teacher educators cannot respond passively to the prospect of change; to do so would be to deny their professionalism. Being a teacher is exciting, challenging and demanding, and if we are committed to engaging in genuine and reflective dialogue with our students, our colleagues in school and the community we serve about the future of education and schooling, then we have to engage in a dialogue with ourselves. The chapters in this book have offered a range of important reflections on that process.

The nature of teacher professionalism will inevitably continue to be re-shaped; new challenges and opportunities in the area of partnership will emerge as will new demands upon the theory and practice of teaching. But while much has been written about the way in which education and schooling has been re-moulded by powerful groups in ways that have seemingly limited autonomy and the exercise of judgement, this need not result in the abandonment of a commitment to social justice and social change in pursuit of a better and more just society. In response to the re-casting of teacher professionalism, Hodkinson and Hodkinson claimed that 'learning can no longer be seen as "lighting fires"' (2005, p.111). Whatever the challenges teacher educators face, they need to find in their professionalism, in the education of student teachers, in their relationships with schools and in their pedagogic practice, a powerful commitment to 'lighting fires'.

References

Alexander, R. (2004). Still no pedagogy? Principle, pragmatism and compliance in primary education. *Cambridge Journal of Education*, 34(1), 7–33.

Alexander, T. (2001). *Citizenship Schools: A Practical Guide to Education for Citizenship and Personal Development*. London: Campaign for Learning/UNICEF UK.

Ayers, W. (2004). *Teaching the Personal and the Political: Essays on Hope and Justice*. New York: Teachers College Press.

Ball, S.J. (1990). *Politics and Policy Making in Education*. London: Routledge.

Ball, S.J. (1993). What is policy? Texts, trajectories and toolboxes. *Discourse*, 13(2), 10–17.

Ball, S.J. (1995). Intellectuals or technicians? The urgent role of theory in educational studies. *British Journal of Educational Studies*, XXXXIII(3), 255–271.

Darling-Hammond, L., French, J. and Garcia-Lopez, S.P. (2002). *Learning to Teach for Social Justice*. New York: Teachers College Press.

Dewey, J. (1916). *Democracy and Education. An Introduction to the Philosophy of Education*. New York: Macmillan.

Fullan, M. (1990). Managing curriculum change. In: B. Moon (ed.), *New Curriculum, National Curriculum*, pp.170–184. London: Hodder & Stoughton.

Hobson, A.J. and Malderez, A. (2013). Judgementoring and other threats to realizing the potential of school-based mentoring in teacher education. *International Journal of Mentoring and Coaching in Education*, 2(2), 89–108.

Hodkinson, H. and Hodkinson, P. (2005). Improving schoolteachers' workplace learning. *Research Papers in Education*, 20(2), 109–131.

hooks, b. (1994). Ecstasy: teaching and learning without limits. In: *Teaching to Transgress: Education as the Practice of Freedom*. New York: Routledge.

Menter, M., Hulme, M., Elliot D. and Lewin, J. (2010). *Literature Review on Teacher Education in the 21st Century*. Edinburgh: Scottish Government.

Sachs, J. (2003). *The Activist Teaching Profession*. Buckingham: Open University Press.

Scott Webster, R. (2009). Why educators should bring an end to pedagogy. *Australian Journal of Teacher Education*, 34(1), 42–53.

206   *Keith Crawford*

Shor, I. (1993). Education is politics: Paulo Freire's critical pedagogy. In: P. McLaren and P. Leonard (eds), *Paulo Freire: A Critical Encounter*, pp.18–34. London: Routledge.

Wallace, M. (2005). *Towards Effective Management of a Reformed Teaching Profession*. Paper presented at C-TRIP Seminar 4: Enactments of professionalism: classrooms and pedagogies, 5 July.

Index

Abbott, A. 17, 20
academic knowledge 19–22, 24, 73, 78, 203
academies 189
access, to technology 178–80
accountability 53, 69, 173
active teaching 44–6, 54, 106, 145–6
activity theory 108, 119, 121
Adler, J. 148
agency 180–2
Alamro, A. 180
Alexander, R. 204
Alibali, M.W. 147
Allen, J. 25
Anderson, B. 9, 166–73
Appleby, Y. 75
apprenticeship 25, 73
Aquinas, T. 45, 47
Arendt, H. 47, 95–100, 166
Arzt, A.F. 148
assessment 37; PISA 32, 41, 59, 143
Atkinson, M. 123
authority 95–6, 100–1; early modern 99–100; freedom 96–7; philosopher king 97–8; Rome 98–9; seminar 101–2; tutor 102–3
Ayers, B. 198

Baker, G. 7, 105–12
Ball, D.L. 145–6, 148
Ball, S. 173, 198
Ballock, S. 84
Bamber, P. 1–10, 126–34
Barden, O. 9, 155–64, 180
Barnett, R. 72–5
Barr, I. 131
Barthes, R. 90, 101
Barton, B. 145
Baumert, J. 145

Belsky, J. 119
Berg, D. 4, 29–38, 70
Bidmead, C. 84
Biesta, G. 59–60
biographies 25–6
biological research 158–60
British Dyslexia Association (BDA) 157
Britzman, D. 25–6
Bromme, R. 145
Brueggemann, W. 62
Buber, M. 50, 62–4
Bullivant, A. 7–8, 126–34
bullying 166–9, 171–3; proactive strategies 170–1; reactive strategies 169–70
Burn, E. 172
Buttelmann, D. 172

capitalism see neoliberalism
Cartesianism 63
challenge 85, 88–90; Hope Challenge 188, 191–5
cherishing 50–1
choice 23
Christian church 98–9
Citizenship 171
Clarke, J. 89
classroom practice 176–80
Coalition government 15, 22–6, 151, 187
Coate, K. 72–5
Coffield, F. 33
Coleridge, S.T. 52
collaboration 87, 90, 134
Collins, A. 182
communicative action 91
communities of practice 78, 107–8, 119–21

208 *Index*

community engagement project 130–2
community of learners 107–8, 134, 202
community, professional 105–12
conflict 89–90
connectedness 65–6
Connell, R. xvii
Conservative government 23, 151
contemplation 46–50, 56; activity 44–6; cultural counter-weight 52–6
Cook, T. 6, 82–91
Corsaro, W.A. 167
Costello, J.E. 63
Cottom, D. 53
Cowley, S. 84
Crawford, K. 197–205
Cremin, H. 170
critical literacy 163–4
critical thinking 45–6, 75, 78, 89–91, 97, 199–200
Cronin, S. 4, 9–10, 15–27, 187–95
curriculum 48, 72–5, 137–9, 143, 176

Daniels, H. 119
Darling-Hammond, L. 38
Davis, B. 146
delivery partnership 87
Denzin, N. 118
Department for Education (DfE) 18, 115–16, 187–8; *Importance of Teaching* 22
Dewey, J. 203
digital *see* technology
Dijkstra, J. 167
disadvantaged families 118–19, 122–3
discourses xviii
Dosaj, A. 179
dually qualified 35–7
dyslexia 155–6, 162–4; biologising 158–60; labelling 156–8; literacy ideology 160–2

early modern authority 99–100
Easen, P. 83
economic theory *see* neoliberalism
Edelman, M. 83
education 50–1, 53, 95; authority 100–1
Education Council of Aotearoa 31
Education for Global Citizenship (EGC) 127–8
Education for Sustainable Development (ESD) 127–9, 137
Education Standards Act 32
educational research 20–1, 24, 73, 78

Ell, F. 30
Elliott, J. 155
Ellis, V. 1, 3, 15, 21–2, 34, 188
emergent learning 181–3
Engestrom, Y. 34, 119
Every Child Matters 115, 171
evidence based research 20–1, 73, 78–9, 127–30, 159–61, 203

Facer, K. 163
families 118–19, 122–3
finance 31
Finland 38
Fisher, J. 61–2
formal courses 78
formal learning environments 176–82
free speech 96
freedom 96–7, 200
Freire, P. 46, 51, 55
Fullan, M. 4, 197
funding 36, 151
Furlong, J. 24, 32, 41–2

Garreau, J. 179
generative partnership 89–91
Gibb, N. 17–18
Gibson, S. 148, 151
Giroux, H. 203
Glendinning, C. 89
global education 127–30; Learning for Sustainability (LfS) 137–40; Wider Perspectives in Education (WPE) 130–4
globalization 32 *see also* neoliberalism
Goldacre, B. 20–1
Gove, M. 17, 20, 22–5
government *see* policy
Graduating Teacher Standards (GTS) 31
Green, B. 194
Grossman, P. 17, 20, 193
Grudnoff, L. 30
Gunn, A. 29–38

Habermas, J. 89, 101–2
Haigh, M. 29–38
Halverson, R. 182
Hargreaves, A. 4
Hargreaves, D. 20
Harré, R. 175
Harris, A. 190
Hartmut, R. xvii
Hatcher, R. 116
Hederman, M.P. 50–1
Hemingway, E. 45

Hiebert, J. 147
Higgins, C. 54–5
Hill, M. 29–38
Hirst, P. 63
Hodgen, J. 145
Hodkinson, H. 205
Hodkinson, P. 205
Hope Challenge 188, 191–5
Hopkins, G.M. 65
Horton, P. 172
Hossain, S. 148, 151
Huebner, D. 65
humility 66
Hunt, F. 129

identity 16, 74–5, 111, 132, 194–5
imagination 91
improvement *see* school improvement
information communication technology (ICT) 177–9
information technology (IT) 176–7
Initial Teacher Education (ITE) 2, 15; mathematics 144, 149, 151; New Zealand 29–38; Wales 41–2
inquiry community 107–8
inspections 15, 20–1, 117, 139, 188–9, 191
instructive/informative partnership 87
instrumental knowledge 100, 202
integrated learning systems 177
interactivity 106
internet 177
intersection 83–4, 88
interviews 108–9

James, A. 167
Johnstone, G. 137–40
Jones, S.W. 41–2
Jukes, I. 179

Kane, R. 32
Keat, R. 94
Kennedy, C. 175
King, B. 137–40
King, M. 30
King, R. 129
knowledge 47–8, 52; academic 19–22, 24, 73, 78, 203; instrumental 100, 202; mathematics 145–8, 150–1; relational 60–7, 72, 203–4; technology 179–80, 183
Kodelj, Z. 96
Korthagen, F. 37
Kraftnick, A.J. 159

labelling, dyslexia 156–60
Laird, M. 47
Lampert, M. 193
Lave, J. 73
Lavelle, L. 55
Le Riche, P. 84
leadership 190
learnification 59
learning difficulties *see* dyslexia
learning opportunities 78
Learning for Sustainability (LfS) 137–40
Leblond, D. 116
Lefevre, P. 147
Lerman, S. 149
lesson study 108–12
Levine, T.H. 107–8
Levy, M. 175
Lewis, J. 41–2
Lichtmann, M. 48–9
Lieberman, A. 106
Lincon, Y. 118
Lindenberg, S. 167
Lingard, B. xvii
literacy 160–4 *see also* dyslexia
Liverpool Hope University xix, 1, 52, 130, 147–8, 188, 191
Lloyd, G. 115
local education authorities 189
Lopes, J. 159
Lortie, D. 25
Lossky, V. 62
Loughran, J. 37
Louth, A. 48
love 66–7
Lowe, B. 129

Ma, L. 146
McClean, M. 31
McCluskey, G. 170
Macedo, D. 46
Machiavelli, N. 99
MacIntyre, A. 54–5
McLaughlin, H. 88
Macmurray, J. 63
McNicholl, J. 1, 3, 188
Maguire, M. 172
maintenance work 21–2
Male, T. 16
managerialism *see* neoliberalism
marketplace 18–19, 32, 53, 69, 94, 100, 189–90
mathematics 143, 145–7, 151–2; SKE 144–5, 147–52
Mayo, M. 84

210   *Index*

measurement 59, 187; PISA 32, 41, 59, 143
Meek, E. 64
Mentor, I. 24
Milbourne, L. 116
Miller, L. 106
mobile learning 178–9
MobiThinking 179
Moore, J. 1–10, 187–95
motivation 55
multi-agency work 115–23, 131
Murray, J. 16
mutual critique 88–9

National Society for the Prevention of Cruelty to Children (NSPCC) 167
neoliberalism xvii–xviii, 22, 51–5, 94, 100–1, 199; measurement 32, 41, 59, 143, 187
New Zealand 29–38
Newman, J.H. 47–8

Office of Standards for Education (OfSTED) 15, 20–1, 168, 179, 189
Olweus, D. 167
openness *see* contemplation
Opfer, V.D. 105
Organisation for Economic Development (OECD) 33, 128
organisational context 73–9
Otago 31
otherness 63–5

Palincsar, A. 107
Palmer, P. 62–6
Papert, S. 179
parents 86–8, 172
Parr, E. 7, 115–23
Parry, G. 72–5
partnership 6–8, 22, 83–5, 94–5, 200–2; challenges 88–9; collaboration 87; generative 89–91; Learning for Sustainability (LfS) 137–40; parents 86–8; uncritical approaches 85–6; Wider Perspectives in Education (WPE) 130–4 *see also* authority
Pearson, M. 9–10, 187–95
pedagogy 60–7, 72, 203–4; pedagogical knowledge (PCK) 145, 148
Pedder, D. 105
peer observation 74
Performance Based Research Fund (PBRF) 33, 36
phenomenology 168

Phillips, D.Z. 67
philosopher king 97–8
Pilkington, R. 5, 69–79
Plato 96–8
poetic 47–8
policy 22–6, 198–9; Coalition government 15, 22–6, 151, 187; Conservative government 23, 151; digital 176–80; New Zealand 32–4
Postman, N. 45
practice 8–10, 74, 202–4; bullying 171–2; mathematics 148–51; technology 179; Wider Perspectives in Education (WPE) 130–4
Pratt-Adams, S. 172
pre-school experience 118, 172
Prensky, M. 175, 178–9
Preschool Service (PSS) 85–9
pressures 21–2, 69–70
Price, G. 178
professional capital 4, 75–9
professional community 105–8, 112; lesson study 108–12
professional identity 16, 74–5, 111, 132, 194–5
professional learning 72–5
professionalism 2, 4–6, 33, 69–71, 197–200; New Zealand 29–31, 33–8; expert 17, 35–7
Programme for International Student Assessment (PISA) 32, 41, 59, 143
PSHE 171
purpose 58–60, 74–7

quality 31
questioning *see* critical thinking

Raffo, C. 116
random controlled testing 20–1
Rastier, F. 51
Reason, P. 91
recognition 96
recruitment 24, 31
reflective learning 73–4
Reidel, C. 178
relational knowledge 60–7, 72, 203–4
relationship maintenance 21–2
research 20–1, 24, 33, 36–7, 73, 78; academic knowledge 19–22, 24, 73, 78, 203; bullying 168–9; dyslexia 158–60 *see also* evidence based research
Research and Teacher Education 21
resilience 3, 191, 194

Index 211

resistance 198
Reynolds, R. 16
Rittle-Johnson, B. 147
Rizvi, F. xvii
Rodrigues, S. 9, 175–83
Rogers, J.N. 15
Roman tradition 98–9
Rose, E. 53–4
Rosenberger, C. 130
Rousseau, J.J. 100
Rummery, K. 84
Russell, T. 37
Ruthven, K. 145
Rutter, M. 119
Ryle, G. 61

Sachs, J. 198
Salmivalli, C. 167
Schofield, S. 180
scholarship *see* research
Schön, D. 192–3
School Direct 18–19, 21–4, 151
school improvement 187–90; Hope
    Challenge 188, 191–5
school-based initial teacher training
    (SCITT) 24, 201
Schwehn, M. 66
science 47–8
SCORED model 77–8
Scotland 137–40
Scott Webster, R. 204
Sellman, E. 170
seminar 101–2
Service-Learning (SL) 130
shalom 60–1, 65–7
Shaull, R. 51
Shor, I. 204
Shortt, J. 5, 58–67, 70
Shulman, L.S. 73–4, 145, 148,
    150–1
Simmt, E. 146
Skemp, R. 146
Smith, P. 168
Smyth, J. 137
Soan, S. 116
Sobrinho, Á. 180
social justice 127–8, 130–4, 137–40,
    166–73, 200, 202
Southworth, G. 16
Special Educational Needs *see* dyslexia
spiritual/moral/social/cultural
    development (SMSC) 128
Steiner, G. 45
Stevenson, M. 8–9, 143–52

subject knowledge enhancement (SKE)
    144–5, 147–52
subject matter knowledge (SMK)
    145, 148
subjectivity 48, 62–5; professional
    identity 16, 74–5, 111, 132, 194–5
Sullivan, J. 5, 44–56, 70
Sure Start 117–22
sustainability 137–40
Sutch, D. 183

Tabachnick, B. 25
Tabberer, R. 42
Taylor, C. 16, 23
Taylor, I. 84
Taylor, J. 48
Taylor, M. 84
Teach First 42
teacher development 105–7, 197,
    202–5; Hope Challenge 188, 191–5;
    lesson study 108–12; multi-agency
    work 115–23; Wales 41–2
teacher educator: features of 16–17;
    New Zealand 33–5; questions for
    17–26
teacher professional community *see*
    professional community
teacher quality 187–8 *see also* school
    improvement
Teaching Excellence Framework
    (TEF) 22
technology 52, 175–6, 182–3;
    development 176–80; emergent
    learning 181–3; literacy 161–2;
    student agency 180–1
Thompson, F. 168
Tomlinson, M. 177
traditional academic 35–7
trust 116
Tubbs, N. 45, 50
tutor 102–3

UCET 24
Ukraine 58–9
UNESCO 129

values 3, 94
Veenstra, R. 167
vocation 194–5
voice 94–5

Waite, L. 52–3
Wales 41–2
Wallace, M. 198

212   *Index*

Watson, A. 145
Wenger, E. 73, 119–20
West, T.G. 162
White, M. 7, 94–103
Wider Perspectives in Education
 (WPE) 130–4
Williams, R. 62–3
Wolterstorff, N. 60–1

Work of Teacher Educators–NZ
 (WoTE-NZ) 33–5
*Working Together to Safeguard
 Children* 115
workplace *see* organisational
 context

Zeichner, K. 25, 29